ROCKONOMICS
The Money Behind The Music

Marc Eliot

Omnibus Press
London/New York/Sydney

Exclusive distributors:

BOOK SALES LIMITED,
8/9 Frith Street, London W1V 5TZ, UK.

MUSIC SALES PTY LIMITED,
120 Rothschild Avenue, Rosebery, NSW 2018, Australia.

To the Music Trade only:
MUSIC SALES LIMITED,
8/9 Frith Street, London W1V 5TZ, UK.

Printed in England by
Camelot Press PLC, Southampton.

FOR MY BEST PAL, DENNIS
. . . with a tip of the Hatlo to Murray, for that watch

"Seest thou a man diligent in his business? He shall stand before kings."
—Proverbs 22:29

"All progress is based upon a universal innate desire on the part of every organism to live beyond its income."
—Samuel Butler

"Only the man who says no is free . . ."
—Herman Melville

"No, no, no, no, no, no, no, no, no . . ."
—The Earls, "Never"

"When we sang for black people, they called it rhythm and blues. When we sang the same songs for white people, they called it rock and roll. The audience was all that changed, not the music."
—Bo Diddley

"The virtual dominance of commercial culture is the immediate ground of America's cultural scope, confusion, banality, excitement, sterility."
—C. Wright Mills

"She is cursed with the catastrophe of parents, and her boyfriends complete her misery by being too young to drive. She sulks behind a screen of bobby pins, slapping at her baby fat, mourning the birth of her acne. She is a worried sixth-grader, an aging child, a frightened girl—and the queen of the $100 million-a-year record industry."

—TIME, *March 15, 1963*

"In any project involving the Beatles we're concerned about the commercial uses of the songs and the use of the Beatles' names and likenesses. That will always be the bottom line."

—*Leonard Marks, attorney for the Beatles*

"If you don't go for as much money as you can possibly get, then I think you're stupid."

—*Mick Jagger*

"The King of Rock and Roll, Elvis Presley, was an overfed, fat monster whose songs were mediocre and had been stolen from black American culture. The fact that the singer was adored by so many Americans is a sad illustration of what Americans are. In the space of two years he became the idol of the public, and twenty years later the public turned him into a winded dog."

—*The Soviet newspaper* PRAVDA *on what would have been Elvis's 53rd birthday*

"Many [Rock and Roll] artists from the '50's and '60's are not very solvent today. These are the performers [who] created the songs we now regard as the standards. Yet, they have little or nothing to show for their efforts because they were not the best money managers. Some signed away their rights to royalties and others were victims of 'creative bookkeeping.' "

> —*From the Starlite Starbrite Foundation Inc. mail solicitation for donations to a retirement home for needy performers*

"The fact of the matter is that popular music is one of the industries of the country. It's all completely tied up with capitalism. It's stupid to separate it."

> —*Paul Simon, in* ROLLING STONE

"I killed Tin Pan Alley."

> —*Bob Dylan*

Table of Contents

Foreword

The Beatles, The Rolling Stones, and The Who shared a common, early fascination with American rhythm and blues of the late forties/early fifties, the roots of what eventually came to be known as rock and roll. The Beatles the so-called "British Invasion" restored a measure of authenticity to American rock with a sound hailed as new, original, and revelatory by the sixties kids too young to remember the original music of Chuck Berry, Little Richard, The Chords, Frankie Lymon, or The Jesters. With the American "top ten" glutted by the post-payola lax-wax of Bobby Vinton, Fabian, Frankie Avalon, and The Orlons, and the pseudo-folk music of the Kingston Trio and Peter, Paul and Mary, The Beatles roared onto the American charts with an R&B influence strong enough to rescue both sides of the pond from the likes of Dick Clark's Kennedy era pop-pap of the early sixties.

And yet by doing so, The Beatles became instrumental in turning the mostly independent, mom-and-pop shop of American rock and roll into the billion dollar international industry of rock. Ironically, the British groups that helped in the grand reclamation of rock's roots also hastened the arrival of the corporate stranglehold by virtue of proving there was, indeed, big money to be made in a business no longer thought to be, to cop a phrase from Elvis Costello, yesterday's headline, today's fish and chip paper. To that end, the history of the Rolling Stones remains incomplete without the story of Allen Klein, The Beatles' saga suffers without an examination of the influence and perspective of Brian Epstein, and Bob Dylan's tale lacks a lot more than luster minus Albert Grossman. ROCKONOMICS, is, therefore, my customized revisionist rag intended to wipe clean the dirty face of rock's hidden history while assessing its loose change.

So please understand, I'm not just one more flabby gaffer looking to nail rock to some self-righteous cross of gold. I believe more strongly than ever in the power and glory of rock, to adore the idealistic in the face of abysmal reality; to celebrate the truth above the cloak of the big lie; and to inspire without commercial interruption the hearts and minds of tomorrow's coming tone-toters. From Brighton, the Bronx, or Beijing, I say let them come, let the music be heard, and let the chumps fall where they may. As my old friend Phil Ochs once wrote: "Ah, but in these ugly times, the true protest is beauty."

I wish to dedicate this edition of ROCKONOMICS to my friends in Beijing and Shanghai. May you live to hear the chimes of freedom flashing, and dance that night away in your best blue suede shoes.

— MARC ELIOT, July 1989

PART ONE

The Old Folks at Home

One

The first American music was hardly American. This disregards native Indians' chants, as the Pilgrims did, in favor of the Elizabethan ballads, madrigals and hymns they brought with them from the Old World. The music was performed without instrumental accompaniment, as it had been in England since the Lord Protector Oliver Cromwell banished all cathedral organs to rid the influence of Roman Catholicism from the Church of England.

The social progressiveness at the turn of the eighteenth century was reflected in music of the day. Most likely the first original American songwriter was Francis Hopkinson (1737–1791), a veteran of the Revolution, signer of the Declaration of Independence, member of the Continental Congress and lyricist. Hopkinson specialized in putting new words to traditional folk tunes, his most memorable being "My Days Have Been So Wondrous Free," and "Yankee Doodle."

The new sense of personal freedom after the Revolution was reflected in the songs of William Billings (1746–1800). Billings traveled from town to town, giving lively sing-along concerts of his bawdy songs to audiences of younger couples attracted by his "Everybody Sing!" fist-thumping gestures. For elder Puritans, Billings was an outrageous sacrilege. Music, they insisted, was meant for church, as a means to commune with God.

As popular as Billings was, no collection of his work exists today. In his time, "pop" music was not written down. A song lasted only as long and far as its composer/performer could perform it.

American musical notation came about as a result of the gradual adoption of English-built organs by New England's churches. In 1823, Jonas Chickering manufactured the first American-made pianos in the back of his Boston woodworking shop. Pianos begun to appear in private homes, and the increasing demand for popular and religious tunes made the printing of sheet music a profitable business. Before long, composers from all over the new country were eager to sell their songs for publication.

Among the most popular was Daniel Decatur Emmet, who was only twenty years old when he sold "I Wish I Was in Dixie's Land," for $500. Although Emmet lived another forty-five years, long enough to hear his song become an American classic, he never earned another penny from his biggest hit.

Others were more prolific, and more profitable. Stephen Collins Foster (1826–1864) composed nearly two hundred songs in his lifetime, and made quite a bit of money doing it. Foster's parents had hoped he'd become a bookkeeper. However, at the age of twenty-two, he sold his first song, "Oh! Susanna," for ten dollars and abandoned forever the world of business. He took his inspiration from Northern minstrelsy, vaudeville harmonies based on the music of plantation slaves, performed for white audiences, and distinguished by the percussive rhythms long missing from America's Cromwellian madrigals.

Northern minstrelsy thrived on the artificial. Blackfaced whites portrayed a sweet spirit and benign sensibility of a black South that in reality had never existed. By day, slaves were forced to sing, to keep them from forming subversive relationships. By night, they sang Protestant spirituals taught by overseers who felt a missionary responsibility to show their captives how to sing for God.

Ironically, much of what came to be known as Negro spiritual music in America was actually based on Puritan hymns.

During the mid-1870s, a second arc of minstrelsy developed produced by and for southern blacks. "Spirituals" such as "Deep River," "Swing Low, Sweet Chariot," "Sometimes I Feel Like a Motherless Child" became standard concert material. Many of the audience were already too young to have experienced firsthand the music's violently oppressive origins.

The turn of the century drew close. Northern ears remained cocked toward the calculated fabrication of the past, while those in the South listened for the coming beat of a different snare.

Two

After the Civil War, America's emancipated slaves migrated north and west to establish new lives on the nation's proliferating ranches and farms, in the industrial factories and mills.

In spite of this cultural cross-fertilization, musical tastes remained inflexibly segregated. Northern minstrel shows continued to perform in blackface for white audiences on the arc of the new sprawl. Black audiences were increasingly appreciative of something called "jazz" as it traveled up the Mississippi to Chicago and from there to New York.

The term "jazz" has been traced to many origins. One version has it that Charles Jazz was a French musician who lived and played in Storyville, the notorious turn-of-the-century red-light district of New Orleans where the end of slavery was celebrated behind the swinging doors and red curtains of the all-night brothels. Jazz, like many of his fellow musicians, soon owned his own club and did double duty as a pimp, offering his customers a chance to "jazz" with his girls. Another version makes jazz the Quarter derivation of the French word *jaser,* meaning to pep up, to exhilarate, to fornicate; to "jazz" someone or to get "jazzed."

Whatever the term's actual roots, Storyville's bluesy, gospel-based music accompanied the lustful pursuits of its night-life patrons. Women, booze, gambling and sex formed an inseparable part of postwar New Orleans revels. The music's improvisational nature became the perfect metaphor for the new freedom.

During the Roaring Twenties urban America was a network of bootleg-supplied speakeasies that supported the post-world war's hedonistic city life. To the God-fearing work-ethic majority, nothing represented the breakdown of America's morality better than the endless partying that carried into the midnight streets of every major city. The jazz of the twenties sat on the night air with a sense of lustful abandon that seemed to mock the social order's puritanical decorum.

Containment was the order of the day, as "red-light" districts occupied a part of each city's downtown, a grudging compromise by city fathers in the hopes of preventing the further encroachment of the amoral worshipers of the night. It was a compromise that proved futile once radio became a reality and networks replaced neighborhoods.

What had been a commercial novelty in 1920 had, by 1927, developed into an industry serving more than seven million American homes. Radio's primary application had been military. At the conclusion of World War I, the corporate armies of General Electric fought to retain the rights to the nation's airwaves.

From 1914 to 1919, General Electric invested more than $10 million in the British Marconi Company, which held the patent on the broadcast system deemed most practical and adaptable for the United States. It then created an American commercial broadcasting subsidiary, the Radio Corporation of America. In response, Secretary of the Navy Josephus Daniels appealed to Congress to keep radio in the hands of the government. However, GE had correctly gambled that President Wilson's problems with Congress over the League of Nations, combined with the scandalous failure of the public railroad system, ensured little official enthusiasm for keeping the airwaves in the hands of the government. Added pressure came from a strong lobby of amateur wireless shortwavers who demanded access to the airwaves under the First Amendment. On October 17, 1919, the Radio Corporation of America was granted a charter as a Delaware corporation.

Appointed to head the commercial division of RCA was former military radio specialist David Sarnoff. His first stated goal was to place, within the time frame of three years, one million GE "Radio Music Boxes" into American homes. Priced at $75 per unit, GE hoped to sell seventy-five million dollars' worth of hardware. Clearly, consumers needed to be able to hear something over the airwaves if those goals were to be met.

So phenomenal was the initial impact of "public" radio that by the end of that third year, the sale of GE's "boxes" exceeded eighty-four million units, with enough back-orders to keep its factories operating in triple-shifts for the next three years.

Westinghouse Broadcasting was RCA's first serious challenger. So popular were Westinghouse's on-the-air announcer Frank Conrad and his broadcasts of the accurate time that requests came in the mail for him to either keep talking or play recorded music between time checks to fill the otherwise dead air so that listeners could be certain they were properly tuned in. Conrad began broadcasting two hours nightly, Wednesday and Saturday evenings. To comply with the requests for music, Conrad borrowed records from a local phonograph dealer in return for identifying his store as his source of the music, a deal that marked the onset of commercial broadcasting.

In 1923, a football game played in Chicago was broadcast live to New York City. The competition for the limited commercial time available during this historic first broadcast was so intense, and the resulting sales figures of products advertised so successful, station owners were convinced that the way to sell the highest priced advertising was to offer listeners entertainment rather than dryly presented information. From that revelation emerged a more powerful commercial radio.

The freedom to electronically enter the sanctity of the American home resulted in the eventual formation of the

Federal Communications Commission. To ensure that freedom wasn't abused, the FCC issued a set of broadcast guidelines designed to legislate the moral context that went out over the air. They excluded any type of sexual suggestiveness, religious blasphemy or political subversity from being broadcast, a morality perfectly suited to the sales ethics of Corporate America determined to focus their advertising appeal directly to the largest segment of the buying public, the mainstream. To that end the popular commercial music of white, industrial America came to dominate broadcasting, while the indigenous music of native and Black America, the jazz and blues of the South and urban Northeast, the music of hookers and junkies and drunks, was, from the beginning, considered commercially unsuited for broadcast.

Which was why the first great "black" star of radio wasn't black at all, but a star of the Northern minstrel arc. Al Jolson began performing in music halls while still a child. By the time he was twenty he had developed into what many considered one of the best minstrelers on the circuit, the preeminent voice of Mammy-mine musicale. His brand of "white jazz," as it came to be known, was about as far as those who controlled American radio were willing to go in presenting the spectrum of the country's various types and styles of popular music.

So charismatic was Jolson that he could have whistled Dixie and it wouldn't have mattered. Which, in fact, he did, as he led commercial white jazz into its next evolution, "big band music," a sound filled with snazzing horns and vocal choruses with no trace left of the authentic American Negro jazz from which it was originally derived. Big band music came to dominate radio, making big stars out of formerly anonymous club musicians who'd eked out a living for years by playing for other people's suppers.

Of these, Paul Whiteman was undoubtedly the biggest, figuratively and literally. Whiteman was a three-hundred-pound former taxicab driver who began his musical career playing the viola at the 1915 San Francisco World's Fair, before joining the navy, where he formed and conducted its first orchestra. Upon being discharged, Whiteman took over the house band at the Hotel Alexandria in Los Angeles, hosting the nightly entertainment at the legendary Indian Grill, where all the movie stars came to dine and dance. Whiteman next headed for New York's Palais Royale, turning that club overnight into the newest "in" nightspot for Manhattan's flapper set.

Whiteman began weekly broadcasts of his evening sets over the National Broadcasting Network, and before long was booked into New York's Palace Theatre, the first time a so-called dance band had reached vaudeville's premiere showcase.

That engagement was followed by a special Carnegie Hall concert. Whiteman used this opportunity to introduce his big band version of George Gershwin's *Rhapsody in Blue.* Gershwin, along with Cole Porter, Irving Berlin and other "name" composers of the day, was attracted to Whiteman's sound, hearing in it a newer, more pulsating sophistication, with just a touch of the "uptown" sound they'd all discovered in their excursions to Harlem. Whiteman, too, had heard it when he went uptown to the Cotton Club to hear the latest, risqué rhythms of the "new" black jazz.

Although Jolson himself was considered little more than a spoiled mama's boy by the music industry, a "Jolson song" virtually guaranteed commercial success. As a result, composers still pitched to him but held back their more intimate, romantic tunes, in favor of such asexual novelties as "Rockabye (Your Baby)," "Swanee," "April Showers." If their pitch was successful, Jolson would do their song in exchange for half their publishing rights in the form of co-authorship credit. Even giving away half their rights, the composers did better with Jolson than they would have without him. And while Jolson may have occasionally complained about the type of songs he was offered, he never complained about the fortune he made doing "Mammy" on his famous knees.

Whiteman continued to promote his sophisticated amalgam of pop tunes, neo-classics and "uptown swing," which led to critics hailing him as "the King of Jazz." He eventually added vocalists to his concert repertoire. On one of the band's swings through Hollywood he picked up a young up-and-comer, Bing Crosby. "Der Bingle" would explode onto the scene the way no one, including Jolson, had done before.

Harry Lillis Crosby was born in Tacoma, Washington to an Irish Catholic mother and a Danish father whose relatives traced back to the Mayflower. Bing (the nickname came from a cartoon character in his hometown paper) became interested in singing while attending high school. After scoring a local success in a performance Paul Whiteman happened to catch, Crosby was invited to join the renowned conductor's orchestra. In 1930, the twenty-seven-year-old Crosby left Whiteman to become the house vocalist at the famed Hollywood Coconut Grove.

The Grove was the closest thing Hollywood had to a speakeasy, catering specifically to the honchos of the film industry. Commercial radio was just reaching the West Coast, and Abe Frank, the Grove's proprietor, decided to broadcast his live shows over the air.

Because of the technical limitations of the Grove's live transmission, Crosby was, by necessity, forced to sing exceptionally close to the mike, a technique that altered his style and delivery. In doing so, he radically changed the direction of American popular music. Crosby, like so many other young singers, had patterned his singing style after Jolson's, belting out lyrics, snapping his fingers, wriggling his hips, all to the delight of audiences. Now he was forced to a more intimate phrasing, to curl into the mike and whisper into the ears of his listeners. He took a cue from the tonal subtleties of the string section to create a sound at once flirtatious and relaxed. The result was as shocking to older listeners as it was popular with younger women.

By 1935, Crosby was radio's most popular performer, his

appeal so strong that Hollywood paid him a million dollars a year to make movies. Kraft offered him their NBC radio program, wanting him to replace none other than Paul Whiteman, whose star, along with his audience's memory of the Roaring Twenties, was slowly fading.

Bing Crosby was the ultimate Depression-age attitudinizer, the idealized pop-star-Everyman whose morning-after rasp became the perfect metaphor for the Depression generation's misspent youth. It was a sound that kept him on top of the commercial heap throughout the thirties and well into the forties, until the mood of the country shifted once more and a new star rose on the electronic horizon.*

The Crosby voice was a major factor in the ever-growing popularity of radio. During the Depression, when the source of entertainment for most Americans came over the free airwaves, the federal government granted more than 750 licenses to broadcast, with more than 600 stations on the air at least eighteen hours of every day. By 1939, Americans had spent more than a billion dollars for equipment on which to hear "free" radio, and another $150 million a year on electricity to keep it turned on.

The widespread popularity of radio led the Federal Communications Commission to revise its standards for broadcast content. In 1939 it issued a list of what it called "Program Taboos." These included fortune-telling and astrology; solicitation for funds; false, fraudulent or misleading advertising; defamatory statements; obscenity, programs offending religious groups and overstimulating kid shows; "booze" glorification; too much advertising; and the playing of too many phonograph records.

The growing practice of playing records over the air was frowned upon by the government as a capricious waste of

---

*Crosby's lifetime sales of a *half-billion* records were surpassed only by Elvis Presley, whose total sales have passed the one billion unit mark. In the fall of 1988, Columbia Records announced a major reissue of sixty-five Bing Crosby songs, available on four LPs or three CDs.

valuable airtime, if not totally deceptive to the casual listener. Often stations pretended they were broadcasting live concerts, with major stars in the studios, when in fact all they were doing was playing records.

There was another problem that threatened to keep records off the air. By 1933, in spite of Bing Crosby's popularity, record sales dropped to an all-time low of five million dollars. Record companies claimed that the public didn't buy records because they heard them free on the radio. They wanted radio stations to pay a performance royalty each time they played a record. Station owners retaliated by threatening to permanently ban them from the air. After all, they figured, if they didn't play them, who'd buy them?

The situation was more serious than either side had realized, and their inability to come to terms led to one of the most intense and bitter conflicts in the history of American media. Before its final resolution, commercial broadcasting would be historically restructured.

Three

Commercial recording became a reality in the last third of the nineteenth century via Thomas Edison's crudely manufactured wax and foil cylinders. Edison's original phonograph inventions were, like his first motion picture equipment, experimental curios, sideshow by-products of the new electric age, invented by a man all but completely deaf. In an article he wrote for the *North American Review* of June 1878, Edison listed a host of practical applications for his new recording device, which included letter writing and dictation, phonographic books for the blind, speech lessons, the "Family Record," music box toys, clocks "announcing" the time, preservation of the pronunciation of spoken language, education through repetition, connection to the telephone for permanent records, and way down the list, almost as an afterthought, the reproduction of music.

It was as if Edison felt the need to justify his new recording invention, offering a tantalizing and prophetic set of applications, every one of which was to prove a reality. Yet, as popular an early novelty as the phonograph was, and as clearly as Edison saw its practical application, he abandoned further work on it in October 1878 to concentrate on the more immediately profitable incandescent electric light.

For the next several years, Edison's phonograph was all but forgotten, and might have remained that way had Bell and

Tainter not introduced their "graphophone" to the general public. Edison labeled this German challenge nothing more than a refined model of his original phonograph. As the graphophone gained popularity, Edison resumed work on his cylindrical sound machine.

The Edison laboratory announced in 1888 a new, more practical machine, even as Bell and Tainter's graphophone was being commercially distributed. The American Graphophone Company of Washington, D.C. marketed the device as the latest advance in office dictation.

That same year the noted pianist Josef Hofmann recorded the first commercial cylinders in Edison's New Jersey laboratory. Other equally well-known performers quickly lined up to perform for the celebrated Mr. Edison and his latest amazing machine.

So popular were Edison's new phonographs and recordings that Jesse E. Lippincott, a Pennsylvania entrepreneur, paid Edison $500,000 for the patent rights. Lippincott agreed with Bell and Tainter that the profit in recording lay in dictation. However, office workers saw the machine as a direct threat to their jobs and did their best to discourage its use. Both Graphophone and Lippincott absorbed huge losses. Lippincott suffered a paralyzing stroke in the fall of 1890 and sold his interest in the recording business back to the inventor.

Edison promptly put his machines onto the general market, at $150 per unit. However, by 1890 the Columbia Phonograph Company, the entertainment subsidiary of the office division of the American Graphophone Company, emerged as the undisputed leader in commercial recording. It was producing hundreds of superior-sounding cylinders daily, an output limited only by the cumbersome recording methodology of the day—a single cylinder was made in a single take. A brass band recording a two-minute march had to play that march over and over again, perfectly, to turn out hundreds of recordings.

The popularity of the new cylinders helped push the price of a Columbia phonograph to nearly two hundred nineteenth-century dollars, cost-prohibitive for most homes. Several ideas were bandied about for a way to lower the price and maintain the profit margin. The company considered selling ad space on each cylinder wrapper, adding spoken "commercials" in cylinders at designated breaks, even cylinders devoted exclusively to advertising, intended for continual play in department stores.

In 1895 Columbia agreed to work with Edison in a united effort to develop a machine that could be sold for as little as seventy-five dollars, in the hope that cylinders would become the most popular household novelty in the country.

The effort failed miserably due to one Emile Berliner. Berliner, a longtime rival of Edison, had invented a telephone mouthpiece that was far more sophisticated than Edison's first attempts at telephone communications. When Edison expressed little interest, Berliner sold it to the Bell Laboratories, a transaction that made him wealthy.

Electricity was Berliner's passion, what he called "the swift and fiery messenger of Heaven's clouds." Once a penniless German immigrant, Berliner used this passion to develop a procession of gadgets, including a way of recording on disks rather than cylinders, a process that also greatly increased the speed of duplication. Berliner returned to his native Germany where he obtained a license to manufacture his new invention, "the phonautograph," from a toymaker, who thought the recording devices might make good Christmas presents for children. Before the winter of 1890 came to an end, the first German "Gramaphones," as they were renamed, began to appear. Secure in his methods and well funded, Berliner returned to the United States to launch what was to become the highly successful United States Gramophone Company.

In 1895 a Philadelphia syndicate put up $25,000 to form a corporation to manufacture the new style of records and the equipment on which to play them. With low-end phonographs now selling for under twelve dollars, the end seemed near for Edison's cylinders.

Unwilling to concede defeat without one more try, Edison

returned to his New Jersey laboratory to develop a spring-driven phonograph to be sold for as little as $20. His model set the cylinder standard for the next thirty years.

Competition over talent came next. Performers quickly learned how to play one company against another. Gramaphone seemed willing to pay any price, and did, offering thousands of dollars for the talents of the evangelist Dwight L. Moody, the spoken philosophies of railway magnate Chauncey Depew, the American actor Joseph Jefferson's recreation of his famous Rip van Winkle, and John Philip Sousa conducting his band. By the turn of the century, Gramaphone's catalog boasted more than five thousand recordings.

So successful was Gramaphone's catalog of records that in 1902 the company debuted an American "Red label" series of higher priced opera recordings that had previously caused a sensation throughout Europe and Russia. The American debut of the "Red Label" was tied to the signing and recording of Enrico Caruso, the legendary Italian opera star. It was now possible. Gramaphone's ads boasted, to hear the world's greatest singer "inside the comfort and privacy of your own home for mere pennies."

By 1903, Gramaphone's annual net profits passed the one million dollar mark, an amount limited only by the company's relatively slow pace in manufacturing records.

Edison, meanwhile, continued to produce what he believed to be the superior recording equipment—the cylinder—and to record the type of music the disk manufacturers felt had no audience. Because he was unable or unwilling to compete with the big dollar offers Gramaphone and others were putting up for talent, Edison turned to the noncommercial music nobody else wanted to record. Appalachian mountain songs, Southern blues and New Orleans jazz formed the nucleus of Edison's cylinder catalog. They were sold at the bargain price of thirty-five cents apiece, compared to the one dollar per record the other companies charged. And, to the amazement of Gramaphone, Victor and other competitors, Edison's cylinders of "Why Bill Bailey Don't Come Home," by Arthur Collins, and "Pretty Peggy," by Edward Rubsam, became best-sellers.

However, in 1911, after having tried for more than two years to compete with his ever-growing competition, Edison finally gave up on his cylinders, putting an end to the continued production of the only authentic catalog of indigenous American music. His invention's demise may have been helped along by Columbia's issuance, in 1908, of the four-minute "Indestructible Cylinder." Edison suspected the scratchy, hissy, poorly recorded devices were actually designed to further destroy whatever market remained for the cylinder.

In 1913 he reluctantly designed his own version of the disk phonograph, but out of a sense of obligation to those who'd purchased his cylinder machines (and a huge stock of unsold units), he continued distributing his cylinders for another ten years to a mostly Southern, intensely loyal black audience.

Columbia and Victor, meanwhile, expanded their catalogs and signed as many "white jazz" acts as they could find, hoping to tap into the more affluent commercial mainstream that couldn't seem to get enough of the music of Al Jolson.

Victor's profits jumped from $13,940,203 in 1913 to $21,682,055 a year later, in spite of a continual voiced outrage by those who felt the new music represented all that was wrong with the country, everything from the escalating problem of drinking among the working class to the newly popular "sport" of contact dancing. Even the Vatican got into the act, issuing a decree from Rome aimed at young Americans, reminding them that the only "good" dance was a tarantella.

By 1919, the phonograph industry had racked annual sales in excess of $159 million. Columbia's net income before taxes that year totaled more than $7 million, which was small potatoes compared to Victor's $37 million, with nowhere to go in the electric twenties but the direction of hemlines—up, up and up.

On January 4, 1929, all outstanding stock of the Victor Record Company was acquired by RCA. The move led observers to believe that RCA intended to broadcast only recordings it manufactured as a way of further boosting sales.

It was a reasonable assumption, but wrong. RCA's real interest in acquiring Victor was to take over the existing manufacturing plants and distribution operation. Not to make records, but to build and sell radios. By acquiring control of Victor, RCA effectively bought out the competition, with designs on limiting the supply of new records, if not completely eliminating them altogether.

It was one more salvo in the developing hostilities between the two industries, records and radio, hostilities about to erupt into a full-scale war.

The business of songwriting had come a long way in the relatively short time between Stephen Foster's death and the Roaring Twenties. Copyright laws amended in favor of songwriters produced a crop of lyricists and composers out to make a quick buck writing the next "hot" tune published on a sheet, recorded on a cylinder, danced to in a speakeasy.

Article I, Section 8 of the Constitution established the fourteen-year renewable copyright, the first legal protection for original music in the United States. The real break for songwriters came one hundred years later in 1889, when the laws were amended to include the concept of performance royalties as a way to protect publishers from counterfeit copies of sheets. In the past, there was no legal requirement for additional monies to be paid the publisher of a song if a purchaser simply passed on a copy of the sheet to a friend, fellow performer, or leader of another band and they performed it. The amended laws extended the responsibility from the point of purchase to performance. Not the purchase price, but a royalty had to be paid each time the music was publicly performed. The law was further amended in 1909 to include

piano rolls and records under the same classification as a
sheet of music.*

From the moment the 1909 copyright amendment went
into effect, composers experienced problems with publishers
who often neglected to pay royalties on time, if they paid them
at all. The solution seemed obvious to at least one songwriter:
simply publish his own music.

The five Witmark brothers began their professional careers
as printers, although like so many immigrant children, the
boys dabbled in business and entertainment. One of the boys,
Julius, liked to write songs and managed to get one published.
When collecting his royalty proved to be all but impossible,
he decided to publish the next one himself. Julius moved
into one small room in the back of his brothers' Fourteenth
Street printing establishment and devoted himself to printing his songs. Soon, all the Witmarks were involved in the
enterprise. One wrote songs, one published them, one performed them, one handled the books, and one did the promoting.

Within two years, they controlled the most popular songs
on Broadway. The secret of their success was to test every
song in the office before taking it on. Everyday, would-be
composers came up and performed for them on the piano or
whatever instruments they carried along with them. The idea
of live performance was a good one, the noise it produced a
bad one, and before long they were evicted.

*The value of a single copyright to a "hit" record may reach extraordinary financial
heights. The Sengstack family, holders of the copyright to Mildred and Patty Smith
Hill's "Happy Birthday To You," have realized from that song no less than one
million dollars a year, every year for the past fifty years. In 1988, the family announced its intention to sell the rights to "Happy Birthday" 's remaining twenty-two
year copyright, for 28 million dollars to Warner Communications. "Happy Birthday"
was not copyrighted until 1938, when the Clayton F. Summy Publishing Company
first published and registered the song with ASCAP. The Summy was purchased by
the Sengstack family. The anticipated price is based on the annual revenues the song
produces. Generally, music publishers sell the rights to a song for up to ten times
its annual cash flow. Although copyright laws have been amended, "Happy Birthday"
was registered to the Summy Corporation, rather than the two sisters who composed
it, allowing for the restriction of protection limited to seventy-five years, under the
current copyright laws.

The Witmarks solved their noise problems two moves later by leasing an entire brownstone on Twenty-Eighth Street. Soon the block became known as Tin Pan Alley for the sound of pianos and drums banging out melodies from the windows, first from the Witmark building, and then the other music publishers who took offices up and down the street. Publishing outgrew the street, and gradually stretched as far south as Fourteenth and as far north as the sunny side of Fifty-Second, the district of ditties.

By 1925, the Witmarks were the leading publishers of popular and classical music in America. That year, they bought out their main competitors, the Tams, and founded the Tams-Witmark Publishing organization, the unchallenged leader in American publishing.

Even the Witmarks weren't immune to lawsuits from composers and songwriters who felt cheated out of their royalties. What had been the original motivation for the Witmarks to enter the publishing business had now become their worst headache. As composers, they never understood why they had so much trouble collecting their due. As publishers, the reasons were obvious. No one wanted to pay performance fees, and publishers couldn't pay out what they couldn't collect.

The amended copyright law was a practical impossibility to implement. There was no way to effectively monitor the performance of every band throughout the country.

On February 8, 1914, a group of nine composers and publishers (out of thirty-five invited) gathered at Luchow's Restaurant on Fourteenth Street in New York City, directly across from the original Witmark office, to see if something couldn't be done. The American Society of Composers, Authors and Publishers—ASCAP—was formed that night, for the purpose of issuing licenses and collecting all due royalties. ASCAP devised a method of collection based on the three methods of income related to the music business. The first was from the performance of songs. Recording artists received income based on the revenue made from the sale of their records.

The second was from the sale of original music to publishers, for an agreed price and subsequent performance royalties from sheets, piano rolls and records. The third was from the money paid to the publishers for their share of sales and performances. Usually, publishers split 50–50 with composers on all performance money.

ASCAP based its system on the successful European method of licensing, donation and distribution. All ASCAP participants would be required to pay a fee for the right to perform published music. The fee to play records was based on a percentage of annual advertising revenues radio stations earned and statistical sampling of actual broadcasts multiplied by preset formulas to estimate total national performances. After deducting an operating fee, the organization would then distribute collected royalties directly to member publishers and composers. The key to the success of the operation was the participation of all venues, from the smallest village bistros to the Metropolitan Opera House.

The early going was difficult for the fledgling ASCAP, with membership in the first years dropping to a low of twenty-two of the more than one hundred publishers in the Alley. The Witmarks belonged from the beginning, and helped to keep the financially troubled organization afloat as it fought off legal challenges by band leaders and club owners who simply refused to pay.

Not until 1917, three years after its formation, was ASCAP's future clear. The Supreme Court in that year validated the organization's right to collect performance royalties and issue membership licenses (*Victor Herbert* v. *Shanley's Restaurant*). It was an even longer time before composers saw any money. ASCAP's first royalty checks to publishers and composers were issued in 1921, the same year radio came of age as a major commercial venue.

While everyone agreed that music played on the radio was an excellent way to sell records as well as receivers, those in charge of the airwaves absolutely refused to even discuss the possibility of paying royalties. Their position was based on the concept of property rights. Echoing the original arguments over sheet music, they contested that once they purchased a record, they owned it, their financial obligation completed.

The stalemate continued for several years. Broadcasters successfully resisted all attempts by ASCAP to collect royalties. Finally, in 1932, the highly influential lobby succeeded in convincing seven states to outlaw ASCAP on the basis of illegal racketeering practices and attempted extortion.

Much of ASCAP's finances were now earmarked to proving not only the viability of its organization, but its legal right to exist at all. In 1940, as many of the contracts ASCAP held were about to expire, the organization threatened to withdraw all member recordings if radio stations didn't agree to a broad-based, cohesive form of royalty payment. To show that it meant business, ASCAP affixed authorization labels to its recordings, warning that it was against the law for any station to play ASCAP-licensed products without paying performance royalties.

In retaliation, broadcasters threatened to start their own organization, to break what they claimed to be ASCAP's monopolistic tactics. In the first weeks of 1939, preliminary meetings were held between broadcast executives and station owners to discuss the possibility of creating an alternative market source of recorded music.

Broadcast Music Inc.—BMI—officially came into existence on October 14, 1939. Based in New York, the new company immediately offered capital stock and overnight raised a half-million dollars in purchasing funds, enough to begin its own playlist. Despite the war chest, ASCAP considered BMI little more than a strike-breaking tactic. ASCAP controlled the cream of the entertainment crop, the mainstream melodists, Broadway blowers and Hollywood hotshots.*

*A third licensing organization, SESAC, is wholly owned by the Heinecke family. It represents about 260 publishers who control about 450 catalogs. SESAC is the smallest of the three major performing-rights organizations. A 1970 judicial decision involving music licensing stated that "BMI and ASCAP are each other's sole competitors of any consequence."

BMI was forced to look to the same source Edison had
turned to when he'd found himself locked out of the mainstream commercial crop. BMI welcomed everyone ASCAP
had specifically excluded from membership: Appalachian
musicians, country fiddlers, blues singers, New Orleans jazz-
men. For the first time in the forty years since Edison's cylinders, professional recognition was given to the vast body of
America's music that fell outside the narrow parameters of
the commercial mainstream.

Anybody who fancied himself a songwriter was able to secure a deal with BMI. An enraged ASCAP announced on
December 31, 1940 that it would immediately press charges
against any station that broadcast ASCAP-licensed music. In
effect, ASCAP pulled its music off the air. (Under the terms
of the 1909 Copyright Act provision, each time a station
played an ASCAP record, it was technically liable for a fine of
$250, for failing to pay royalties.)

Overnight, radio stations revised their record libraries to
include only BMI's available catalog of songs. Popular commercial music vanished from the airwaves. Much to ASCAP's
amazement, as Edison had discovered thirty years earlier, the
public was only too eager to listen to and accept America's
"other" music.

Thus encouraged, BMI sought to increase its inventory and
paid more than a million dollars in advance royalties for popular Edward B. Marks Publishing Company's catalogs. Marks'
switch from ASCAP to BMI was a crucial one. A founding
member of ASCAP, Marks had become disenchanted by the
organization's house politics. His defection to BMI gave it
even more credibility, along with some much needed new
music.

BMI was now in a position to guarantee an average $20,000
advance for the right to license a composer's music. In addition, it offered more equitable contracts to newcomers, as
opposed to ASCAP's nine-point favored-nation method of
payments with rates based on frequency of play and length of

membership. In addition, ASCAP membership was not offered to anyone who hadn't published at least five songs.

In the summer of 1940, a suit was instigated by the Justice Department under the Sherman Anti-Trust Act, which accused ASCAP of restraint of trade, monopolistic tactics, and discrimination against nonmembers. It was this suit that finally succeeded in bringing ASCAP to its negotiating knees. Twenty-six years of doing battle with station owners had drained the organization's finances and broken its morale. By November 1941, it was over. ASCAP settled for the same two and three-fourths percent of radio stations' annual advertising revenues (a standardized method of royalty payment, distributed directly to publishers and composers in amounts based on actual monitored play) the stations had willingly given to BMI, far below the seven and a half percent ASCAP had always demanded.

There were those who saw in the settlement a major victory for ASCAP, which had never before earned so much as one cent in broadcast royalties. Others saw it as a Pyrrhic victory. ASCAP's hard line of negotiation had brought about the existence of BMI, whose roster of talent signaled to many the end of Tin Pan Alley's golden era.

Animosities continued to smolder. In 1942, James Petrillo, president of the American Federation of Musicians, called a strike and pulled the federation's musicians out of all recording studios to prevent the manufacture of new records. Petrillo's union had sought for a long time to break the back of the recording industry. The proliferation of recorded music had made a considerable dent in the amount of live music performed on the air. The new settlement threatened to cut even further the dwindling and highly lucrative airtime of union musicians. Petrillo claimed patriotism as his only motivation, citing the nation's wartime need for shellac, which just happened to be the main ingredient in the manufacture of records. No one took this rationale seriously, or the real threat of any type of walkout. Nevertheless, the strike Petrillo called on August 1st lasted for more than a year and all but halted the manufacture of any new records.

As a result, many "newly discovered" BMI blues, folk and jazz musicians were prevented from recording. ASCAP benefited from the rerelease of much of its substantial catalog, making 1943 a watershed year for the organization and guaranteeing its continued existence.

Eventually the strike ended, and so did the war, the big one. The boys came home again and found that everything they'd left behind had changed—appliances, cars, homes, hairdos. Nothing was like it was when they'd left.

Not even music. Especially music.

Four

The financial health of the country was finally restored by the supply-side economics of World War II. The flourishing economy saw the growth of a new consumer demographic, that age range when young men were too old to be children but too young to be soldiers, and young girls were too old to be baby-sitters but too young to have babies. American adolescents had gained a new handle: they were now teenagers.

The consumer potential of the new "teenagers" grew faster than any other segment of the population. In the thirteen years following the end of World War II, teenage buying potential grew to an estimated ten *billion* dollars. The weekly allowance became an American obsession, a way for teens to compare financial status among themselves as a group. In the first years after the war, every teenage boy had to have his own jalopy. Once he had wheels, the local drive-in became the perfect place to take his girl.

After the movie, they needed some place to go. The newest "in" spot became the neighborhood soda shop, the stained-glass ice-cream palace where kids went to relax, have a snack and check out the latest records on the jukebox.

The origin of the term *jukebox* may have come from the fictitious name "Jukes" given to a real family that was the focus of a nineteenth-century sociological study of the inheri-

tance of feeblemindedness and its correlation with social de-
generacy. Southern brothels were often referred to as "juke
joints" by outraged civic leaders who linked immorality with
feeblemindedness, a way of condemning both as enemies of
a God-fearing community. In the years before the war, every
corner bar had a box; the poor man's nickel orchestra, the
hooker's seductive accompaniment.

Jukes had been popular in the South for years before they
caught on up North because they were the only available
outlet for the "race" music that almost never got played on
the radio. After the war, if a Southern "race" record did well
on a juke, it occasionally found a slot in the new mob-con-
trolled boxes up North, giving the postwar teens their first
exposure to a sound most had never heard before. When it
came to spending money on music, boys fed coins into the
jukes, but statistics showed that records were mostly bought
by teenage girls.

During those years one unmistakably sensual voice oozed
from radios kept constantly on for reports from the front. The
voice was younger, more adventurous and sexier than the
familiar groan of the aging patriarch of pop, Bing Crosby.

The difference between Crosby and Frank Sinatra was the
way the younger crooner laid it on the line, with an agitation
in his voice America's eight million manless women could
immediately relate to. Unlike Crosby, Sinatra became their
fantasy boyfriend rather than their huggable papa.

Sinatra began his career on the radio as a "Major Bowes
Original Amateur Hour" winner. That prize helped him land
the spot as Harry James's new vocalist, and from there he
joined Tommy Dorsey's band. Sinatra left James because of
the bandleader's continuing problems getting his records on
the radio, a result of this ACAP affiliation. Due to a lack of
radio play, Sinatra's recording of "All or Nothing at All," with
the Harry James Orchestra, sold only eight thousand copies.
Rereleased after the settlement, the same recording went on
to sell three million copies.

Sinatra stayed two full seasons with Dorsey, fronting vocals for $125 a week. Dorsey encouraged his singer to listen to Bing Crosby records. It was advice well taken. In 1941, Sinatra replaced Crosby at the top of the *Downbeat* poll for favorite vocalist, a spot Crosby had held for six undisputed years. After being voted 1943's top band vocalist by *Billboard* magazine, Sinatra left Dorsey to pursue a solo career.

Columbia Records offered Sinatra a recording contract, and he quickly learned the rules of the hit-making game. Paul Colby, the legendary Greenwich Village club owner and onetime song plugger for Sinatra in the forties, recalled how Sinatra refined a practice first introduced by Al Jolson: "I went to work for a publishing firm called Barton Music, which was one-third owned by Frank Sinatra. It was a smart move on his [Sinatra's] part, no question, to have a piece of the songs he sang. Our first hit was 'Saturday Night Is the Loneliest Night of the Week,' and after that he had one hit on top of another. We were all making money hand over fist. That was the whole purpose of having a publishing company, to record unknown songs by new writers, make them hits and keep a piece of the action. It became a standard part of the business, if you were big enough, and Sinatra, on Columbia at the time, was the biggest."

Sinatra's chosen repertoire cleverly reflected the heartbreak of separation the wives, girlfriends and young mothers in his audience experienced during the war. "I'll Never Smile Again" and "I Walk Alone" were typical of the songs that made him the ultimate female fantasy, a position highlighted by his legendary personal appearance in 1943 at New York's Paramount theater.

Not that the famous engagement was everything the Sinatra legend now recalls it to be. Singing on the radio was one thing, performing live for Sinatra was something else again. Whereas Crosby's manufactured patriarchy had benefited from his familiar movie-priest persona, Sinatra had no strong visual identity. George Evans, Sinatra's press agent, noticed the occasional moans and swoons during Sinatra's initial performances and promptly hired a dozen young "bobby-

soxers'' for $5 apiece to create what amounted to orches-
trated pandemonium. Newsreel cameras were conveniently
on hand to record the event.

Evans dressed Sinatra in a flashy, style-of-the-moment zoot
suit, and rehearsed ad-libs and arm movements with the
singer, perfectly coordinated with timed head tilts and eye
squints.

By the end of the extended engagement, Paramount's first
in twenty-five years, Sinatra had entered the big time. Having
received $1,250 a week for the Paramount appearance, Sina-
tra was able to quadruple that for a return engagement.
Weekly singing appearances on radio's "Your Hit Parade"
brought in $2,800 a week, with freelance one-shots on any of
the variety weeklies bringing in another thousand per. Movies
were next. Sinatra sang for $100,000 a film, big money for
what amounted to a couple of days' work. By the mid-forties,
Sinatra had carefully crafted his image into every lonely girl's
dream lover.

A far cry from reality. Bluntly put, Sinatra was a mama's
boy. As a child he almost never left Dolly Sinatra's side, gaining the reputation in childhood as "a sissy," a reputation he
carried with him into the world of show business. Wherever
he went he heard the whispers, and perhaps as a way to offset
them, obsessively pursued both show girls and mobsters. His
accomplishment as the first pop idol to cash in on youthful
vulnerability was all the more remarkable in a decade when
most young men his age were in a uniform fighting in the war.

Sinatra fell as meteorically as he'd risen, his decline coincid-
ing with the disappearance of his youthful looks behind a
crackling face and prematurely balding dome. Just six years
after his legendary appearance at the Paramount, Columbia
Records released him from his recording contract. By 1952,
Frank Sinatra was unable to get a deal with any major label
until Capitol finally agreed to a one-year look-see. It could
afford to take a chance on Sinatra. It was the new kid on the
record block, not yet able to compete with Columbia and
RCA, the two "majors" dominating the record industry. Capi-

tol had nothing to lose with Sinatra, especially since it got him for a very good price: less than nothing. In addition to receiving no advance, Sinatra agreed to pay his own studio time.

It was a bitter downfall for the one-time idol of millions of young women, due at least in part to the developing mind-set of the postwar teen. The new kids may have simply rejected what their older sister war-widows had been so crazy over. Sinatra was yesterday's news. Further, as big sisters' husbands and boyfriends returned, their need for fantasy figures evaporated.

In many ways, Sinatra represented the last of the old-style ASCAP idols. The music business was changing, as were its methods of discovering talent. BMI's emergence as a power in the industry led to the exposure of a type of music almost never heard in most regions of the country. By the time of his death at the age of twenty-nine. Hank Williams, a country boy who could barely read or write, succeeded where no one had before. His songs became the first to cross the border separating Tin Pan Alley from the rest of America.

Interestingly, like Jolson and Sinatra before him, Williams was a mama's boy. Abandoned by his father at the age of seven, he became psychologically umbilicaled to mama Lillian for the rest of his life. Lillian had been a fairly successful musical entertainer in her day, but when Hank began to show signs of real talent, she forfeited her own career in order to take over the personal management of his.

Almost from the moment he arrived on the country/western scene, Hank Williams was a phenomenon. Within a year of turning pro he was invited to perform at the prestigious Grand Ole Opry, the pinnacle of the Southern music scene. The Opry paid its members scale, but any song performed on the show quickly found its way onto the country charts, so no one ever complained.

As for Hank Williams, everyone, audience and performers alike, marveled at his ability with a lyric. His songs were nothing like the usual sweet fiddle-filled serenades that made lis-

teners grin as they squeezed their sugar's hand. Williams'
songs made them want to squeeze sugar's something else, a
phenomenon not lost on Fred Rose.

Rose was half of Acuff-Rose Publications. For all intents
and purposes they were the Southern music publishing industry. As such, the partners had a lock on the Grand Ole Opry.
Roy Acuff supervised the selection of hopefuls who got the
nod to perform, and almost without exception those who
were lucky enough to be chosen were those whose music was
published by Acuff-Rose.

It wasn't long before Williams began writing hit songs "in
collaboration" with Fred Rose, forming a songwriter partnership published by Acuff-Rose. Hank Williams was very happy,
and Rose became very rich. "Pappy," as Williams called Rose,
was someone to replace his manager/mother, someone he
could trust like a father. Rose took over all of Williams's
finances, bookings, recordings and personal appearances,
leaving Williams to concentrate on performing and writing hit
songs.

In 1947, Pappy scored a major coup by signing Williams to
a recording contract with the newly formed MGM Records.
The company's parent film company was interested in the
possibility of turning him into a singing cowboy movie star in
the tradition of Roy Rogers and Gene Autry. The studio
signed Williams to star in a projected series of musical west-
erns, none of which ever got made.

Rose's next goal was to get Hank Williams a major hit
record—not just a regional country breakout, but a national
pop hit, all but unheard of without ASCAP connections.
Which Rose had. Acuff-Rose was among the first publishers
to sign with BMI, after having been continually rebuffed by
ASCAP. After it became clear that BMI was here to stay,
ASCAP signed what amounted to an insurance policy's worth
of country publishers, either as an investment or as a way of
squeezing BMI by narrowing the rapidly dwindling pool of
unsigned talent and publishers.

Rose, anticipating just such a move, kept one of his

publishing subsidies, Milene Music, out of the Acuff-Rose stable. When the time was right he assigned it to ASCAP. Hank William's first single, released in June of 1947, was "Move It On Over." The Milene song was a moderate country hit. "Lovesick Blues," a year and a half later, was the success Williams and Rose had been looking for. William's version of "Lovesick Blues" hit number one on *Billboard's* national "Folk Record" chart.

"Lovesick Blues" was not a Hank Williams original (and therefore not an Acuff-Rose/Milene song, something that made Pappy less than happy). The tune was a Friend-Mills collaboration written in the twenties, "countrified" in the thirties by Yodelin' Emmett Miller, recorded again in the forties by Rex Griffin and finally by Williams on MGM, in late 1949.

Mitch Miller, the head of music direction at Columbia, heard something in one of Hank Williams' ASCAP songs that he felt set it apart. But he wanted it for a Columbia artist. It wouldn't be the first time Miller mix-matched performers with material. He'd scored with his hot pop singer, Johnnie Ray, by having him record the gospel song "I'm Gonna Walk, Walk, Walk with My Lord." He'd given Frankie Laine "This Old House," another gospel chestnut that shot to number one on the pop charts. He approached Tony Bennett with Hank Williams's "Cold Cold Heart."

Bennett at first refused to record it, objecting to what he referred to as the barnyard sound of the fiddles. Miller urged him to concentrate on the lyrics and assigned Percy Faith to come up with a more sophisticated arrangement. Tony Bennett's version of "Cold Cold Heart" shot to number one on the pop charts, and Miller quickly made an arrangement with Rose that in exchange for "first looks" at any Williams material, he'd see to it that the label's top pop vocalists recorded them.

"Cold Cold Heart" made country and western music commercially viable to the mainstream. So much so that Miller decided to reverse his experiment, taking a sophisticated Tin

Pan Alley tune and matching it with a legitimate country star. The result was Marty Robbins's hit recording of "A White Sport Coat and a Pink Carnation." The next logical step for Miller was to create a "Columbia cowboy." Guy Mitchell was chosen over Hank Williams, who was still considered too much of a bumpkin to make it with Columbia's mainstream audience.

Meanwhile, Fred Rose continually pushed Williams for more hit songs as good as "Cold Cold Heart." The only problem was, Williams hadn't written that one either. "Heart" was a song Williams had bought from one Paul Gilley, a basketball player at Morehead State College, for a handful of cash before putting a new tune to it and giving it to Pappy.

It wasn't the first time Hank had "bought" a song. "Long Gone Lonesome Blues" and "I've Been Down That Road Before" were originally co-written with Vic McAlpin. McAlpin sold all his rights to Williams for $500 per song.

Nevertheless, Hank Williams (and Fred Rose) had Williams put country music on the pop charts. Even if he wasn't seeing very much of the half-million dollars plus his music had so far earned for Acuff-Rose, it didn't matter to him. He really wasn't in it for the money. He was rich enough when his pockets were filled with cash and Pappy told him he'd done well.

When Hank Williams died at the age of twenty-nine, New Year's Eve, 1953, he had a total of $4,394.80 on deposit in the only bank account he ever had. The combined assets of all his jewelry, costumes, hats, guns, guitars and belt buckles were valued at a little more than $13,000.

Williams was married three times in his life, but he married his third wife three times. It was a nifty little scam dreamed up by one Oscar Davis. Davis planned to sell tickets to the Hank Williams/Billie Jean marriage, to take place in New Orleans' Municipal Auditorium, even though the couple had already wed. The plan was to charge 75 cents to $1.50 for seats. Sales were so strong that an extra matinee had to be added to the one already planned. The day's total gross exceeded $30,000, not including the freebie "wedding" gifts exacted in return for advertising displays in the lobby.

Davis was a slick promoter who almost never missed a trick. When Williams passed away, he lost no time in looking for another singer he could cash in on. Originally a carny with an eye for talent and how to make money off it, he became the first to see the potential in a young truck driver from Tupelo. The youngster was going absolutely nowhere and fast doing local Memphis radio station jingles for the "Red Foley Show."

It was October 1954, and Davis was hungry for action. He turned to a fellow carny to see if he could help get the young singer booked. It so happened, although Davis had no way of knowing, that his carny friend had tried and failed to steal Hank Williams away from Rose after Williams' string of hits eclipsed the carny's own country act, Eddy Arnold. Now Davis's friend took a look at Elvis Presley and all at once saw the gold in them thar hips.

Five

It took three years and three months for "the Colonel" to finally snag his prey, but only weeks after that for the phenomenon called Elvis Presley to explode onto the national scene. For many, Presley represents the birth of rock and roll, and in a way, they are right. In the years between Hank Williams's death and Elvis's arrival, the first great rush of mostly black rhythm and blues had come and gone, transfigured in the '56 mania that engulfed the young, white guitar-slinger who sang what he called rock and roll.

Rhythm and blues first gained national exposure during the thin stack of years between the end of World War II and the outbreak of the Cold War. They were years when racial tolerance flashed through a nation still recovering from the racist cancer of Fascism. The new "Jackie Robinson" brotherhood combined with postwar prosperity revived the basic American belief that anyone could start his own business, be his own boss and make his own fortune. One of the easiest businesses to get into was the latest "boom" industry, popular music.

For nearly thirty-five years after the introduction of the phonograph, the American record industry had been dominated by the two majors. Product came to the listener from one direction, the manufacturers. Corporate marketing rather than the public's taste controlled the flow of music to the mainstream. To be a successful composer or entertainer meant to be recorded by Columbia or RCA.

A third major company entered the field in 1934, when Decca Records opened its American branch. Decca's European parent lured Jack Kapp, head of a Columbia subsidiary label, to take over the company. Kapp made his brother Dave a partner in the operation. Their first act sent shock waves through RCA and Columbia. The Kapp brothers cut the price of a record from seventy-five to thirty-five cents and broke all previous industry sales records. Having succeeded in broadening their potential market, they then looked to expand their roster.

While at Columbia, Jack Kapp had signed many major names to long-term personal management deals. Now that he needed additional artists, Kapp simply brought his Columbia roster with him. The Decca roster soon included Bing Crosby, band leader Guy Lombardo, the Dorsey brothers, and Hoagy Carmichael.

With three majors now actively competing and airplay threatened by ASCAP's ongoing battles with station owners, the search began for other commercial outlets. For the first time, the majors seriously considered the financial potential of jukeboxes, long the primary venue for the few, mostly Southern independent labels unable to break their product over the nation's mainstream airwaves.

Within five years, more than 350,000 jukeboxes were in operation across the country, with the majors taking up 45 percent of their revolving racks. The remaining slots were taken by the independents. Records by such artists as the Mills Brothers, the Ink Spots, Duke Ellington and Cab Calloway began to receive their first mass exposure.

Not that this exposure was entirely welcome. Many blacks felt that these performers had somehow sold out. Calloway was a longtime star on the "chitlin" circuit. Directly as a result of his records being in jukebox, he was offered the part of Sportin' Life in a Broadway revival of George Gershwin's

Porgy and Bess. Earlier productions of the show had brought angry cries from black entertainers who considered it exploitative and derivative, little more than modern-day minstrelsy, and Calloway a sellout for agreeing to appear in it. Still, the year after he appeared on Broadway, Calloway grossed three quarters of a million dollars entertaining mostly white audiences. After twenty-five years barely making ends meet, Calloway had become mainstream America's newest overnight sensation.

Others made the most of their new exposure. Nat "King" Cole became known as the "Sepia Sinatra" and landed a contract with Capitol Records. Jesse Stone, whose 1942 "Idaho" became a jukebox favorite, saw his song make the national pop charts after being rerecorded by Benny Goodman.

Independent recording became the newest growth industry. Two technological developments played a crucial part: the introduction in 1948 of the "unbreakable" LP record and the development of high-quality, low-cost recording equipment, making it possible for anyone to enter the business of popular music for an initial investment of less than a thousand dollars. Recording costs, operating expenses and performer royalties could now be paid from sales as low as fifteen hundred units. Benefiting from BMI's catalog of largely unrecorded music, the independents became the first serious competition for the majors. Which is not to say they had any great social stake in the music, or the careers of performers. It was simply an easy way to make money, without having to make much of an initial investment.

Between 1948 and 1954, more than a thousand new labels went into business. As a result of the distribution system used by jukeboxes, "race" records and "hillbilly music" began to gain some degree of national attention.

More and more, black entertainers crossed over into the mainstream. Bob Keen, a white musician and founder of Keen Records and Del-Fi who eventually discovered and produced Ritchie Valens, remembered how he first came to record Sam

Cooke: "There were three or four majors and that was it. The rest were independents, one-shot jobs, putting out blues and what they called race music. Everything in the business was segregated; if you put out blues records as an independent, that's all you put out. Or country, or Latin. Or gospel. 'Pop' was still Sinatra, and rhythm and blues was the thing mothers were afraid their sons and daughters were going to be seduced by. I'd jammed a lot with Nat Cole's guys and played with Duke Ellington's band. One of the guys had this friend, Sam Cooke, who'd recorded a couple of solo tunes for Specialty Records, under Art Rupe. Specialty was an independent 'soul' label, with Little Richard their biggest act. Cooke doubled as lead singer for the Soul Stirrers, a happening gospel act. Rupe didn't want to release Sam Cooke's single because his backup was done by the Modernaires, a white pop group that had gained a following doing vocals with the Glenn Miller band during the war. No one had ever released an integrated pop record before, and Rupe didn't want to be the first to try. He owed 'Bumps' Blackwell some money, and used the Sam Cooke single as payment. Blackwell was a friend of mine and knew I was looking for new talent. He brought Cooke and me together, and I released his first hit, 'You Send Me,' on Keen Records. 'You Send Me' sold a couple of hundred thousand copies on the strength of jukeboxes and what were then known as the 'colored' radio stations. We sold eighty thousand copies in Los Angeles before it was ever played on a white station. Once it broke through, and white kids heard it, they put it through the roof."

Keen was one of the new breed of white independent label owners who produced "race" records. Ahmet Ertegun was another, a young Turkish immigrant whose family settled in Washington, D.C., the capital too, of the Negro vaudeville circuit. Ertegun, then a student at Georgetown University, and a friend, Herb Abramson, decided to form their own independent label to try and put some of the music they'd heard in their neighborhood clubs on record. They formed a partnership (with a third, silent investor, a Turkish dentist by the name of Dr. Sabit), moved to New York City and formed Atlantic Records, recording every unsigned black act they could find.

They had their first hit in 1949, with Stick McGhee's "Drinkin' Wine Spo-dee-o-dee," which sold 400,000 copies. In spite of placing number three on *Billboard*'s "race music" chart (changed in 1951 to the R&B chart), the record was considered a novelty by most industry observers.

Atlantic broadened its repertoire, often combining musicians with other people's music, adding a studio producer, to create a desired "sound." Jerry Wexler was initially brought in to soften the hard edge of rhythm and blues, to make it more palatable for white audiences. Wexler put together the then unknown former lead singer of the Dominoes, Clyde McPhatter, with the Drifters, Atlantic's breakthrough crossover group. Propriety had long been the chastity belt of pop lyricism, romantic longing and unrequited love the favorite subjects of such mainstream pop crooners as Sinatra, Dean Martin, Tony Bennett, Perry Como, and Mel Torme. One of Wexler's goals was to combine the lyrical content of mainstream pop with the smooth vocal stylistics of rhythm and blues.

The initial success of Atlantic Records brought scores of other white-owned independent record companies into the game, helping to move R&B into the commercial mainstream.

Chess Records in Chicago had been recording rhythm and blues since 1946, when it first began to preserve the sounds of Muddy Waters. The blues guitarist's style of play recalled the legendary Delta Blues stylist Robert Johnson. By 1950 Chess was releasing a more urgent, grumbling R&B, fronted by guitarist Ike Turner and his Delta Cats, a group formed in Mississippi that migrated north via the blues club route. Turner connected with Chess via Sam Phillips, who owned a recording studio in Memphis. Phillips had had no luck placing any of his records with the majors, something that would have paid off handsomely for him as he always included as part of the price for the use of his studio a piece of the records made in it.

Eventually, Chess broke Chuck Berry onto the R&B charts, along with Bobby Charles, Johnnie and Joe, the Monotones, and on its Checker subsidiary, Bo Diddley and the Flamingos. Jubilee hit with Edna McGriff, the Orioles, the Four Tunes, the Cadillacs, Bobby Freeman, the Royaltones, Harold Ember, Faye Adams, the Nutmegs, the Five Satins, the Turbans, the Mello-Kings, the Silhouettes, and Charlie and Ray. Rama introduced the Crows, the Harptones, the Valentines, the Cleftones, and formed the Gee subsidiary for Frankie Lymon and the Teenagers. Gone/End had the Dubs, the Chantels, the Flamingos, and Little Anthony and the Imperials. Old Town had the Fiestas, the Solitaires, the Valentines, the Harptones, Robert and Johnny, and Billy Bland; Vee-Jay had the Spaniels, the El Dorados, the Dells, the Magnificents, and Jerry Butler and the Impressions. Aladdin produced Helen Humes, the "King" Cole Trio, saxophonist Lester Young, the Five Keys, the Teen Queens. Specialty gave the world Little Richard. Imperial delivered Fats Domino.

Talent was told to bring their own music or were given a topic, such as Christmas or summertime, and told to come up with a song. Often these "composers" were paid five or ten dollars for their songs, along with a case or two of whiskey, considered payment in full. The list of artists who willingly made these deals runs as long as the rolls of R&B. The most notable composers and performers include Lightnin' Hopkins, John Lee Hooker, Etta James and B. B. King. Some, like Little Richard, whose records went on to make millions, pursued royalty claims in court cases that in some instances remained unresolved for more than thirty years.

In 1952, independent labels grossed over $15 million, almost all of it remaining at the "executive" (white) level. Tours were set up, acts put on the road, living in cheap motels, traveling in dilapidated buses and receiving almost no money for their efforts. As late as 1955, the five El Dorados toured the Eastern states for three months, performing in dozens of venues, and received, after "expenses" were deducted, a total of $134 to be divided among them. [See Appendix A]

By the mid-fifties, 80 percent of all music played on the radio was licensed by BMI. The $15 million worth of performance fees this translated into was enough to convince ASCAP to reverse its position and pressure the majors to record the R&B and country music it had begun to license. At least one label, Columbia, immediately sought out ASCAP country music, leading to Mitch Miller's deal with "Pappy" Rose for the music of Hank Williams. (Columbia also co-produced the Broadway musical *West Side Story* and released the original cast album. The show's equation of rock and roll with juvenile delinquency perfectly suited Mitch Miller's feelings as to the credibility and quality of rock, while the popularity of *West Side Story* contributed handily to the company's coffers.)

By this time there were six majors. RCA, Columbia, Decca, Capitol, MGM and Mercury were all eager to jump on the lucrative R&B bandwagon. Capitol created a Memphis division exclusively for the recording and release of rhythm and blues and what it still referred to as "hillbilly." Their plan was to mine the still largely untapped lode of talent of the Fred Rose–Roy Acuff–Grand Ole Opry circuit. RCA established Bluebird, what it called its "race" label, to release its big new "find," Sonny Boy Williamson.

Still, those who worked at the majors expected R&B music to quickly fade into the great discount bin; an expectation that disappeared in 1954, when Atlantic went to the bank with its release of "Sh-Boom," by the Chords, on its subsidiary Cat Records.*

---

*It wasn't unusual for labels to release records on "affiliate" or "subsidiary" labels. For one thing, it made good economic sense to diversify in this fashion. It widened a company's exposure without saturating a market. It also allowed for individual producers to develop acts and "sounds" on satellites, which tended to widen the market. (That it made it more difficult to track royalties didn't hurt either.)

"Sh-Boom" became a number one record in L.A. off the exposure it received on Art Laboe's radio record hop. Laboe was one of the first deejays in the country to feature R&B for a general, i.e., white audience. Hill and Range Song Publishers noticed the popularity of "Sh-Boom" and traced its copyright back to Atlantic.

Hill and Range was the brainchild of Julie and Jean Aberbach, two Jewish Viennese World War II immigrants who, while fairly new to the country, were veterans of German music publishing. As they settled in Tin Pan Alley, they quickly realized that the cheapest available music was R&B, a sound that had an energy not so unlike the lusty beer hall music they'd published in Germany before the war. They became interested in "Sh-Boom" because it had the potential for broad crossover, with its fool's paradise of encoded sexual lyrics. They struck upon the idea of redoing the record with one of the majors. To that end, they made an offer to Atlantic, which controlled the publishing of "Sh-Boom," for the right to remake it and share in the publishing revenues generated by whatever sales the new version produced. While "Sh-Boom" had done well in Los Angeles, it was nothing like a national hit. Atlantic Records, figuring the song had run its course, sold 50 percent of "Sh-Boom" 's copyright to Hill and Range for six thousand dollars.

Hill and Range immediately took the song to Mercury and struck a deal for a "cover" version to be recorded by the Crew-Cuts. The collegiate-image Crew-Cuts were a salaried group signed to Mercury. As such, they received a couple of hundred dollars for their "covers" of the Penguins' "Earth Angel," Nappy Brown's "Don't Be Angry," the Charms' "Gumdrops," and the Chords' "Sh-boom," which, weeks after its Mercury release, shot to the top of the pop charts, the first legitimate "white" R&B hit.

Mercury Records had given Hill and Range half the six thousand dollars needed to purchase the publishing rights to "Sh-Boom" from Atlantic. However, it soon became clear in the industry that it really wasn't necessary to invest in the usually murky copyrights that may or may not have existed on R&B material. Often a song was copyrighted by an indie company in its own name after it was recorded. The singer/songwriter was completely cut out. In most instances, the name on the record was enough to establish legal ownership of the copyright. Even if a legitimate copyright did exist, a record could still be worth a fortune to a company making a successful cover, as it was (and still is) perfectly legal to copy, or "cover" the arrangement of any recording.

"Sh-Boom" ushered in the era of white covers and helped establish the careers of white cover artists like Bill Haley (Joe Turner—"Shake, Rattle and Roll"), Georgia Gibbs (LaVern Baker—"Jim Dandy"), Pat Boone (Little Richard—"Tutti Frutti"), Ricky Nelson (Fats Domino—"I'm Walking"), and later on the Beatles and the Rolling Stones (numerous covers by Chuck Berry, Little Richard, Robert Johnson, Solomon Burke, Smokey Robinson). More often than not, white publishers owned the independent labels that controlled the original versions. They shopped the songs to the majors, hoping to score a large enough advance to take the money and run, in some cases selling their entire publishing backlog as part of the deal. Having sold their company they were free to open up the next day around the corner, start signing up new talent and begin the process all over again. The very same group of publishing hustlers who helped break authentic R&B onto the pop charts were also the first to sell it out to the majors. They simply had no interest in whatever social significance the music, by its very presence, might have offered. The only thing that mattered was the money they could make from it, and many of them made fortunes.

As did organized crime. Mob control of the jukebox industry played a significant role in breaking R&B north of the Mason-Dixon line. The Anastasia-controlled faction of the New York City Five Families moved into jukeboxes shortly after World War II, establishing territorial control, as well as what songs went in to which jukeboxes. The mob initiated the notorious red-nickel practice, whereby businesses that took mob jukeboxes had to show a certain amount of coin play per unit, or make up the difference monthly. Proprietors were forced to purchase so many indelibly red-striped coins to use whenever giving change for the jukebox. The red coins were then recycled and exchanged at a mob-favored discount, with the proprietor in effect giving the organization a double-cut of the action.

The mob kept its own "charts," constantly shuffling boxes so popular titles got the most exposure. It didn't matter what label the record was on, who was singing, or what color he or she was. If an R&B or a country song was big in one region, it was shipped to another. Eventually, the most popular R&B records made their way to the neighborhood soda shops up north, frequented by America's newly affluent teens.

In 1957, the FBI identified five members of New York's Anastasia family as having "substantial involvement" in illegal jukebox operations, with connections that stretched all the way to Chicago's Sam Giancana. It was around this time that Wurlitzer, the largest manufacturer of jukeboxes at a time when the industry was grossing nearly a quarter billion dollars a year, decided it had had enough. Competition with other companies was one thing, muscle from the mob another. Rather than taking on organized crime, Wurlitzer picked up its marbles and got out of the jukebox business.

As popular as the jukes were, radio had one thing they didn't: the human touch, the voice of big daddy. In a decade whose youthful heroes were reflected in the tilted torsos of Marlon Brando and James Dean forever in search of father figures, a metaphor for teenagers whose fathers had been taken away first by World War II and then Korea, one paternal deejay from the Midwest emerged to play pied piper to a generation more than ready to fall in line behind his very big beat.

Alan Freed was born in 1926 to immigrant parents newly settled in Johnstown, Pennsylvania. His musical interests were cultivated in high school, where he played in the school orchestra and organized his own band, the Sultans of Swing. He began his professional broadcasting career at the age of twenty. For seventeen dollars a week he played classical music and swept the floors at WKST in New Castle. His next job was at WAKB, in Akron, Ohio, playing pop hits.

There, a local department store, looking to boost its sales of record players, sponsored an Alan Freed "Request Review" program. That show proved so successful that Freed took it to Cleveland, his first major market. Once established, he planned to bring the concept to television, as the first "tee-jay." Before long, he got a chance to do just that on Cleveland's WXEL-TV. However, the show bombed, and Freed, under contract and therefore unable to work for any other radio or TV station, was forced to accept the job as host for the late movie. Lance Freed, Alan's son, recalled that period of time in his father's life: "We lived in a part of town called Shaker Heights, and there was a place where the road split around a little island with some trees and a little gully. One night, after the late show, my father fell asleep at the wheel and went right into one of those trees. It was a pretty bad accident; bad enough that my father was in the hospital for six months. Not only was he severely lacerated all over his body, but he had a ruptured liver, ruptured spleen, internal bleeding, the kind of injuries most people just don't survive. I'm not sure he ever fully recovered from the effects of that accident. I'm not saying he never had a drink after that—my father was a man who lived his own life and did pretty much what he wanted to do—but the doctors told him that the way his liver had healed, with all the scar tissue and such, that even a single drink could be very serious. But he did drink, and he probably shouldn't have, although as a child I just don't remember him ever being drunk. His liver just couldn't tolerate it."

By June of 1951, with his health somewhat restored and his contractual obligations worked out, Freed was back on Cleveland radio, once again playing classical music. This time his sponsorship was a record store, which wanted Freed to play

R&B records and increase their surprisingly strong sales. Freed resisted, not wanting anything more to do with pop, until he visited the store to see for himself what all the excitement was about. There, he witnessed firsthand the phenomenon of dozens of black R&B records being bought mostly by white teenagers.

A week later, he convinced his station manager to let him add a second program to the schedule. Following his classical show, he hosted a show devoted exclusively to R&B.

While generally credited with introducing the phrase "rock and roll," Freed certainly wasn't the first to play R&B on the radio. Art Leboe had done it at least five years earlier in Los Angeles. There, the heavily Hispanic population made his show number one in its time slot. Among the dozens of others calling their radio shows "rock and roll parties" were Dewey Phillips in Memphis, Gene Nobles and John Richbourgh in Nashville, "Daddy" Sears in Atlanta, and "Jack the Cat" Elliott in New Orleans.

What Freed was first at was playing "race" records for a major-market white teenage audience. His success, combined with the racism of the times, caused a backlash in the broadcasting industry. Rumors began to spread among other deejays that Freed was a lightskin black who could pass, a rumor that gained credibility through Freed's sonorous voice (partially the result of polyps), kinky hair and broad nose. Another attack throughout his career was that he was Jewish (he was one quarter Jewish on his father's side), a thinly veiled slur suggesting he was conspiring with the independent labels largely controlled by eastern European immigrants.

Either undaunted or unaware of the industry hostilities toward him, Freed started his own record label and christened it "Champagne Records." The first act he signed called themselves the Crazy Sounds, a name he changed to the Moonglows. Like many who began their own label, Freed either penned songs for the group or took co-credit for writing he did not do. Composing and publishing, as always, were where the money was.

Dave Freed, Alan's brother, had a small distribution company, Lance Distribution, which specialized mostly in R&B,
and eagerly took on Champagne. George Goldner first heard
of Alan Freed through Dave Freed.

Goldner was the founder of Rama Records. The New York–
based independent specialized in selling records by Tito
Puente and Joe Cuba to the Puerto Rican population of the
barrio. Goldner, an original, was a street kid and among the
first to recognize the commercial potential of doo-wop, hearing in its glorious harmonies the sense of freedom it gave to
teenage boys doing four-part under the corner streetlight.
Goldner began to record doo-wop and quickly gained a reputation for his ability to promote these records. This reputation attracted promoter Morris Levy, known and feared in the
industry for his long-time involvement in music and organized crime.

Levy began his career in the music business allegedly handling jukeboxes for the Genovese family in the forties, before
running Birdland, the famed New York City jazz club, with his
brother, who was gunned down there by purported gangland
rivals who mistook him for Morris. Levy became Goldner's
partner after attempting a takeover of Rama Records. According to those familiar with the incident, Levy tried muscle on
Goldner before actually buying in when Goldner refused to
be intimidated, a quality Levy admired.

The stories surrounding the Morris Levy legend are endless. They are also endlessly revealing as to the nature of the
man and the business of rock and roll in which he was, and
is, so much a part. Levy's attitude toward talent is best
summed up by what he used to tell his acts when they'd come
looking for their royalty checks, which he was notoriously late
in paying, if he paid them at all. "Royalty? You want royalty,
go to England!"

In 1965, both Goldner and Levy were after Tommy James

(and the Shondells) to sign with Roulette, after hearing James's version of "Hanky Panky," on James's own label. Goldner offered James $10,000 plus 5 percent of the gross, and firmed the deal with a handshake. A little later, Goldner received a phone call from Levy, eager to tell Goldner about the hot young act he'd signed, for only $5,000—Tommy James. "I offered him ten," Goldner said, to which Levy replied, "Yeah, but I gave him eighteen points!" When Goldner asked how he could give that much, Levy laughed and said, "What difference does it make, I'm not going to pay him anyway!"

There are stories about George Goldner as well. One of the most colorful and in its way indicative of the state of record promotion in the early fifties tells of his style of record promotion at a big deejay convention in Cleveland. Goldner hired hookers to service the deejays. He had the girls arrive a day early, to sit them down and go over his new releases with them. The idea was for the girls to whisper the names of those records in the jock's ear while they were making love.

Goldner decided he wanted to meet Alan Freed after he'd made headlines with his first live R&B show, putting Freed and R&B on the front page of every newspaper in America. The 10,000-seat Cleveland arena Freed rented to showcase his Moonglows, among other R&B acts, sold out in one day. Freed, sensing a financial killing, permitted the overselling of the arena to the tune of 18,000 tickets. It was the inability of some of the audience to gain entrance, and not the music, that caused the first rock and roll "riot." The night ended with Freed being arrested for deliberately overselling the house. The charges were later dropped, but the incident earned Freed a national reputation.

An impressed Goldner contacted Freed and brought him to New York. Gee Records (later Gone/End) was created especially for Freed to "produce" the Dubs, the Flamingos, and Little Anthony and the Imperials. While Goldner and Freed hit it off well from the start, both socially and in business, Levy didn't trust the new member of the team—he never trusted anyone or anything he didn't or couldn't buy—and searched for a way to gain control. It didn't take him long to notice that Freed liked the occasional drink, or its effect. Levy reportedly kept an underling assigned to Freed at all times, to see to it that Freed always had a few before business meetings, presumably to make him easier to manipulate. It wasn't long before Freed had sold his interest in Gee Records to Levy.

Levy eventually gained total control of all Goldner's labels and masters. He liked to brag that Goldner was a compulsive gambler, and sold everything he had in order to play the horses, a bankroll Levy was more than willing to put up, in exchange for Goldner's record holdings.

Producing was understood between Goldner and Freed to mean that Freed's name appeared on anything he helped to promote. Already hip to the profit structure of popular music publishing from his Moonglow days, this was business as usual to Freed.

There was no shortage of "talent" looking to make records. Doo-wop singing was so popular that any group of kids who could do it at all were good enough to get a recording contract.

Frankie Lymon and the Teenagers, discovered singing on a corner under a lamppost, were brought to George Goldner by Richard Barrett. Goldner recognized their talent immediately and guided them through the recording of some of the greatest doo-wop sides of all time.

More often, talent was "discovered" when a studio was booked for a day and open auditions were held. As a rule, every group that walked through the door was signed and recorded, sometimes receiving as much as twenty dollars, other times nothing. To the kids, having a song on the radio was their only goal. Most of the time all they got out of it was the street glory and the best girls on the block.

Johnny Maestro, originally the lead singer of the Crests and later the Brooklyn Bridge, recalled recently what it was like to make a record in the fifties: "The Crests signed their very first

recording contract in 1957 with Joyce Records, and I'm proud
to say that I'm one of the few artists who did receive royalties.
I still have the check at home. Seventeen dollars and fifty
cents, for our recording of 'My Juanita.' "

By 1953, after only a few months in Manhattan, Alan Freed
was broadcasting on New York radio. His nightly "Rock and
Roll Party" on WINS was so popular that his salary rose
within two years from a base of $15,000 (plus 25 percent of
the advertising revenues from his show) to an annual income
in excess of $750,000. By 1955, Freed was starring in a series
of cheaply made rock and roll movies made for a couple of
hundred thousand dollars that never failed to gross in the
millions. They usually played between the live rock and roll
shows that Freed hosted two, sometimes three times a year.

Alan Freed's New York stage shows gave many teenagers
their first look at the faces that belonged to the voices they
listened to on the radio every night. The Easter 1957 show at
the Paramount theater, Freed's fifth, broke all existing house
records, including Sinatra's. The stomping and shouting by
the opening day audience was so forceful that the theater's
management feared the building might collapse. The show
was halted and the second balcony cleared, so city building
inspectors could check the structural support system.

The February 23, 1957 *New York Times* treated the opening-
day pandemonium outside the theater as a major news event.
A front-page story headlined "Rock 'n' Roll Teen-Agers Tie
Up the Times Square Area" detailed the eighteen and a half
hours thousands of teens stayed on line, in the hopes of
getting in to see the show. The record-breaking opening day
take was $29,000. Freed was quoted backstage in a remark-
ably concise summation of the phenomenon: "Rock and roll
began on the levees and plantations, took in folk songs, and
features blues and rhythm. It's the rhythm that gets the kids.
They are starved for music they can dance to after all those
years of crooners."

No less than a half-dozen articles inside the paper chronicled the various aspects of the new "craze." One highlighted the new dress of the rocking teen, noting that blue jeans and leather jackets were now the "in" clothes. Another noted that American rock and roll had spread all over the world, even to Leningrad, where Elvis Presley records were reportedly being bootlegged on X-ray plates and selling for $12.50 a copy.

The *Times* interviewed several psychologists on the subject. One educational psychologist was quoted as saying that what happened outside the Paramount theater on opening day was "very much like the medieval type of spontaneous lunacy where one person goes off and lots of other persons go off with him." Another "noted" psychologist drew a parallel between rock and roll and Saint Vitus' dance disease.

However, the most intriguing article to appear that day in the *Times* had to do with the financial bonanza that rock and roll had produced. Record companies such as RCA, Elvis's label, were reported to be operating twenty-four hours a day in order to fill all the outstanding requests for rock records. Seventy thousand pairs of jeans had been sold in the metropolitan area in the weeks before the opening of the Easter show. Coca-Cola and Schaefer beer were considering using rock and roll to sell their products. The Ralston-Purina Company had already commissioned an "original" rock song to sell its cereal products:

> Who-ho-ho-ho
> Rock that rock
> And roll that roll
> Get that Ralston in the bowl

The Christmas '57 show broke all previous box-office records with an opening day take of $32,000. Over the twelve-day Christmas holiday, Freed's show grossed over $300,000. Most of the acts were paid scale, and none ever complained. An appearance in an Alan Freed show guaranteed a hit record. The bulk of the profits went directly to Freed, Levy, Goldner, and WINS radio.

To Freed, it was only the beginning. In his immediate future he saw national television, bigger films, books, records, merchandising deals and whatever anyone could think up to cash in on. Nothing, it seemed, could stop him now.

Perhaps it was his unbroken run of successes that blinded him to what was happening in the rest of the record industry. As early as 1955, Freed's most profitable year, the dark clouds that would eventually block his place in the sun had already begun to form. Rock and roll radio was shifting away from original R&B, in favor of the white covers produced by the majors. Country/western, lost in the first wave of R&B's dive into the mainstream, now sounded a viable alternative to the "black-black" sound of what those in the business referred to as R&B.

The top ten records of 1955, in descending order from ten to two were Nat "King" Cole's "A Blossom Fell," Gale Storm's "I Hear You Knocking," the Four Lads' "Moments to Remember," Pat Boone's "Ain't That a Shame," Frank Sinatra's "Learnin' the Blues," Roger Williams's "Autumn Leaves," Mitch Miller's "The Yellow Rose of Texas," the Four Aces' "Love Is a Many-Splendored Thing," and Tennessee Ernie Ford's "Sixteen Tons." The only legitimate rock and roll song in the top ten happened to be the top-selling single of the year, Bill Haley's country/western–flavored Decca release, "Rock Around the Clock." "Clock" spent thirty-eight weeks on the *Billboard* top 100 chart, twenty-five of those in the top ten, eight of those at number one. Of the remaining top ten, two records, those by Gale Storm and Pat Boone, were covers, three were movie themes, and Tennessee Ernie Ford's "Sixteen Tons" was considered part of the new C&W wave. Nat "King" Cole was one of the very few authentic black performers to make the national charts, along with Al Hibbler, Sammy Davis, Jr., and Chuck Berry. Forty-two of the top fifty singles were released by the majors: eleven by RCA, eight by Columbia, eight by Capitol, eight by Decca, and seven by Mercury. Certainly not R&B's best year.

But definitely Bill Haley's. "Rock Around the Clock"

spurred back-sales of his previous records, including "Crazy Man Crazy," a minor-league tune except for the fact that it was the first of what was now being called "rockabilly" records to break into the *Billboard* pop 100 chart.

"Rock Around the Clock" had become an iconic fifties street gang anthem via *Blackboard Jungle,* (causing the film to be banned in England for eleven years). It was the first rock song to reach number one on the *Billboard* pop chart and eventually sold 25 million copies, making it the best-selling rock single of all time (the second best-selling pop record, behind Bing Crosby's rendition of Irving Berlin's "White Christmas," which has, to date, sold more than 170 million copies). "Rock Around the Clock" was released twice to lukewarm receptions and moderate sales. Its third release came about because of its last-minute addition to the 1955 film by way of its composer. Sixty-three-year-old Jimmy De Knight was working on the New York location parts of the film and suggested his own song to the producers as an appropriate theme.

The film's Bronx locale marked New York as the capital not only of rock and roll, but of the growing problem of juvenile delinquency. By all logic, the theme song of the film should have been something more R&B or doo-wop in its sound. Haley's spit-curl rockabilly/C&W was about the farthest thing from the Bronx it was possible to get, but very close to a sound the rest of the country was tuned into.

Like Freed, Bill Haley began his career in radio before turning to performing as "the Rambling Yodeler." He changed the name of his first band, the Four Aces of Western Swing, to Bill Haley and His Comets when they began to record on Essex, an independent label that specialized in "white" rhythm and blues, a sound combining the driving beat of urban R&B with C&W lyricism. Haley and the group moved to Decca in 1954 as white cover artists (Big Joe Turner's "Shake, Rattle and Roll") and a year later exploded onto the national scene with "Rock Around the Clock."

In spite of his having appeared in several Alan Freed movies, at the insistence of the film studios, Haley resented Freed's reluctance to play Bill Haley and His Comets records on the radio. Freed refused to play any whites who covered original R&B tunes, including Haley. In response, Haley claimed it was he, not Freed, who was the real king of rock and roll.

In one sense, they were both right. Freed had championed R&B, while Haley had helped popularize rockabilly, and together they'd given rock and roll to America's teens. In another sense, they were both wrong. The year 1955 belonged to them, but only as pretenders to the throne. The real king was about to ride in on the next royal wave.

Six

At the 1955 BMI Awards, sixteen of the twenty-eight songs that had made the most money were R&B, even if some were cover versions. "Sincerely," the original Alan Freed/Moonglows tune, had been a modest hit in its original Champagne Records release but a smash when the McGuire Sisters covered it. Chuck Berry had burst onto the scene with "Maybellene" (another Freed "co-authored" tune, with Berry to this day angry about Freed's forcing him to share credit and income) and Little Richard had made his debut with "Rip It Up," both BMI-licensed smashes.

As early as 1953, ASCAP resistance to R&B had polarized the music industry. Three of ASCAP's most prestigious members—Alan Jay Lerner, Ira Gershwin and Paul Cunningham—decided to "get" BMI (Bad Music Incorporated, as ASCAPers liked to refer to the rival licensing organization in private). As official representatives of ASCAP, they filed a $150 million anti-trust action against BMI, accusing it of conspiracy to dominate the market.

It was highly ironic that ASCAP, which for years had considered itself the industry watchdog, employing restrictive covenants and highly selective membership requirements to ensure the "quality standards" of its elitist organization, now accused BMI of doing exactly the same thing.

The lawsuit dragged on for years, with considerable industry support. Frank Sinatra sent a support telegram to ASCAP in 1956, recalling a dispute he'd had with Mitch Miller when he, Sinatra, was at Columbia. Sinatra's telegram implied he'd left the label after being forced to record inferior BMI tunes instead of more commercial ASCAP songs, the reason for the poor sales of his last albums. Miller, certainly no friend of BMI, nevertheless ordered CBS's lawyers to investigate every recording made at Columbia during his tenure.

The results revealed that 95 percent of all the songs Mitch Miller had committed to record were licensed by ASCAP. Moreover, the overwhelming majority of songs that Sinatra had recorded for the label were ASCAP. Two that BMI licensed happened to be published by Sinatra's own company.

As the lawsuit dragged on, ASCAP's powerful Washington lobby successfully prodded Congress to launch a full-scale investigation into BMI's business activities. This investigation lasted nearly two years, with the focus eventually narrowed once more to the original question of BMI's ownership. ASCAP's position was that radio stations had a vested interest in playing BMI music, since they were, in effect, the principals of the organization. Further, ASCAP suggested that the rise of what was now being called rock and roll had come about as a result of the music having been forced upon the public by station owners for the sake of making huge profits.

The station owners' position was simple. Yes, they owned stock in BMI, but the organization had yet to pay a single cent in dividends. Further, they insisted, radio, particularly top 40, was based on *Billboard*'s and similar publications' charts, making what they played the reflection of the popular musical taste of the day.

The hostilities continued, even as popular taste underwent a drastic change under the guidance of one Southern colonel about to invade the North.

Oscar Davis first heard of Elvis Presley in 1954, a year after Hank Williams's death. Davis had been working at Memphis radio station WMPS in October 1954, when he heard a new record on the "Bob Neal Show." Neal, in addition to being one of the most powerful and influential jocks in Memphis, did the audience warm-up at the Grand Ole Opry and owned a thriving country music record store in the heart of Memphis, so there was little that passed the scene without his knowing about it. Presley had made some noise on the Opry's chief competitor, the Louisiana Hayride, which was where Neal had first heard him.

Presley's first recordings were made at Sam Phillip Sun Records studio in Memphis. Initially Elvis wandered in to make a private recording, but after several weeks rehearsal his trio came up with a revolutionary arrangement of an old blues song called 'That's All Right' which launched him on to the "Hayride" broadcast.

Still, it was standard operating procedure for Sam Phillips to sign all his acts to at least a publishing agreement, if not full personal management contracts. Knowing that, Neal contacted Presley to find out the terms of his deal. Presley had a recording agreement with Phillips, but no management deal, and quickly signed a one-year contract with the popular deejay. Neal would receive 15 percent of personal appearance fees and 15 percent of the performer's share of recording royalties.

Neal soon discovered something about Elvis that wasn't immediately apparent on his records. No matter where the young singer performed, girls went crazy for him. Figuring that the best way to "sell" Elvis was to let audiences see him, Neal booked Elvis into over one hundred shows, two a week for a solid year, and used his radio program to hype the appearances every chance he got.

Left out of all this was Oscar Davis, who lamented about his latest loss to the "Colonel." A carny pal, the Colonel's name was Tom Parker, but he was born Andreas Cornelis Van Kuijk, in Holland, to Dutch parents. It's believed that as a teenager "Parker" illegally emigrated to the USA and joined the Southern carnival circuit. It was there he first heard "hillbilly" music. By 1948 he had developed into a successful enough promoter to be awarded the honorary title of colonel by the governor of Louisiana, Jimmy Davis, himself a one-time country singer.

After commiserating with his carny pal, Parker decided to check the kid out for himself, to see if he really was as good as Neal thought he was. Calling in one of his markers, the Colonel sent Jimmy Rodgers Snow, the son of the legendary Hank Snow and a country singer in his own right, to check out one of Elvis's live shows. Snow did, and raved about Presley to the Colonel. A short time later, Parker signed a deal with Neal to have Presley as the opening act for a state tour the Colonel had booked starring Bill Haley and His Comets.

Parker personally joined the tour in order to observe Presley's relationship with Neal. The Colonel treated Neal harshly, hoping it was obvious to Elvis that his current manager wasn't strong enough to handle it. At the same time, he lavished Elvis with cash, clothes and carny-blarney the likes of which the young singer had never seen.

The Colonel obtained a copy of Neal's contract with Elvis by calling in another marker. Studying it, Parker saw that the agreement was only for personal services, independent of Sam Phillips's recording deal. The Colonel decided to take Neal into his "confidence," telling him that he'd gotten word that Elvis's recording contract with Phillips was about to be purchased by a major record label. Neal laughed and told the Colonel exactly what he needed to know, that offers for Elvis's recording contracts came in every day. Decca had already offered Phillips $5,000. Dot Records, the upstart independent whose unorthodox distribution methods forced the majors to change theirs, offered $7,500.* Atlantic had offered $25,000. Even Columbia had made inquiries into Elvis.

All of which made the Colonel shrug and announce he could get $50,000 for Elvis's contract. Neal stopped laughing.

The Colonel wasn't shooting blanks. Before making his move with Neal, he'd made a deal with Hill and Range. The

---

*Dot, formed in 1950 by Randy Wood, offered records with a 100 percent return for unsolds, which became the new industry standard.

Colonel would deliver Elvis, for a piece of every song of theirs he recorded. Although the rest of Tin Pan Alley considered it a maverick house run by immigrants, Parker thought it the perfect publishing house for Elvis. In the early fifties, Aberbach had personally gone to Nashville to meet with record producer Owen Bradley, who worked with many of the top country acts, for advice about signing acts. The result of those meetings was a series of publishing deals between Hill and Range and many of the top country acts, including Johnny Cash and Lefty Frizzell. Aberbach offered them a piece of whatever original music the company published, or a piece of whatever songs the performers recorded already controlled by Hill and Range. When the Colonel approached Hill and Range about getting a deal for Elvis, Aberbach jumped at it, giving the Colonel something to bring to Elvis, something Parker kept under his hat until he felt the time was right to make his move.

That time came on August 15, 1955, when the Colonel persuaded Neal to sign over management rights to Elvis for the guaranteed annual sum of $2,500, plus attendance bonuses. He pointed out to Neal how much more money Elvis would bring in personal appearances signed to a major, at this point probably RCA. Further, Parker assured Neal that no matter what, his cut would always be there, without his having to do a lick of work for it. "Just leave everything to me," was the Colonel's snake-oil soothant. It was enough to convince Neal to surrender Presley's contract to the Colonel without getting anything up front.

Elvis, impressed with Parker, eagerly signed a new contract that gave the Colonel 25 percent of all earnings for an initial ten-year period, renewable by mutual consent in 1967, at which time the Colonel's commission automatically doubled to a full 50 percent. (Another 10 percent went to the William Morris Agency for their involvement in film negotiations.)

Having signed Presley, the Colonel now set about to place him with one of the majors. Steve Sholes of RCA had heard about Presley and was interested. Sun's release of "Baby Let's

Play House" had made it to number ten on the *Billboard* country and western chart, and Sholes was ready to deal.

He offered Sam Phillips $20,000 for Elvis's contract and Sun recordings. A $5,000 cash bonus would be split 75–25 between Elvis and his new personal manager. An additional $15,000 was put up by Hill and Range, for RCA, in return for 50 percent of anything Elvis recorded that they published. The net result was RCA's cash layout reduced to $10,000, making Elvis a very cheap, and therefore safe risk. Out of all of this, Elvis's personal take was about $3,000 in cash and a Cadillac convertible, a "bonus" from RCA.

The Colonel saw to it that Hill and Range formed two separate publishing companies for Elvis. Presley Music (BMI) and Gladys Music (ASCAP) ensured that no matter what the outcome of the on-again, off-again licensing wars, Elvis would be protected. As previously agreed, Hill and Range arranged to have Elvis's name added to the writing credits of any songs that he recorded in return for his "exclusive" right to the material. As a kicker to the deal, for managing the two Elvis subsidiaries, Hill and Range received 50 percent of Presley Music/Gladys Music earnings.

With this kind of incentive, Hill and Range immediately went to work creating a pool of Elvis "writers." Six salaried pros were hired, among them the songwriting team of Jerry Leiber and Mike Stoller, a California duo whose earlier hits included "Black Denim Trousers (And Motorcycle Boots)," and "Smokey Joe's Cafe," the springboard for their own independent label, Spark Records. One of their early R&B tunes for Atlantic, "Hound Dog" had already been covered by Elvis.

Also brought on board was Ben Weisman, a Brooklyn boy who began his musical career as a classical pianist. As part of the personal songwriting tutelage of Irving Berlin, he was introduced to Aberbach. Hill and Range was looking to expand its interests into country music and needed writers not only able but willing to write "hillbilly." According to Weisman, "Aberbach wanted me to write country songs. 'Gee,' I said, 'I'm a Brooklyn boy, what do I know about country songs?' He held up a check in his hand and said, 'You see this, Weisman? You're writing country!' I first met the Colonel when I wrote a Hill and Range song for Eddy Arnold, 'Mills of the Gods,' and that led to my getting onto the writing team for Elvis.''

Elvis' singing style was derived from the white Italian middle-class singers who dominated radio and records in the late forties and early fifties. Often, he'd do impersonations of Frank Sinatra and Dean Martin for his friends. He was also influenced by Johnnie Ray, a pop sensation in the early fifties, whose one-knee style of crooning soon became a part of the standard Presley presentation. Hill and Range's pool of writers were instructed to create music that would appeal to a wider pop audience, rather than strictly country or rockabilly. Nowhere, however, was there any obvious R&B influence or direction in Elvis's career. Whenever he was asked about how he developed his singing style, he was always careful to avoid any mention of black music, a position whose significance was not lost on those in the industry taking a very close look at rock and roll.

In fact, Elvis's association with "race" music stemmed from the famous remark by Sam Phillips that if he could find a white singer who could sing like a black man, he, Phillips, could make "a billion dollars."* That Elvis's first recordings were mostly covers of "race" music was more the result of those he played with in the studio than anything else, as his own musical knowledge was limited. The shift in Elvis' singing style and choice of material came about after his deals with Hill and Range and RCA.

Ironically, Presley's shift of musical style and ASCAP affiliation were what saved him from the coming payola scandals. In spite of the occasional outrage expressed against Elvis by

*Phillips's best shot at the big time was Elvis, whose contract he sold in a minute, an action that says more about his ability to define talent than anything he ever said or did. As for his being the forerunner of modern rock, the sign that hung outside his storefront recording studio in the fifties said it all: "We Record Anything—Anywhere—Anytime."

parents, columnists and evangelicals, Elvis was seen by industry heavies, particularly those affiliated with ASCAP, as the Mickey Mantle of pop, the Great White Hope of the fifties. As early as 1957, ASCAP venerables such as Bing Crosby, who privately expressed annoyance at the latest "new thing," were prevailed upon to give Elvis the official endorsement needed to bring him into the mainstream. Crosby, ever the good soldier, did so, making it easier for Sinatra, who'd been among the most vocal in his revulsion at Presley's gyrations, to be the official TV greeter of Elvis upon his return from military duty. In a time when the music industry came under its heaviest attack from the government, when payola became a household word and the lives and careers of rock and roll performers were destroyed, Elvis Presley's name was never brought up, his business practices never questioned, his finances never examined. Presley remained safe from the 1959 ASCAP-led industry purge, even though it was no secret that his deal with Hill and Range was based on the very same publishing-sharing concept that became one of the original definitions of payola.

In 1956, his first year in the Bigs, Elvis Presley sold 10 million singles, still the largest sale ever by any performer in a one-year period. His various hit singles dominated *Billboard*'s pop charts at number one for more than twenty-five weeks. In the first three months he was with RCA, he was selling 75,000 records *a day*, accounting for half of RCA's total sales. From the sale of these recordings alone, Presley and the Colonel earned over a million dollars. Their share of airplay and performance royalties earned them even more. "Don't Be Cruel" alone sold more than 6 million copies while on the charts, and "Love Me Tender" was the first record to ever go gold before selling a single copy, thanks to a guaranteed one million copy advance sale. "Heartbreak Hotel," recorded in '56, sold 38 million copies the first five years it was released, resulting in thirty-eight "gold records" (the industry issue to the artist, publisher and producer for one million units of sale of a single). In his first ten years at RCA, Elvis

Presley records sold over 115 million units. Eventually, Presley's sales figures approached a billion units, more than double those of the previous record holder, Bing Crosby.

Wasting no time, the Colonel quickly signed a marketing deal with Special Projects, Inc., of Beverly Hills, a special subsidiary of H. G. Saperstein and Associates, for the purpose of merchandising the Presley name and logo. Eighteen separate licenses were granted, leading to the creation of lines of clothing, costume jewelry, sodas, guitars, greeting cards, stuffed pillows and hound dogs, teddy bears, and hundreds of photos, books and magazines, with a first year's total gross of more than $55 million, more than twice Saperstein's original estimate.

That same year Elvis received $100,000 to star in *Love Me Tender,* a film which made back its million-dollar negative cost in three weeks. The Colonel jacked Elvis's new personal appearance fee to $20,000 for as little as three songs.

He also made sure that no one got too close to his living gold mine. Not that Parker was afraid of competition. He'd already proven himself irreplaceable to Elvis. What the Colonel feared was someone discovering that Presley's swaggering persona had little to do with how the boy acted in real life.

For just as with Jolson, Crosby and Sinatra before him, Elvis was transfixed on the maternal. He was a mama's boy, possessing those peculiar qualities shared by the century's biggest pop stars, which somehow translated into a personal appeal that cut across gender, age, economics and class. With Elvis, it made real mothers want to smother him and teenage girls want to mother him. It also allowed teenage boys to like him, instinctively knowing that Elvis was no threat to take away their girlfriends. The flip side of Elvis's momism was his lifelong dependence on the Colonel, something Parker may have picked up on. Parker was in for the long haul, and to that end he shrewdly concealed Elvis's dark side while guiding his career toward the mainstream.

Parker's canny ability for self-preservation was nothing if

not focused and perceptive, the very opposite of Alan Freed's impulsive, lurching, track-jumping career. Freed's rock and roll shows may have shaken the foundations of the theaters they played in, but it was the Colonel who finally brought the house down.

Seven

In 1958, America's nineteen million teenagers spent nearly nine million dollars a year on themselves, and a lot of that on rock and roll. BMI was now referred to in the industry as Big Money Incorporated, a state of affairs that so outraged ASCAP it used its Washington connections to help instigate a congressional investigation into the financial practices of the rival organization. However, the most that Emanuel Cellar's Antitrust Subcommittee of the House Judiciary was able to come up with was the introduction of a bill designed to limit the amount of BMI stock broadcasters could own.

Some of the industry's most loyal holdouts added rock to their rosters. Columbia's Mitch Miller broke his public vow never to record a rock and roll record by signing Dion to a multiple-album contract. Miller dropped the Belmonts from the act and ordered a slate of pop tunes for Dion's first album. His objective was to mold Dion into the next Sinatra.

Things seemed better than ever for Alan Freed, whose Christmas '58 show proved to be another record breaker, with $300,000 grossed over a ten-day run. As the new year began, Freed planned to open a string of rock and roll nightclubs as venues for mini-versions of his big theater rock shows.

His plans failed to materialize. As ever, Freed did not see the implications of his actions. The previous May, an incident had occurred at one of his rock and roll shows that activated the series of events which led to his professional downfall.

Freed had begun to export his shows to major cities in the northeast. An incident at the Boston show seemed to release all the destructive elements that rock and roll was thought to inspire: riot, anarchy, drinking and sex. It began when Freed supposedly announced to his audience, in response to an unusually heavy number of police covering the event at the direct request of the Catholic Archdiocese, that "the cops don't want you to have a good time!" The alleged comment resulted in Freed's arrest for inciting the ensuing riot.

According to Lance Freed, Alan's son, the facts of the Boston "riot" are not what they've always been reported to be: "My father was definitely a victim, in the sense that he was set up; there's just no question anymore about that. He was seen by many at ASCAP as the leader of the movement that made BMI a viable organization. ASCAP was certainly one of the organizations effective in convincing people there should be some investigation into how those 'nigger music' records could get to be hits. FBI documents and memoranda we've gotten our hands on, is pretty disturbing stuff . . . suggesting there was communication between the Archdiocese and the FBI, on the order of 'We can get him there . . .' Who knows how they became involved, or why."

An organized conspiracy to "get" Alan Freed wouldn't have met much industry resistance. As popular as he was with teenagers, Freed was disliked within the record industry because of his refusal to play records he considered "unfaithful" to rock and roll. Some felt he restricted his playlist because it was more profitable for him to push records in which he had a financial interest, in either the publishing of the music or the personal management of the group.

In March 1958, two months before the Boston incident, Mitch Miller addressed a convention of "top 40" disk jockeys and used the occasion to lament the demise of creative radio programming, accusing deejays of playing to an audience of eight- to fourteen-year-olds.

Freed took the attack personally and went public with his

reply. In an interview in *Billboard,* Freed called Miller's attack "sour grapes" and declared his intention to ban all Columbia records from his show. Columbia Records had little to lose by Freed's threat. Mitch Miller told associates he was so sure rock and roll was a passing fad, that if it showed any signs of lasting he'd kill himself. Still, the gauntlet had been thrown. Freed had taken on a powerful adversary. Miller, one of the most well liked executives in the record business, also had strong connections to ASCAP.

Miller began his career as music director of Mercury Records, where he "discovered" Vic Damone, Patti Page and Frankie Laine. He moved to Columbia in 1950, after the label's annual gross slipped to fourth place among the majors in the wake of Sinatra's release. His job was to restore Columbia to the top of the corporate heap.

He accomplished that goal in two years. Columbia's sales had increased 60 percent by 1952, and the label was once more the recognized leader. Miller had significantly realigned the label's priorities, beginning with the dissolution of its newly formed R&B division.* He was adamant about his feelings for rhythm and blues, often referring to it as "musical illiteracy," and coining the term *leerics* to describe the sexual content of its songs. Throughout the fifties, Mitch Miller became ASCAP's unofficial spokesman in condemning rock and roll, a position that increased his prestige and power in the music industry.

Alan Freed's public avowal to ban Columbia records from his show proved to be an empty threat. WINS, the radio

*Columbia had recorded Duke Ellington and Bessie Smith, primarily through the efforts of John Hammond. However, these recordings were considered archival, intended for a limited audience. Hammond continually fought to bring the more indigenous sounds of American music to Columbia, whose executives much preferred the more central, commercial sounds of the popular mainstream. Hammond's career at Columbia was overshadowed in the fifties by the arrival of Mitch Miller, and once again in the sixties with the emergence of Miller's successor, Clive Davis. Although responsible for the signing of many of Columbia's biggest recording stars—Benny Goodman, Duke Ellington, Bob Dylan, Aretha Franklin, Bruce Springsteen—Hammond never received the full in-house recognition he deserved and was considered by many to be the "company flake," whose fingers were anywhere but on the pulse of commercial American popular music.

station he worked for, absolutely refused to allow any such practice, having no desire to make enemies with Columbia's powerful leader.

Although it shouldn't have, the radio station's failure to back him took Freed by surprise. Then, two months later, after news of his arrest in Boston hit the front pages, he was called into the office of the president of WINS and told that his services were no longer required.

When the end came, Freed was, according to someone at the station the day the firing took place, "struck dumb for one of the very few times in his life." Especially since his contract with the station gave it 25 percent of whatever his stage shows earned, a deal that had put a half-million-dollar profit into the station's coffers. Far from being fired, Freed had counted on the station's paying for his defense. If anything, he considered himself a "goodwill ambassador" for the station. [See Appendix A]

Not exactly the way the station viewed him, as they invoked the morals clause of his contract and banned him from the airwaves. With his contract about to expire and up for renegotiation, WINS may have felt that the time was right to disassociate itself from Freed, who would become one of the prime targets of the industry's worst-kept secret, the coming federal investigation into the practice of payola. Everyone knew something big was about to break and that heads were going to roll. One of the most enthusiastic supporters of that investigation was Mitch Miller, and one of Miller's worst enemies was Alan Freed.

Shortly after Freed's firing, Miller leaked the story to the press that a well-known host of a rock TV show had refused to play a Four Lads record unless publishing rights were shared with him. While the show was not named, it was generally understood in the industry that he was referring to Alan Freed. Freed had joined WABC radio and was also hosting a local TV rock and roll "dance party" on WNEW patterned after the successful Dick Clark "American Bandstand."

Miller continued his public diatribe. He declared in *Bill-*

board that payola was rampant in the industry, and that Columbia Records refused to participate in the illicit practice. Overnight, *payola* became a household word as the infamous pay-for-play scandals of 1959 broke onto the front pages of every newspaper in the country.

Although it was treated in the press as the inevitable result of rock and roll, payola wasn't anything new to the music business, nor had the word been coined by Miller. The term first appeared back in 1916, when *Variety* published a front-page editorial condemning the widespread practice of influence peddling, what it called "direct-payment evil."

Payola had become a fact of industry life, encouraged by Alley publishers as a way to sell music. Drinks, dinners and gifts were regularly given to performers to influence their choice of songs. "Pluggers" regularly rewarded department store salespeople who pushed the right songs when asked by customers what new music to buy for the home piano. As early as 1863, composer Walter Kittredge had given Asa Hutchinson, head of the Hutchinson Singing Family, a share of the royalties of "Tenting Tonight on the Old Camp Ground," for singing the song at the group's very popular concerts. In 1892, composer Charles K. Harris paid J. Aldrich Libby to put "After the Ball" in his musical, *A Trip to Chinatown.* In 1905 alone, Tin Pan Alley paid more than a half million dollars in payola.

Over the years it became a regular practice to secure a name performer's "run-of-the-act" loyalty to certain songs by guaranteeing his exclusive right to it and padding that guarantee with payments of up to $25,000. If the song became a hit, it would sell more than enough sheets to offset the "guarantee" and show a profit. Competition for certain performers' services became intense, so much so that on more than one occasion a publisher found himself the target of violent retaliation from an act that failed to secure a wanted song. On at least one occasion, a song plugger was beaten to death in the back alley of a famous vaudeville theater, the victim of a payola deal that went bad.

In 1916, *Variety* organized the first voluntary organization to curb the practice of this growing blight on the industry. By now, payola was so out of hand that payments outstripped profits. *Variety*'s interests weren't totally altruistic, however. The money which publishers once used to announce new songs in the trades now went to payola. John J. O'Connor, *Variety*'s business manager, realized the link between his paper's diminishing ad revenues and payola and was instrumental in the formation of the Music Publisher's Protective Association. The stated goal of the organization was to put an end to the practice of paying financial tribute to performers.

Almost immediately payola ended, as the vaudeville circuits were informed they were to use music only from member publishers of MPPA, or they wouldn't be allowed to use any music at all. But payola soon resumed, the only difference being the method of payment. What had previously taken place out in the open now occurred behind closed doors. Everyone in the industry knew about it, including the officers of MPPA, who continued to publicly condemn the practice while privately acknowledging there was nothing they could do about it.

In 1934, another organization was formed to combat payola, this time on the airwaves. It had become commonplace for gifts to arrive at radio stations wrapped in lists of songs the bearer of such good fortune wished to have played. At least two instances are on record of ASCAP's direct involvement in payola. During the thirties, Harry Richman and Paul Whiteman both received financial tribute from ASCAP to perform certain songs. In 1938, the Federal Trade Commission notified ASCAP that payola was a form of bribery and therefore unethical. The FCC pressured ASCAP to come out publicly against payola and advise its members to desist from continuing the practice. ASCAP heeded the FCC and advised its membership accordingly, advice that had absolutely no effect.

Also in 1938, the Professional Music Men, a union of song pluggers, was organized to fight payola. Pluggers had complained for years that the practice amounted to unfair competition. The organization formalized a system of penalties for "giving or offering a consideration of any kind for the purpose of inducing anyone to render or to permit the rendition of any musical composition." Unfortunately, the system proved unenforceable.

In 1950, *Billboard* reported that payola to disk jockeys was at an all-time high. A year later, *Variety* reporter Abel Green led off a series of articles detailing payola with the headline "PAYOLA—WORSE THAN EVER."

Despite ASCAP's own history, payola became a new weapon in its ongoing battle with BMI for control of the country's popular music. Behind ASCAP's strong urging, the government began an investigation into payola.

In 1951 under the chairmanship of John S. Wood, Congress launched a major investigation to seek out Communists in the entertainment field. The war in Korea had stirred the fires of America's anticommunist passion, leading to a series of investigations into American film and theatre. However, in practice the targets were less Communists than rebel "independents." Subversive politics became the public "sell," for what was, in reality, a battle over corporate control of the film, music and later TV industries.

The film industry was effectively controlled by seven major studios, each of which produced, distributed and exhibited its own product. Beginning in the late forties, the first effective independent movement in Hollywood organized itself to fight for the right to exhibit in studio-owned theatres. The result was a consent decree that decided the studios were guilty of monopolistic tactics and that forced them to divest of one of the three branches of the film business. Most protested loudly as they shed their movie houses. Independents considered the war over, but within months the first rumblings of communist infiltration echoed through Beverly Hills. To many who took the side of the majors, an attack on Hollywood's way of doing business was an attack on the American way of life. The film industry became polarized into two factions. "Old" Hollywood was made up of the hard-line studio moguls and their star contract players, represented by Screen Actor's Guild President Ronald Reagan; while the "new" Hollywood of independent actors, producers and directors lined up behind the leaders of the Directors Guild and the Writers Guild.

Round one went to the independents, as the 1951 Wood investigations into subversive activities in the motion picture industry failed to establish a single instance in which the Communist party had found vocal expression in any American work of film or theater.

Round two was something else again. In 1953, Congress opened another series of hearings into communist infiltration in the entertainment field. The investigation expanded into the field of musical entertainment. This time heads did roll, as the notorious Hollywood blacklist came into use, making it impossible for many of those who'd previously supported the independent movement to get work at the studios. The timing of this investigation coincided with BMI's rise to prominence in the wake of the postwar boom in independent record production.

Among those called to testify were bandleader Artie Shaw, radio "folk" personality John Henry Faulk, and folksingers Lee Hays and Pete Seeger. Hays and Seeger, along with Ronnie Gilbert and Fred Hellerman, were members of the Weavers, a highly popular folk act whose style recalled the Almanac Singers of the thirties. The Weavers' 1950 Decca recording of "Good Night, Irene" (BMI), a Huddie Leadbetter and John Lomax folk tune, sold a million copies and was followed by "On Top of Old Smokey" (traditional), "So Long, It's Been Good to Know You" (BMI) and "Kisses Sweeter Than Wine" (BMI). By 1952, the group's total record sales exceeded five million units. Yet, as a result of Hays and Seeger's testimony, the Weavers were dropped by Decca Records and effectively blacklisted from recording. This move forestalled the popular acceptance of folk music in America for nearly a decade.

The 1959 payola "scandal" was actually the second tier of

a federal investigation whose initial target was the fixing of television quiz shows as a way of protecting the networks from "upstart" independents.

In the twelve years of its commercial existence, television had come under the control of three major networks who controlled all aspects of what was broadcast over the air. However, in the late fifties, a generation of young, aggressive producers looked to break what they perceived to be the networks' monopolistic hold.

Among those who came under the closest scrutiny during the quiz show scandals were Jack Barry and Dan Enright. Together this pair of producers had built an independent television empire on the strength of their highly successful quiz shows, which included "Twenty-One" and "Tic-Tac-Dough." There was talk that Barry-Enright Inc. planned to start a fourth network or resurrect the defunct Dumont operation. Barry and Enright had structured their corporation in such a way as to prevent any single sponsor or network from being in control of either the content or sale of commercial time.

The investigation focused on the "fixing" of the Barry-Enright series of quiz shows. The most popular of these was "Twenty-One," which combined isolation-booth questions with the gambling tactics of blackjack. Barry and Enright had originally secured the single-sponsorship of the Revlon Corporation for its package of prime-time programs ("The $64,-000 Question," "Tic-Tac-Dough"). The relationship between the sponsor and the producers deteriorated as Revlon pressured Barry-Enright to emphasize the personality rather than the intellectual prowess of their contestants. The producers, looking to break away from Revlon and expand their TV empire, were reluctant to cooperate, until early in 1959 when Revlon threatened to cancel its sponsorship. Almost immediately, Charles Van Doren emerged as the perfect combination-of-ingredients contestant—a certified "intellectual" (the son of famed Columbia professor Mark Van Doren) with the good looks and easygoing manner of a matinee idol. Van Doren defeated a long-running champ Revlon had considered too "unpopular" and went on to a months-long reign as "Twenty-One" 's undefeatable champion. In spite of the show's conspicuous jump in popularity during the Van Doren run, Revlon continued to battle the producers over control of their growing stable of programs.

When Van Doren was called before the congressional committee, he admitted to having been given the answers to questions prior to broadcast. Revlon immediately dropped its sponsorship of all Barry-Enright programs; although the sponsor's involvement with the "fixing" of shows was quite extensive, they were never investigated by the committee and continued to sponsor other programs on network TV.

The two producers didn't fare as well. In a single week, all Barry-Enright product was removed from the network. Overnight, the independent producer became persona non grata in television, a subversive threat to the moral content of programming that entered the American home.

At least one congressman felt the need to put the investigation into some kind of perspective. Oklahoma Democratic Senator A. S. Monroney admitted that the "scandal" had little to do with whether or not contestants were supplied with answers. What was really involved, he insisted, was "the struggle for rating supremacy [leading] to [the] rigging of TV quiz programs." The purging of the independents sent a clear message through the TV industry that the major networks in collaboration with corporate sponsors were firmly in control, and intended to stay that way.

It happened that Barry-Enright owned a couple of top 40 radio stations. It was all ASCAP and the majors needed to link the fixing of quiz shows to the illegal practice of payola. Once and for all they planned to break the back of BMI, rock and roll, and the independent record movement. All that was needed was a dramatic way to break the scandal, something to make the public sit up and take notice. A villain was the key.

Someone to personify everything that was wrong with the music industry. Someone to take the fall from grace.

And so it was that rock and roll's first patriarch, Alan Freed, entered the unredeemable hell of professional extinction.

Eight

By early 1960, the payola scandal's reverberations echoed through the halls of the White House. President Eisenhower, sensing some great political, if not moral deficit in the revelations concerning pay-for-play in the music industry, personally requested Representative Oren Harris's subcommittee of legislative oversight to look into the possibility of introducing a bill making payola a crime. Ironically, nothing anyone had done was against the law.

Nevertheless, the scandal resonated too, in the executive offices of WABC radio, which had picked up Freed after he'd been dropped by WINS. ABC demanded that Alan Freed sign a statement saying he'd never received any money or presents to promote records. Freed refused to sign and was fired. A few days later, WNEW-TV also fired Freed from the afternoon dance show he'd hosted for two years. On his final telecast, Freed looked directly into the electronic eye and spoke the last words he would ever broadcast to New York City. Smiling, and rolling his trademark 45 between his thumb and fingers, Freed said softly, "I know a bunch of ASCAP publishers who'll be glad I'm off the air."

Freed not only could not get a job on the air, he was unable to continue his concerts. His acquisition of talent had been based on an exchange of performance for airplay, never paying an act more than two hundred dollars for an entire run.

Unable to complete his part of the bargain, he was forced to cancel his upcoming holiday tour, too late to get out of the commitments for the rental of theaters. Still, he made good on the advance guarantees, a move that sent him into personal bankruptcy.

As the payola investigations continued. Manhattan District Attorney Frank Hogan, allegedly under pressure from ASCAP, subpoenaed the books of all New York City–based record companies. When several major discrepancies were found, the outcry reached election-year Washington, and the House Committee on Legislative Oversight, coming off the political bandwagon of the quiz show scandal, announced its intention to fully investigate payola.

It was determined that the independent record companies singled out for investigation had paid over $250,000 to 207 disc jockeys in 42 cities. It became clear that the targeted fall guys were going to be deejays, in those days the men who selected which records made it to the air. The record companies, station owners, A & R (Artist and Repertoire) men and entertainers would remain outside the parameters of the investigation.

Some of the revelations were ludicrous, such as the discovery of "stockola." One indie, anxious to have his records played, included stock options in his company with each promotional disk he sent to deejays. RCA, although untouched by the committee, canceled its planned "Special Millionaire" promotion for the Miami deejay convention, in which each deejay who attended was to receive a million dollars in play money to be used to bid on cars, trips, clothes, TV sets and steroes. Deejays were able to increase their holdings by $5,000 each time they visited RCA's booth and were encouraged to come back as often as they liked.

The committee made public what the record industry had known for years: that banquets, prizes, women, drugs and cash were all part of the music business game, and not that different from every other industry. One record executive described the situation this way: "It was bizarre, that's the only word I can think of, that one American business was singled out for industrial gift giving. At the same time record people were being thrown in jail, professionals in Washington were doing the very same thing. They're called lobbyists. Maybe they weren't paying anybody, but parties? Send your family to Jamaica for a week? Lest anyone forget, entertaining a client was a legitimate tax-deductible business expense, the government's way of encouraging corporate gift giving. Only in the music industry did it become a crime to take the client out to lunch. The payola scandal had nothing to do with payola. It was a very successful attempt on ASCAP's part to regain control of the music industry. In the end, like everything else in America, it was a question of corporate politics, with morality the vehicle used to sell the public."

Although Freed fell the hardest, he wasn't the only one. Tom Clay, the leading deejay in Detroit (WJBK), admitted to taking $6,000 from several independent record companies to push their music. He was summarily fired, along with his station manager, who insisted that nothing wrong had taken place. Deejays, the manager held, were paid for their knowledge and expertise, so what difference did it make who paid them? Junkets, another dismissed station manager insisted, were simply "a part of the game." Across the country, in every major market, deejays either resigned or were fired. In the initial weeks following the first stage of the investigation, many station owners demanded that deejays submit to and pass lie detector tests and take FCC-approved oaths of honesty, or face instant dismissal.

The next phase of the investigation concentrated on where the money to pay off deejays came from. One company after another admitted to "borrowing" money from the royalties owed to talent to pay deejays, usually with nothing left to pay the performers. Frankie Lymon, leader of the Teenagers, a group that sold millions of hit singles in the late fifties, earned twenty-five dollars a week at the peak of his career. The rest of his money was "witheld," the record company claimed, for promotional purposes—payola—or put into a trust account for the thirteen-year-old, an account that was later revealed to have never existed.

The committee then focused on Alan Freed's connection to Frankie Lymon's independent record label, Rama Records (Roulette), and his relationship to the label's owner, Morris Levy. It became clear that Levy had cut Freed in for a healthy share of Lymon's income. Further, Levy held two mortgages on Freed's Connecticut house, at the very least a conflict of interest, and probably, the committee suggested, indicative of a lot more.

The Levy/Freed connection did indeed go back to Freed's first days in New York, and they'd been involved in a lot of business together. Some of it had proven profitable, as with Frankie Lymon; some was just plain ridiculous, as when they tried to copyright the term "rock and roll."

Freed was subpoenaed by New York State Attorney General Louis Lefkowitz, who began an investigation into the business practices of Alan Freed and Morris Levy. Freed, already bankrupt, had little cash left for his mounting legal expenses and quickly racked up a half-million-dollar legal bill he was unable to pay. According to Lance Freed: "I think the thing that hurt him most was not being able to do what he loved to do, which was to be on the radio. Eventually, he just couldn't get a job. I don't think he ever felt the investigation would result in the end of his career. Had he known that, maybe he would have done things differently."

The stories of Freed's glory days are rich with tales of high living and generosity, as if he felt that the money could come his way forever. If Freed received a hundred dollars in cash, he'd likely take the fellow who delivered it out for dinner and spend a hundred and a quarter on him. A close associate of Freed recalled the pride he took in "Greycliff," as he called it. The lavish, secluded Wallachs Point, Connecticut sixteen-room mansion overlooked a private view of Long Island Sound. It was a home custom-built so that if Freed chose to he could broadcast his radio show directly from it, a home from which he could conduct his little-known but extensive involvement in the battle against childhood nephrosis supported, he liked to tell friends, entirely by the money he made from payola. "Over there," he'd say, pointing to the den, "you see that room? That was built by Frankie Lymon! And there, you see the bedroom? Chuck Berry did that for me . . . over there, that's Atlantic Records' pool . . . " Every room in the house had been personally dedicated by Freed to the star whose publishing or promotion money had built it.

According to Lance Freed: "Atlantic Records' Ahmet Ertegun built this huge pool with flagstone all around it, for the house, which my father used to say all the time was the most expensive part. Morris Levy told me that Ahmet was a little annoyed because my father wasn't playing enough Atlantic Records and reminded Dad that Atlantic had put the pool in, so why wasn't he playing any Atlantic records? And my father's answer was that he didn't think they were releasing anything good enough, at the moment. He promised when a good one came along he'd play it. Levy said you can't do that and reminded him again of the pool, to which my father told him if he didn't like it, he could fill it in."

When it came time to testify before the Oren sub-committee, Freed, in the hope of gaining leniency, in his own words, "sang like a canary." Freed's biggest fear was to be incarcerated and unable to get proper medical treatment for his failing liver. Although he later claimed he was misquoted, Freed gave a New York reporter an interview immediately after his closed-door session in Washington, implying they had the wrong guy; that he, Freed, was small potatoes, and that the one they really wanted was Dick Clark. Lance Freed relates the following: "Joe Smith [of Capitol Records] tells a very funny story, I don't think it's true, but nevertheless it is revealing of the times. The story goes that my father testified, and Dick Clark testified. Clark, unlike my dad, who always came out front to face the reporters to let them know he wasn't trying to avoid them, left through the back in a dress and wig. He was whisked to a waiting limo, taken to the Washington airport and [put] on a plane back to Philadelphia before anyone could get to him. Things got so bad, though, that on one flight the stewardess came by and said, 'Mr. Clark, would you like something to drink?' 'How do you know I'm Dick Clark?' he said. And the stewardess replied, 'I'm Alan Freed.''

Dick Clark made a name for himself in rock and roll by developing what came to be known as the "Philadelphia sound," the derivative sound of white working-class Philadelphia, all that remained of crossover R&B. Philly rock was best represented by Fabian, Frankie Avalon, Bobby Rydell, Connie Francis, Bobby Darin and Annette Funicello, all connected, in one way or the other, to Clark.

Clark was born and raised in Mount Vernon, New York. Like Freed, he began his career in local radio, as a staff announcer for a small station in Syracuse, New York, doing station breaks and occasional live commercials before moving to Philadelphia and WFIL radio in the spring of 1952. At the time, WFIL-TV had a program called "Bandstand," a series of promo clips and interviews played between records. Bob Horn hosted the show, until he was fired for public drunkenness and replaced by Clark, whose clean, youthful good looks appealed to the station's management.

In 1957, "Bandstand" became "American Bandstand" when the show joined the ABC television network. In a matter of months, the daily ninety-minute live afternoon show was reaching a target audience of better than twenty million teens per broadcast. Clark's power within the music industry expanded when it became clear that the playing of a song on "American Bandstand" guaranteed its breakout as a national hit. The show became the single most powerful record promotion since the advent of top 40 radio and sold more records than any previous avenue of exposure.

In addition to "American Bandstand," Clark created and was the sole owner of Arch Music Publishing, January Music Publishing and Sea Lark Enterprises. He also held a 50 percent interest in Swan Records, a 25 percent interest in Jamie Records, a one-third interest in Chips Record Distributing, sole ownership of Hunt Records, musical copyrights to 160 compositions, half ownership of the Mallard Pressing Corporation and sole ownership of Globe Record Manufacturing. In spite of his naive, choir-boy good looks (or because of them), he was singled out from the pack, along with Freed, and came under the scrutiny of the Harris subcommittee. Like Freed, he was called to testify. Even before being subpoenaed, although everyone knew he would be, Clark put two of his three publishing companies up for sale (Sea Lark, which was bought by BMI, and Arch, which was bought by ASCAP) and divested himself of Mallard. One of the vice-presidents of Mallard was also an executive at Cameo, Parkway and Swan labels. Clark was a one-third partner in each label, which respectively recorded Bobby Rydell, Freddy Cannon and Chubby Checker. All three had records played on "American Bandstand" that became huge hits.

Clark's relationship with Checker reveals much about the power of the Clark empire and the personality of the man at the helm.

Hank Ballard was an up-and-coming artist with a couple of charted hits, including "Finger-Popping Time" and "Let's Go, Let's Go, Let's Go," before his original recording of "The Twist." According to one informed source, Clark booked Ballard onto "American Bandstand" to promote "The Twist." Ballard, who had a reputation for being a ladies' man, failed to show up on the day of the live broadcast, having gotten himself into a situation with a couple of young "fans." Clark reportedly was furious. He decided to get revenge by taking Ernest Evans, an unknown singer who was then earning his living as a chicken plucker, changing his name to Chubby Checker (wordplay on Fats Domino), and having him cover "The Twist." Checker's version, played on "Bandstand," went to number one.

By the time Clark testified, he felt safely distanced from his other interests, well prepared to deal with the probing questions of the committee. He'd already made his record-business philosophy public in a 1958 *Billboard* article, in which, in response to his various financial interests in music, he had replied: "What's wrong with it? The matter depends on the individual. If a man knows what's good for him—what side his bread is buttered on—and he's intelligent and honest with himself, then there's nothing wrong with it at all."

Clark used the newly revised list of his personal holdings as a defense of his innocence, suggesting that a hundred-dollar bribe to get a song played on "Bandstand" was not only immoral, it was just plain bad business. Under oath, Clark declared, "I want to make it clear . . . that I have never taken payola . . . I have never agreed to play a record or have an artist perform on a radio or television program in return for a payment in cash or any other consideration."

This was in contrast to Freed, who confessed under oath to having received more than $30,000 in payola.

Still, Congressman Peter Mack of Illinois condemned both men, labeling Clark the "top dog in the payola field." The early testimony was damaging to Clark, with stories of how records that were going nowhere got to be played on "Bandstand," and how Clark personally benefited from their becoming hits. The Crests' "Sixteen Candles," for example, was cited as having gained frequent "Bandstand" exposure after one of Clark's publishing companies had acquired it, and "American Boy" composer Orville Lunsford's tune became a hit only after his label gave Mallard the pressing business.

Things began to turn around for Clark when the president of the TV network division of the American Broadcasting Company, Leonard Goldenson, came forward to testify on Clark's behalf, referring to Clark as "upright" and of "good character." Goldenson had good reason to be proud of his star. Clark had single-handedly put ABC on the daytime map. Annual "Bandstand" ad revenue billings had reached an unprecedented $12 million, while Freed's billings on ABC radio were approximately $200,000. Predictably, Freed received no such corporate endorsement. After Goldenson's testimony, the committee's attitude toward Clark began to change. He was now being cast as the embodiment of the postindustrial

American dream. Privately, there were many in the industry who believed that Clark had never been a serious target, that his presence was meant to underscore by contrast the real "villain," Freed.

By the end of the hearings, Clark was being praised by Oren Harris as "an attractive and successful" young man. "Yeah," Clark allegedly remarked to his lawyer, "how successful do you think he'd feel having to dissolve thirty-two corporations in one day?" In his autobiography, *Rock Roll and Remember,* Clark sums up his experiences with the committee this way: "The hearings taught me a lesson about politics and business. I learned not just to make money, but to protect my ass at all times." In a 1981 interview, Clark expressed his continued bitterness toward Washington officials: "I have a deep hate for most politicians. In status, I rate politicians in the same class as pimp[s]." As for Freed, Clark has this to say: "I never knew Alan Freed during his radio heyday, only after the bubble had burst. During the payola thing, we weren't close, and I think it was partly because I was going on to other things. I won't say anything bad about him. It's not nice. He was an extraordinary man, irascible. He was generous, bright, abrasive, a rebel. Without his insight that white people would listen to black music, this whole industry might have never gotten off the ground."

As a result of the hearings, legislation was passed by Congress making payola a federal criminal offense, punishable by a fine of up to $10,000, imprisonment for up to one year, or both. The Federal Trade Commission outlawed payola as unfair competition, and the Bureau of Internal Revenue declared that firms which engaged in payola had committed bribery and therefore the payments were not deductible as legitimate business expenses.

Radio stations lost no time in revising the role of disk jockeys in order to take payola out of their hands. No longer considered musical "experts," they were forced to work off preselected playlists. All across the country, those deejays

who'd been on the air before the hearings were put under the
closest scrutiny. Art Leboe, one of the pioneering deejays on
the West Coast, recalled the way it was:

> By the time the FBI got to the West Coast, the stations
> were asking for 'loyalty statements.' At the time I owned
> Original Sound Records, two publishing companies here
> and one in England. I was making quite a few legitimate
> bucks. Still, I went to my lawyer and told him they
> wanted me to sign this statement. He took one look at it
> and said, "You're not going to sign that statement,
> you're going to give them a sworn affidavit which is going
> to list everything you own. You own this company, you
> own this company, etc. The records you play on your
> show are going to go through the programming depart-
> ment, and any records you own are not going to be given
> any preferential play." The whole thing with payola, and
> the legislation that was passed, the so-called '317 rule,'
> dealt with the surreptitious [nature] of payola. Not what
> you do, but the way you do it. Records now had to be
> logged for the FCC, and any tie-ins such as personal
> appearances and dances advertised on the stations had
> to be paid for. In effect, the deejay could no longer walk
> into the station with a record under his arm and play it
> on his show because someone had paid him to do so.

The end of the hearings marked the end of an era. Almost
overnight, independent rhythm and blues records disappeared from the airwaves. Coming on the heels of Buddy
Holly's death, Jerry Lee Lewis's marital problems, Chuck
Berry's arrest for violating the Mann Act, and Little Richard's
conversion to gospel, the glory days of rock and roll seemed
over.

The number one song of 1960 was the movie theme "A
Summer Place," by Columbia Records' Percy Faith. The next
two were Elvis songs recorded prior to his entering the army,
followed by the Everly Brothers, another Presley, Johnny

Preston's country novelty "Running Bear," the Drifters' "Save the Last Dance for Me," Mark Dinning's "Teen Angel," and Connie Francis's "Everybody's Somebody's Fool." Elvis Presley's music was by now running on ASCAP automatic, while Mark Dinning and Connie Francis were both part of the Philly sound. The Drifters were the only legitimate R&B act to make the top 10, and only after they'd radically changed their sound, adding strings and lush melodies to emulate the more acceptable, safer sound of pop.

Annual record sales fell 5 percent from 1959 to 1960, the industry's first decline in five years. Total sales of pop records in America in 1960 were approximately $600 million, down nearly $30 million from the year before, although nowhere near as low as it had been in 1950, before R&B's initial breakthrough, when total sales were in the $250 million range. With rock and roll able to generate that amount of revenue, no one in the industry really expected the music to die. Rather, those in positions of power expected to separate the small-timers from the big profits. To that end, rock was about to become prime product. The majors prepared to restyle it into the fashion of big business.

Dick Clark was at the forefront of that restyling. He emerged from the payola scandal young enough to rebuild his rock and roll empire into one of the most powerful in the entertainment industry, while Alan Freed remained an outcast, a professional leper in the industry he'd helped to create. Clark concentrated on his professional relationship with ABC. He used "American Bandstand" as the point of departure for several new production deals with the network, involving radio and television rock and roll "specials." He also produced a new daytime rock program to precede "Bandstand" on the network schedule. In addition, ABC produced a couple of feature films which starred the youthful-looking Clark and placed him as a guest star on a couple of its sitcoms. Joe Smith, a leading record executive, put it this way: "Clark was middle America, nice, a white-bread face. Freed was gruff, a street man, New York rock and roll, tough." One repre-

sented the future of rock, while the other remained tethered
to its inglorious past.

To the end, Freed insisted he never took money in advance
to play a record. Still, unable to get a job in New York, he
headed west, where he attempted to rebuild his failing career.
No sooner had he arrived in L.A. than he was arrested in May
of 1960 on federal bribery charges and indicted for receiving
$30,650 from six record companies. He eventually pleaded
guilty, was fined $300 and given a six-month suspended sen-
tence. In 1964 he was indicted again, this time for evading
income tax on that money. A year later he was dead of uremic
poisoning.

Art Leboe, who tried to get Freed on the radio after he'd
come to L.A., recalled those last days: "Alan came out here
in 1960 and we worked together at KDAY. I took him around
to my dances and whatever I was doing. He loved being on
the air again but was frustrated because he wasn't able to
make the impact he had in New York. Kids liked him out here,
but not the way they'd loved him in New York."

Lance Freed adds: "He never made a cent after 'the shit hit
the fan,' as my father used to say. Even today, all the performance money collected on the publishing of his music goes
directly to the IRS. Originally, the debt wasn't quite a hundred thousand dollars, but with all the interest accrued over
the years, it's headed towards the millions. There was nothing
left at the end except the house in Palm Springs, which he was
able to keep through the California Homesteading Act. Without that we all would have been out in the street. Right up to
the end he continued to make plans to someday return east.
When the Beatles hit, he saw it as a great thing, especially
because of the fifties stuff they were doing at first, and to my
dad it signaled a turning point, and maybe for him a way back
in."

Ben Weisman recalls this encounter: "I remember seeing
him in Martoni's, a local restaurant in Hollywood where a lot
of music people hung out, sitting at the bar, nursing a drink.
He looked awful, and hardly recognized me at first. Once he

did, though, he was the old Alan, with a smile, a handshake and a genuine interest in what I was doing. When I asked him what he was up to, he told me he had all kinds of plans for coming back. A month later he was dead."

Freed's downfall meant nothing and everything. As a show business personality, he was just one more fifteen-minute opportunist. But as the man who brought rock and roll into the mainstream, he changed forever the parameters of American pop, the way it sounded and the way it was sold.

PART TWO

Dear Landlord

Nine

By the end of 1960, rhythm and blues was a fading memory. In the aftermath of the payola scandal, most independent labels sold their catalogs of master recordings to the majors for whatever they could get. Jac Holzman, founder of Elektra Records, one of the few independents to survive the period, summed up the results of payola this way: "The music was co-opted. The reversion toward the large corporations was economically motivated, the music that came out of it a reflection of those economics. In other words, rock and roll had become big business."

Very big business. In 1959, the last year before payola, the record industry had grossed a record $600 million, triple what it had earned just five years earlier, with a very high margin of profit.

The average studio cost to make a rock single in 1960 was between $1,000 and $3,000. To press 1,000 singles cost an average of $110, about 11 cents each, another $100 for the labels, the sleeves usually thrown in free by the printer. To release 20,000 copies of a potential hit single cost an average of $5,000, with a potential return of $17,500. After publishing fees and distribution costs, a label could show a healthy profit on a modest hit; a profit that skyrocketed in proportion to the relatively fixed costs of a hot-selling single. Yet this investment was too risky for most of the postpayola independents, who preferred to get out of the business before the committee came knocking at their door.

The music industry was back where it had been before the glory days of BMI, in the hands of ASCAP and Tin Pan Alley. The majors prepared to claim as much of the annual $9 billion teenager market as they could get their hands on.

Irwin Pincus, at the time the head of Alley-based Gil Publishing, remembers those days: "It became a writer/publisher business servicing the majors all over again, rather than an independent record operation. A writer would come up to our office at 1650 [Broadway], play his song on the 'house' piano, and if we liked it we'd take it, have a demo made and make a record deal with one of the majors. We financed the demos, usually at a studio in the same building. For a hundred bucks, a hundred and a half tops, I could get a really decent demo made, piano, drum, rhythm, lead, bass guitar and singer, twenty-five bucks apiece, fifty or so if they were union on-the-books and I had a demo I could sell.

"It was a contact business, all based on who you knew. That's how records got made. I remember in the early sixties I'd taken a song called 'A Hundred Pounds of Clay' to a great producer of the time, Snuffy Garrett, who was with Liberty Records, a subsidiary of MGM. I played it for Snuff, hoping to get him to do it with Bobby Vee. Snuff loved the song, but for one of his own acts, Gene McDaniels. 'Trust me,' he said, 'McDaniels is going to be a big star.' So I let him have the song, he produced it with McDaniels, and it was a smash. And that's the way it worked. The publisher was the link, the available ear, the conduit for the majors and the material, the one who would listen to anyone off the street and through whatever contacts he had, try to get a song made, without necessarily knowing who was going to be singing. The labels picked songs from demos, matched them with artists, decided who should arrange it, how it should be packaged, when it should be released. Artists weren't writing much in those days, and for the most part writers weren't performers. You had writers such as Neil Diamond, Carole King, Gerry Goffin, Barry

Mann, Neil Sedaka, Leiber and Stoller, Cynthia Weil, Ellie Greenwich, Ben Weisman, Doc Pomus, all of whom were terrific young songwriters, getting a foot in the door because the older Alley boys still didn't want anything to do with rock and roll, maybe because they couldn't write in that style. The new kids were a breath of fresh air, strictly musical office workers, none at the time in any way performers. They didn't even sing on their own demos. No one outside of the business ever knew who wrote what song, or cared. The performer who recorded the song was the sole identification factor."

Which, in most cases, suited the writers just fine. They were young, mostly from New York's outer boroughs, looking for a way to get into the music business. Jeff Barry, one of the best of the breed, recalls his Alley days: "I started in the business around 1959, 1960, the Kitty Hawk era of rock, when the economics were completely different from what they are now. Everything was on a different scale. You could probably buy the best American car for five or six thousand dollars, and you could make a record for maybe a thousand dollars. I was one of those kids who always loved music and always loved singing and wanted to be an entertainer. I was born and raised in Brooklyn, and the idea of making records and making a living from making records was something that never really occurred to me. I never studied music, I knew two chords, but I always loved singing. As it happens, someone in my family knew a publisher, at E. B. Marks Music, who published 'Wonderful! Wonderful!,' the Johnny Mathis hit, 'Malaguena,' stuff like that. I made an appointment to go up and see them, as an artist, to see if they liked the way I sang, using my own two-chord songs, the only stuff I really knew. Being publishers, they were naturally more interested in those two-chord songs than they were in me. They asked me if I had any more, which I did, all built on those same two chords, and that was it, I was in the business. I quickly learned that once you were a songwriter, it was almost impossible to jump out in front, on stage, and be a performer. There were performers who did that, only that, and it was your job as a writer to supply them,

not replace them. The big thing, I remember, was the difference in the music itself, from what Frank Sinatra had done,
Tony Bennett, all of that generation. I was just a kid writing
songs for other kids to record, and for kids to listen to. That
was the difference. I wasn't working in a room with a bunch
of older men composing what they thought rock and roll was
about; I was writing, really, for myself, for what I liked, for
kids who were like me, my age, who could relate to the music
instantly and honestly."

"The real action was taking place behind the scenes," Irwin
Pincus recalls. "Any good publisher had a relationship with
a number of A&R men, arrangers, disk jockeys, and the nature
of selling product involved lunches, gifts, favors, etc., none of
which was even looked at or explored by the payola investiga-
tors who were more interested in nailing Alan Freed and
knocking out the independents than anything else. A lot of
people got shafted, just like before. In many ways it was business as usual."

Ben E. King, lead singer for the Drifters before going solo
with a string of hits that included "Stand By Me," remembers
those days of trying to make a living as a singer and songwriter at Atlantic Records: "I got started in the business in
1958 after a fellow called Lover Paterson, who was managing
a group called the Five Crowns, heard me singing doo-wop
on the corner and the next thing I knew I was a member of
the group. In 1959, we were appearing at the Apollo Theatre,
in Harlem, with the Drifters, who were breaking up that same
week. We were approached by their manager, George Treadwell, to become the new set of Drifters, which we did. It's hard
to say who actually owned the name 'the Drifters,' but I believe it was George Treadwell. At the time, no one really knew
who owned the name or the group, and as of this day no one
knows, in spite of twenty-five years of court battles. The first
'Drifters' record we recorded was 'There Goes My Baby.' "

"Baby" was an attempt by Atlantic owner Ertegun to actively change the sound of the group, to remove any lingering
suggestion of R&B in favor of a more lush, popular sound. He

wanted to keep the Drifters from being relegated to the "ol-dies" heap, as so many of their R&B contemporaries had. "Baby" was notable in its time for being the first rock and roll song to add strings, unheard of in traditional R&B.

"We were on salary when we became the Drifters," King says. "That was the agreement I signed, and in doing so I forfeited my performance fees for the songs that I'd written. My publishing was handled by Progressive, which was the publishing arm of Atlantic Records. All I eventually got was my composer fees. In effect, I gave away half of everything I did because I didn't know anything about publishing; I was a kid and I wanted to sing. I gave them 'There Goes My Baby,' 'Save the Last Dance for Me,' 'This Magic Moment,'* and one or two others, before I left the group in 1961 to go solo. At the height of my career with the Drifters, when we were hav-ing one hit record after another, I was making about a hun-dred dollars a week, including all tours and personal appear-ances. It was the saddest time of my career. And when I did tell them I was leaving, they just shrugged their shoulders and said fine. There was always someone else to take over the singing. When I walked, I thought the group would come with me. After all, we'd started together before the Drifters, and one of the guys in the band was my best friend. None of them backed me up or left. It was an amazing thing to see. The only thing I have to say about Ahmet is that he saw me walking into a situation with the Drifters and never warned me about things like publishing, or how to look out for the sharks."

In 1962, Artie Butler was an Alley-based studio musician with a desire to get into arranging and composing: "I started out as a sideman, a piano player, doing sessions in the Alley wherever I could get work. The sessions paid fifty-six dollars union scale, then went to sixty-five. The leader would get double scale. I became a button-pusher, what they call a sec-ond engineer now, at the old Bell Sound Studios in New York, in that five square blocks or so that made up Tin Pan Alley. The first record I made by myself was off a song that Abner Spector had. Spector owned Tuff Records, which was dis-

* There remains some confusion as to who actually wrote these songs. Sources differ, some claiming that they were written exclusively by King, others citing Leiber and Stoller as co-authors.

tributed by Chess. The song was not the greatest. But I heard
something in it, and asked if he'd mind if I went into the
studio and made a demo of it. He agreed, and I went to the
Broadway Recording Studios at 1697 Broadway, laid down an
organ track, then added a drum track. Every time I put another color on, I went another generation. This was well
before the days of the twenty-four track, so the sound got
worse with each generation, somehow getting better in its
'worseness.' When I finally finished with it, the record had a
definite 'sound.' 'Sally Go 'Round the Roses' was the name of
the song, by the Janettes. I brought it back to Spector, who
listened to it and said it was a piece of garbage. I brought it
to Leiber and Stoller and they said it was a smash, and wanted
buy it. I went back to Spector and told him I'd just seen Mike
and Jerry fifteen minutes ago and they wanted to buy it. Spector said no, the record was his. Now, I'll tell you about the
facts of life in the music business. Everybody gets it once. I
never got a nickel off that record. I got paid union scale which
I think was fifty-six dollars. After the record was a hit [it
reached number 26 on the *Billboard* top 100, in September of
1963], Spector told me he wanted to give me something and
said I should meet him in front of the Colony Record Shop.
When he got there he said he wanted to thank me for what
I did, and he put something in my hand. I didn't want to be
rude and look at it right in front of him, so I waited until he
left. It was three dollars. He gave me a 'bonus' of three dollars
for creating the record for him."

   "The split between songwriter and publisher was an indus-
try-standard 50–50 split," Pincus explains. "The monetary
value in those days was two cents for the songwriter and two
cents for the publisher. So if a song was a hit and sold a
million copies, a gold record, that meant twenty thousand
dollars for the writer and twenty thousand dollars for the
publisher, plus whatever money there was from performance—you know, airplay, jukeboxes and sheet music. The rest
of the money belonged to the singer, whatever his deal was,

and the record company. Obviously, it was the record companies that made the most out of a song."

One of the many Alleymen who found work in the post-payola/pre-Beatles era was Bobby Darin. Like most of his contemporaries, he started as an entertainer, with little or no knowledge of how the music business worked. However, by the time the Beatles arrived in America, Darin had successfully rewritten the rules of the game, the first rock and roll singer to completely own his own publishing.

Bobby Darin was born in the Bronx, the child of Italian immigrants. With the enthusiastic encouragement of his mother, Darin set out to make his mark as a singer.

One of his first professional associations was with Don Kirshner, a high school friend with whom he wrote jingles for TV commercials. In 1956, they signed with George Scheck, a small-time Alley producer always on the lookout for a way to make a fast buck. In addition to the jingles he wrote with Kirshner, Darin wrote a couple of rock tunes by himself for Scheck, all of which did poorly. Darin blamed the songs' failure on the singers and went into the studio to record one himself. "My Teenage Love" was picked up by Decca and died.

A year later he got another shot when Atco, an Atlantic subsidiary label, signed him. Atco put Darin into a series of Apollo rock shows hosted by then upcoming deejay Murray Kaufman. Kaufman gave Darin "Splish Splash," which Ahmet Ertegun personally produced. It was around that time Darin first met Dick Clark, who invited him to appear at a "Dick Clark Record Hop." That appearance led to Darin's doing "Splish Splash" on "American Bandstand." "Splish Splash" went on to become the thirty-ninth top-selling single of 1958.

Feeling his career stalled after "Splash," Darin switched management. In the summer of '59, under Steven Blauner's guidance, Darin recorded Kurt Weill's "Mack the Knife," which became the number one song of the year and earned Darin two Grammy Awards. Shortly after, he was subpoenaed by the Harris subcommittee and questioned at length about the authorship of "Splish Splash." "Murray the K" as Kaufman was known at WINS, where he was hired to replace the just-fired Alan Freed, had given "Splish Splash" extensive exposure on his show. Harris wanted to know if Kaufman had actually written the song or had accepted the publishing as a form of payola. Both Kaufman and Darin maintained that Kaufman's mother had come up with the title and that the jock had written the song, helped out in the rewrite by Darin. The subcommittee also questioned Darin about his relationship with Dick Clark and the circumstances involved in the record being exposed on "American Bandstand."

Kaufman and Darin both emerged unscathed from the hearings. Darin resumed making records, and by the age of twenty-four, had sold eight million singles and two million albums.

In 1962, Darin left Atco to accept an offer from Capitol that made him the highest paid pop singer in the history of the recording industry. Darin signed for a reported $750,000, with a $2 million guarantee against album sales, more than thirty times what Presley and the Colonel had gotten from RCA only six years earlier with no guarantee. Instrumental in putting the Capitol deal together was Joe Csida, who had once managed Darin and who recently had taken a position with Capitol to develop and manage a stable of performers that included Nat "King" Cole, Judy Garland, Peggy Lee, Dinah Shore, Dean Martin and Frank Sinatra.

At a party to celebrate his signing with Capitol, Darin met the man who was to make him more money than he had ever thought possible. Allen Klein was a young accountant looking for a way into the big business of entertainment, and he figured Darin was his meal ticket. Walking up to Darin, he handed the performer a check for $100,000. When Darin asked what the money was for, Klein answered, "For nothing."

It was the culmination of a well-planned scheme to get Darin as his first celebrity client. Klein had made it his business to become friendly with some of the personnel who worked at Darin's accounting firm. He somehow managed a look at Darin's books, conducted his own audit, found a six-figure discrepancy, and pointed it out to the grateful company, who allowed him to personally deliver the check in exchange for saying "nothing," which was exactly what he did. Darin, impressed with Klein's style, fired his accounting firm and turned all his holdings over to the man who proceeded to build a mini-empire for Darin and himself.

Klein went back to Capitol and renegotiated Darin's deal. As part of the inducement to sign, Klein wanted Csida to sell the singer Trinity Music for $350,000 cash. Csida wanted Darin on Capitol badly enough to say yes. As a result, Darin (and Klein) gained total control of 700 Trinity Music titles, only 70 of which Darin had personally written.

As a result, by 1963, Bobby Darin was a multimillionaire. Because of his publishing acquisitions, his career was by far the most financially successful of the early sixties pop-rockers. Even after his records stopped selling, his movie career bombed, his TV shows fell off the Nielsen charts, and his nightclub career floundered, Darin continued to amass a fortune. The million-dollar difference between Bobby Darin and Ben E. King was the control of their respective publishing. Darin's experience became the object lesson for the coming generation of sixties singer-songwriters determined to keep the Alleymen's hands out of their pockets, by taking rock and roll out of the Alleymen's hands.

Ten

Rhythm and blues finally broke the color line in American popular music in the late 1940s and in doing so supplied the material impetus toward independent record production. At the same time, country and western lent an indigenous charm to the hard edge of R&B. To these two aspects of modern rock a third was added in the sixties. As post-payola rock and roll searched for a pulse, folk music, declared brain-dead a decade earlier, rose from the dead like Lazarus with a hit single.

American folk music was linked to the fortunes of the progressive left ever since the first years of the twentieth century, when the Chicago-based Industrial Workers of the World (IWW) attempted to organize all workers whose lack of specific skills excluded them from the growing union movement. The IWW, whose members were known as Wobblies, welcomed all blue-collar, migratory and agricultural workers otherwise left with no individual negotiating power at the hands of their respective employers. The essential "tool" the Wobblies used to spread their message was folk music, infused with new, topical lyrics. Ralph Chaplin, an early organizer for the IWW, used "John Brown's Body" as the basis for "Solidarity Forever" and "Darling Nelly Gray" as the music for "The Commonwealth of Toil." Harry McClintock rewrote the hymn "Revive Us Again" as "Hallelujah, I'm a Bum," which became one of the most popular songs of the Depression.

Without question, the greatest talent produced out of the folk/union movement was Woody Guthrie. Heavily influenced by "The Little Red Book" of Wobbly songs, Guthrie wrote the first of his great American chronicles, "Talking Dust Bowl." Late in the thirties, after Guthrie had migrated to California, he landed a job on live radio, KFVD, hired to perform as a "hillbilly" for twenty dollars a week.

While at KFVD, Guthrie met Ed Robbins, commentator for "The People's World." The owner of KFVD was a staunch believer in free speech and had no problem with a Communist broadcasting once a week. This was not an uncommon occurrence during the days of the Depression, when some form of toleration for, if not affiliation with, the radical left was considered by some to be patriotic. Robbins invited Guthrie to sing at a rally for IWW organizer Tom Mooney. Guthrie had written a song about him and sang it on his radio show the day after Mooney was released from prison by the newly elected governor of California, Culbert Olson. Mooney's release was a payback from Olson for the IWW's endorsement, part of the Communist party's support of the entire Democratic slate from President Roosevelt down, one reason that Washington officially tolerated the IWW in spite of its affiliation with the CP.

Guthrie entertained at the rally and later agreed to let Robbins become his booking agent. For the next several years, while continuing his radio program, Guthrie often entertained at various communist rallies, touring occasionally with his friend Will Geer and writing songs that supported his growing commitment to the American left.

The Roosevelt era of communist tolerance came to a sudden, unexpected and inglorious end with the announcement of the 1939 Hitler-Stalin Pact. The "Popular Front" was fatally discredited in the United States. The ramifications of the German-Soviet deal were felt everywhere in America, from union organization to commercial broadcasting. Woody Guthrie's radio show was no longer considered necessary, and its cancellation marked the end of his commercial broadcasting career.

Guthrie remained dedicated to his causes, and played whenever and wherever he was asked. One such appearance, late in 1940, at a rally organized by Will Geer to benefit the John Steinbeck Committee for Agricultural Workers, happened to be attended by Alan Lomax, the assistant director of the Library of Congress's Archive of Folk Song. So impressed was Lomax that he arranged for Guthrie to record his songs for the noncommercial Library of Congress collection (where they remained for twenty-five years before becoming widely available to the commercial, record-buying public).

In the mid-forties, Guthrie formed the Almanac Singers, a consortium of New York folk singers in the tradition of the Wobblies. The Almanacs worked out of the Greenwich Village apartment of Pete Seeger. Guthrie, Seeger, Lee Hays, Millard Lampell and Sis Cunningham, as the Almanac Singers, played for factory workers, at union meetings and at antifascist rallies.

In the immediate aftermath of the war, a feeling of optimism rose among the organized unions. Proper recognition was long overdue for their part in the war effort. The Almanacs enthusiastically supported this position and entertained various chapters of the Congress of Industrial Organizations (CIO), hoping to make "If I Had a Hammer" the official anthem of the union movement. However, the onset of the Cold War led to organized labor's rejection of the ever-hardening Communist party line and its most eloquent spokespersons, the Almanacs.

The folk-song movement was delivered another blow, literally and figuratively, when Paul Robeson's appearance in Peekskill, New York, in June 1949, resulted in a riot to protest his communist loyalties. The incident marked the end of Robeson's commercial career, and with it, whatever remained of the public's tolerance of leftist folksingers.

The same year Robeson was given his commercial walking papers, a new folksinging group made its first, cautious appearance. Although the official name of the group was the Weavers, they liked to refer to themselves as the No-Name Quartet. Pete Seeger was the founding member of the group and wasn't anxious to have it thought of as the "son of Almanac."

Much to Seeger's surprise, both Decca and Columbia expressed interest in the Weavers, after initial positive scouting reports came back from both companies. Seeger approached Harold Leventhal, a former song plugger who, in Seeger's view, held views that were politically correct, and asked him to take over the group's management.

Leventhal agreed and signed the Weavers to Decca. Part of the deal called for the group to sign over a portion of its publishing to the label, which is why the name of Gordon Jenkins, a house arranger for Decca, shares publishing credit on some of the original Weaver songs. This type of payola was standard procedure among the majors, a part of the industry for nearly fifty years. Folk music may have concerned itself with idealistic causes, but the business of recording it remained corrupt and unsung.

Against all industry expectation, the Weavers' recording of "Irene" became a huge hit, *Billboard*'s 1950 "Song of the Year," number one for thirteen incredible weeks. The group followed up with a most eclectic string of hits, including "On Top of Old Smokey," "Wimoweh," "Kisses Sweeter Than Wine," and Woody Guthrie's "So Long It's Been Good to Know You" (Guthrie's first hit record). By 1952, the Weavers had sold more than five million records, impressive in any category and for any label.

Still, many in the traditional folk community were put off by the Weavers' commercial success and considered them sell-outs for rearranging their music to make it more commercially acceptable. Legally, questions were raised as to the extent traditional music in the public domain could be altered and then copyrighted for the purpose of collecting royalties. "On Top of Old Smokey," one of the Weavers' biggest hits, was a well-known traditional folk song in the "AAAAAAA" pattern, the melody and pattern of the first verse repeated throughout. In order to make the song more commercial, Decca requested they add a "BBBBBBB" pattern. Once this was done, the record company added the name "Paul Campbell" to the writing credits, a code name created by Decca for the purpose of collecting royalties on legally questionable folk music copyrights of altered songs.

It didn't take very long for the majors to realize the potential profit in "traditional" folk music, one of the principal reasons folk music emerged into the mainstream in the aftermath of the payola scandal. With a sudden gap created in the supply of music caused by the demise of rhythm and blues and fifties-style rock and roll, the majors turned to the ready catalog of "free" material they'd spent a decade acquiring. The economics of survival overruled the politics of economics once Capitol's Kingston Trio scored with "Tom Dooley." Before that song was off the charts, a new wave of major label "folk" groups appeared. The Cumberland Three, the Chad Mitchell Trio, the Gateway Singers, the Limelighters, the Dauphin Trio, the Wayfarers, the Travelers, the Tarriers, the Babysitters, the Balladeers, the Folk Singers, and the Brothers Four were just a few of the ersatz folkies who rode the crest of folk's early sixties commercial wave.

Ironically, the group that had started the fifties folk revival, the Weavers, were excluded from its second wind. Singled out as victims of the fifties red-baiting that fanned the political sentiments of a nation. Even as their records continued to make the charts, jokes like the following spread throughout the industry: Three party members met for the purpose of arranging their next rally. Each was assigned their respective designated duty: one to bring the Negro, one to bring the Jew and one to bring the Weavers. Walter Winchell, one of the most obstreperous tabloid columnists, wondered in print how the Weavers were able to reconcile their "righteousness" with their royalties.

It didn't take much to persuade Decca Records to allow Pete Seeger to resign. Although the Weavers survived in one combination or another into the early sixties, they never again enjoyed the popularity they'd had with Seeger at the helm.

While the fortunes of the Weavers might have been different if there had been no politically inspired resistance, the commercial success of folk music in the fifties, no matter how brief, did help to bring some new long-players into the music business.

Jac Holzman had always been fascinated by the technology of broadcasting and recording, as much as with the music itself. As a young man, Holzman spent many hours in the broadcast control rooms of WLIB in New York watching his grandmother perform. When he realized that advancements in technology—the LP, magnetic audiotape equipment—had made the recording industry cost effective, allowing manufacturers to inexpensively turn out small quantities of relatively unbreakable disks, Holzman decided to get into the business. While most of the others entering the record business at the same time were interested in pop, rhythm and blues or country, Holzman's personal obsession was folk music.

With six hundred borrowed dollars, he went into business. Elektra Records was set up to build a stable of salable recording folk artists. His first acquisition was John Gruen, whose eclectic piano work opened Holzman's catalog, followed shortly by the more traditional music of Jean Ritchie's Southern Appalachian Mountain tunes. Buoyed by Ritchie's success, Holzman acquired Frank Warner, Cynthia Gooding, Tom Paley, Hally Wood, Josh White, Ed McCurdy, Sonny Terry and Brownie McGhee, Theodore Bikel, among many others. Weaver Fred Hellerman served as principal music consultant for the fledgling label while continuing his performance duties at Columbia.

"Five years after the label began," Holzman recalls, "I began to draw a salary from Elektra for the first time, a hundred dollars a week. Up until then I supported myself making money any way I could, usually installing hi-fi equipment. And I could live on the hundred bucks, I could make do, getting from record to record. Rents in New York in those days . . . I paid five dollars a week for a fifth-floor walk-up and put all my money into getting the next record. It was treading water while moving forward. You moved an inch, and an inch, and an inch . . . My theory was, if I could hang in, I had to be in the right place at the right time once, and once would be enough, that would make the difference.

"Nineteen fifty-six was the first year we broke even. The economics of the business in those days was that nobody knew from banks. Anyone who started a record company before 1960 wasn't financed by any bank. Our banks were the pressing plants, the printers and the album jacket manufacturers. We'd pay them a little every time, the debt would grow, but we'd always send them a check. The secret was, if you told them a check was going to be there on Tuesday, you had to make sure it was there on Tuesday. If you did that you could get credit, if they had any faith in you whatsoever. You kept the suppliers involved in the process. You invited them to the parties, made sure they got concert tickets, and when it finally did hit for Elektra, someone like Peter Strauss of Pilgrim Press continued to press Elektra jackets for me for years, and eventually made a lot of money with us. Because he was there when we needed him. And we needed him, and a lot of others. It's like we had one foot in a boat and one foot on the dock, and the boat's moving away, and you're just about to fall in the water, and the boat comes back a little, and you're not so stretched . . . like that. I guess we were gamblers in those early days; we shot from the hip with no financial smarts about what we were doing. All we were trying to do was stay in business long enough for the magic to happen; call it the angst of start-up. That's the way it was at Atlantic, and a couple of years later, I'm sure that's the way it was at A&M. It was always basically the same. The economics of the independent record business was a major juggling act. Royalties? No one paid more than five percent royalties, and some, particularly with black artists, paid a lot less than that. And some paid in drugs and no cash at all."

By 1963, Elektra had established itself as one of the giants of the independent movement, specializing in folk and what was now being called folk-rock, with such quality artists as Judy Collins and Phil Ochs.

But Holzman claims: "The time I loved Elektra most was when I could put my entire staff of fourteen people around a Chinese banquet table."

One of the staff was Paul Rothchild, Elektra's recording director from 1963 through 1969: "I came to Elektra at the start of the singer/songwriter era, having cut my teeth signing a bunch of people to the label I'd previously worked for, Prestige-Folklore, where I'd signed up a lot of people from the Cambridge/Boston folk scene. In those days I was very much a part of the ignorantsia, understanding little of the commerce of the music industry. It was a time of great naivete, to me, to the people I was signing. We were doing it to reach a small audience. It never occurred to us it was anything more than a job, a salary, a way to make ends meet. When I returned to New York, my home, I got involved with the folk movement in the Village and found there was an enormous amount of talent. Dylan, of course, was the benchmark. As a result, I was in no rush to sign a lot of talent, even though everyone was looking for a label. I'd be sitting in the Kettle of Fish, one of the major clubs of the Village, and Dylan would come in and the whole atmosphere would change. He would come up and ask what you thought of a song, play it for you literally the minute he wrote it, and that would start off a chain reaction. Phil Ochs would insist you hear his song, and one after another. It was a phenomenon, really, the early days of the singer/songwriters."

And their managers. Albert Grossman arrived in New York a year before Dylan. Both gravitated to Greenwich Village looking for their futures, but their inspirations were worlds apart. For Dylan it was the social progressiveness of Woody Guthrie combined with the musicality of Hank Williams. For Grossman, it was the solid gold fob that bounced from the Colonel's big hip.

Eleven

So much has been written about Bob Dylan that there is little anyone can add to or take away from his musical reputation or literary abilities. As a spokesman for his generation, he wrote on an anthemic scale, managing as no other rock figure, with the possible exception of Elvis Presley, to forge a public persona so uniquely suited to his style of music. Dylan looked as if he lived his songs rather than merely wrote them. The primal sixties folk-rocker, Dylan managed to idealize the image of Woody Guthrie on acid. His persona became the youngest world-weary folksinger in history.

Dylan's off-mike personality was another story. The product of the familiar pattern of dominant, doting mother and passive, distant father, Dylan creatively reconstructed his family to conform with his own idealized version, casting Joan Baez as the Madonna and Albert Grossman as the father. Two stories offer tantalizing insights into Dylan's early self-image, and how it affected his ability to make decisions regarding the management of his money and his career.

Various New York clubs claim to be the one where Dylan made his professional New York debut. It actually took place September 28, 1961, at Mike Porco's Folk City. New York's cabaret laws made it necessary for all club performers to be bonded and licensed. This included the village coffeehouses and nightclubs that offered folk, even though most of the clubs were, at first, little more than bars with a single mike hooked up to an amp. Porco had put music into his club as a last-ditch attempt to save his failing restaurant, a victim of the massive redistricting that all but eliminated the regular clientele that had frequented Gerde's (the club's original name, taken from the first owners) in the evening. Izzy Young, head of the Folklore Center, who'd been looking for a place to showcase some talent, approached Porco about using his restaurant as an informal club in the evenings. Porco would get the bar business and the cover charge would be split by the entertainment.

Although Young's association with Porco proved a brief one, the music stayed, and soon Gerde's Folk City moved to Third Street. This Greenwich Village street became the main drag district of the burgeoning folk clubs, which included the Bitter End, the Gaslight, Cafe Wha and the Night Owl. Complaints from the neighborhood about noise and traffic led to the city's issuing entertainment licenses to the clubs, to go along with the familiar cabaret "cards" all New York performers were required to have. Cabaret cards were a holdover from the Mayor LaGuardia era of New York politics, one of the laws he put into effect in his battle to rid the city of illegal speakeasies.

When Porco told Dylan he'd need a cabaret card to play Folk City, the young singer went to city hall to apply for one. There, he was told that because he was still a minor, he'd need a parent to cosign his application. Dylan told the clerk he had no parents, that he was an orphan, an itinerant, a wanderer. When he returned empty-handed, Porco offered to act as Dylan's official guardian, signed the appropriate papers and secured a card for his "son." Porco then took a personal interest in the young Dylan, fed, helped to clothe, and at times even sheltered him.

Immediately after playing his first gig at Folk City, Dylan asked Porco to manage him, something Porco considered but ultimately declined.

Not that long after his memorable debut, Columbia Rec-

ords, in the person of John Hammond, offered Dylan his first
contract. Once again, the record company needed a parent's
signature, and once again Dylan claimed he was an orphan,
his only living relative a blackjack dealer in Vegas. Dylan
assured John Hammond, the next paternal figure in Dylan's
career, that Hammond could "trust" him.

Dylan often tested professional relationships by asking
those in a position of authority to trust him. In a very real
sense he conducted what amounted to a series of auditions,
a way of testing the loyalty of those he sought out as surrogate
fathers to help guide his career. Professional loyalty became
Dylan's personal metaphor for parental love, which may have
been the subtextual motivation for his choosing Albert Grossman as his personal manager, and the reason he found it so
difficult to separate from Grossman when it became obvious
their professional relationship had deteriorated.

Albert Grossman remains in death (from a heart attack,
February 1986) one of the most enigmatic figures in the history of rock and roll. Cold, ruthless, shrewd, intellectual, he
was a resident of the night in every sense of the word. Those
who will speak now of him, and there aren't many, remember
a man whose instincts were brutally on the money. Grossman
was more influential than any other manager of the sixties in
shaping the liberal ideals of those who made the music, while
tilting rock toward the multimedia billion-dollar industrial
complex it was to become. One who worked closely with
Grossman recalls him this way: "He always had such a stature,
and at the same time such ease. He became the next obvious
father figure, perfect for someone like Dylan to have to gravi-
tate toward, because he, Grossman, was such an iconoclast.
He was irreverent, but he was very solid. He had the mood of
the folkies, and he wasn't that much older than them, but he
seemed generations removed. His inspiration may have been
the Colonel, but Grossman, no question, was a general. No
bullshit. I literally saw him huff and puff and blow the house
down a number of times. He came off at first glance as a
sweetheart of a guy, but underneath that charming veneer, he

was a killer, through and through. If he was on your side, you never saw that. You saw the jovial, friendly, dope-smoking safe haven."

Grossman's agreeing to manage Dylan was the best evidence of his ability to read not only talent, but the direction of the times. Early on, Grossman was aware of the potential the "new" folk music out of Chicago, Boston and the Village held as the next alternative to rock. It was clean, middle-class, white and nonpolitical. The Kingston Trio proved all of that with "Tom Dooley." At first, Grossman believed his fortune was in a folk trio, one he sought to build from the right components. He liked Carolyn Hester, and considered Bob Gibson, whom he eliminated because Gibson's blacklisting problems in the fifties made him a tough sell. However, once Grossman laid eyes on Dylan, he knew he'd found his future.

John Hammond came upon Dylan at a session rehearsal for Grossman's Carolyn Hester. Unaware of the talk in the Village about "the new kid in town," it was on the basis of Dylan's background guitar for Hester that Hammond signed him to Columbia. Dylan, at this point having been in New York for nearly nine months, and rejected by all the folk labels, including Elektra, Vanguard and Folkways, was desperate to get a deal, no matter what he had to do. One close friend at the time recalled Dylan's initial arrival in New York in a three-piece suit and tie, in the image he believed he needed to approach the men who controlled the record business. The friend recalls Dylan's subsequent jeans and boots look as a well-thought-out image calculation, one that gave him status and authenticity in the downtown folk community, where his taste in music and poetry naturally led him.

Dylan's initial meeting with John Hammond at Carolyn Hester's rehearsal has gone through many interpretations and retellings. One thing remains certain, however: Hammond's signing of Dylan to a five-year contract. Although there was very little in the way of an advance, the signing was significant because it represented the first sixties Village folk act to make it to a major.

It was a deal met with skepticism at corporate headquarters. "Hammond's folly" was the way Columbia executives referred to Dylan, after his first album barely flickered in the wind. The first album contained only one original Dylan song. Hammond, hoping to boost sales, pressed Dylan to go with more of his original material. To that end, he advised Dylan to look into a formal publishing deal with Lou Levy, who signed Dylan to Dutchess Music, a BMI-licensed company, with a cash advance of five hundred dollars. Dylan, reportedly down to his last coins, signed "immediately," as the story goes, taking cash as the ink dried on the contracts.

Grossman, dissatisfied with the deal, set about to change it. He was tight with Artie Mogull, of M. Witmark and Sons Publishing, the inveterate Tin Pan Alley publishing giant. Witmark was old-line ASCAP, committed to its still exclusive roster of music. Nevertheless, Grossman broke him down. Very likely, Dylan had no idea of the historical significance of signing with Witmark. Six months after Dylan had signed with Dutchess, Grossman had Dylan personally sing his catalog for Mogull, who offered to sign Dylan for a thousand dollars. At that point, Grossman suggested that Dylan simply buy back his publishing from Levy, shrewdly choosing to keep out of the direct negotiations.

Levy proved no problem, having made nothing from Dylan's first album, and released Dylan for the return of his original five hundred dollars. During the next three years, Dylan wrote more than 225 songs, making millionaires several times over of Mogull, Grossman and himself. Grossman continually pushed Dylan's songs onto other performers, encouraging them to record cover versions. Stories are told of Mogull's offering cash to various folk labels if they would have their artists record Dylan's songs; while Grossman piggybacked his stable of performers, which included Odetta and Peter, Paul and Mary, to cover a lot of Dylan. Judy Collins, Manfred Mann, the Byrds, the Animals, Sonny and Cher, and the Turtles, had hits with Dylan's songs.

Dylan's Witmark contract expired in 1965, at which time

Dylan agreed, at Grossman's urging, to start his own publishing company, Dwarf Music. The move eliminated Mogull and doubled Grossman's take to 50 percent of all Dylan's publishing income. This was in addition to his managerial piece, said to be 20 percent of everything, including Dylan's 50 percent share of his own publishing. Having accomplished that, Grossman promptly hired Mogull to handle the new company's business affairs.

Grossman next set his sights on isolating Dylan from his other "paternal" relationships, particularly Mike Porco and John Hammond. With Porco, it was simply a matter of getting Dylan onto the Village circuit, into the other clubs, which greeted him with open arms and profitable bookings. As for Hammond, he was disposed of after producing Dylan's first Columbia album, whose sales made Grossman "furious," and resulted in Hammond's being replaced by the time Dylan was ready to return to the studio. While this was taking place, the talk on the streets of the Village was of Dylan's having been "taken in" by Grossman, having willingly (and unnecessarily) signed away a thick slice of the publishing pie to a man whom he thought he needed and could trust. There seemed to be no other way to explain Dylan's mute devotion to the older, calculating manager who controlled the otherwise arrogantly outspoken performer's every business move.

Grossman, meanwhile, having successfully restructured Dylan's publishing, now attempted to get Dylan's contract with Columbia renegotiated. Grossman had Dylan sign a letter informing Columbia that since he'd been under age when he signed his contract, he considered it invalid. Further, Dylan demanded the immediate return of all his masters.*

The letter was given to Clive Davis, a middle-level Columbia lawyer, who studied the situation and advised the company to take the position that, because Dylan had been in the

---

*Masters are the physical equivalent of a musical copyright. Control of a master means control of future use of the recorded material. In most instances, publishing rights and masters remain the property of recording companies and are subject to rerelease, unless specific arrangements have been made in advance for their eventual return to the artist, something which rarely happens.

studio since turning twenty-one, his complaint had no legal
basis. The result of this was the opposite of what Grossman
wanted: an extension of the year and a half left on the original
contract, an option Columbia decided at that point to exercise, as if in retribution, without any increase in royalties or
bonuses. It seemed to many in the business, Dylan especially,
that Grossman's plan had backfired, and badly.

It's possible, however, that Grossman's intention all along
was to get Columbia to extend its commitment to Dylan,
because in spite of all the accolades his young star was receiving, Dylan records just weren't selling very well. By forcing
Columbia's hand, Grossman insured Dylan's remaining at
Columbia for at least three more "no-cut" years, plenty of
time to put Dylan over into the big-time side of the musical
tracks. Once again, Grossman seemed to know something
everyone else didn't. Within weeks of "renegotiating" Dylan's
deal with Columbia, "Like a Rolling Stone" became his first
hit, the number one song of the summer of '65.

Dylan's "Like a Rolling Stone," debuted live at the Newport Folk Festival, threw the big switch and electrocuted the
sixties resurgence of folk music. Dylan's decision to go rock
gave his audience of middle-class plebeian teens a new, socially aware rock, a lyrically oriented brand of music.

Dylan dominated American rock and roll for the next two
years, right up until the time Columbia opened negotiations
to renew his contract. By this time, however, Grossman was
eager to move Dylan to MGM, which made no secret of its
desire to sign him and its willingness to pay handsomely for
the privilege.

Grossman was already quite well connected at MGM, having signed several acts to the Verve/Forecast subsidiary, including Ritchie Havens, Gordon Lightfoot and Ian and Sylvia.
It's possible Grossman had an eye toward one day owning the
label, which would have given him absolute control of his
roster of talent, including the ability to negotiate contracts for
them with himself. He may have been comparing himself to
Allen Klein, who already controlled substantial MGM stock.

Klein, who literally invented the singer-songwriter of the sixties through Bobby Darin, expressed public disdain for Dylan and Grossman. Some involved with the MGM negotiations recalled that Klein was vehemently against the label signing Dylan, probably out of fear that it made the possibility of a Grossman takeover one step closer to reality. It's believed that Klein made a complete study of Dylan's finances, and considered wooing him away from his over-protective manager. Some say he considered Grossman's rank amateurism was displayed nowhere more clearly than during these negotiations with MGM.

At the same time Dylan began to pull back from his association with Grossman. Those who remember him in those days talk of his near-obsessional preoccupation with just how much money he'd "given away" to Grossman through the series of publishing deals that so generously favored his manager. Now, Grossman was about to sever the final link to the early, New York glory days. Leaving Columbia was something Dylan, according to his friends, was totally against, no matter how much money was involved.

The extent of Dylan's famous motorcycle accident in July 1966 remains unclear. Several sources have expressed some doubt as to the severity of the accident in which Dylan allegedly broke his neck and was forced to cancel more than 150 concerts. Equally suspect was the radically altered voice that Dylan used three years later on his first postaccident album, *John Wesley Harding*. Others strongly suspect the accident never happened at all.

Dylan, living in Woodstock, New York, in the summer of 1966, was at increasing odds with Grossman over the "Rolling Stone" performance at Newport '65. Grossman, one of the original backers of the festival, had gotten into a fight with folk purist Al Lomax over whether or not Dylan and other musicians should be allowed to plug in at all. Apparently, Lomax wasn't the only one opposed to the idea. There were many others behind the scenes at Newport that day who correctly believed that if Dylan played rock music, the momentum of the folk movement into pop would be severely hurt, if not totally lost. Before Dylan's scheduled appearance, the Paul Butterfield Blues Band, a white group out of Chicago that Grossman had taken over and was looking to break at the festival, received a lukewarm reception from a crowd that resisted the rock infusion into the traditional sound of the blues. Backstage, Grossman and Lomax duked it out after Lomax's bitter introduction of the Butterfield Band, just as Dylan launched into what was considered the most shocking performance of his career, the electric debut of "Like a Rolling Stone." Coming off the stage, Peter Yarrow ordered Dylan to go back out, apologize and do an acoustic set. Dylan did return to the stage, grabbed a guitar and sang "It's All Over Now, Baby Blue." The performance left the audience stunned into silence, an audience that included Albert Grossman. In spite of having gone to blows to defend Dylan's right to play the song any way he wanted, Grossman nevertheless felt that his star attraction had committed commercial suicide and let him know it in no uncertain terms.

From that moment on, perhaps interpreting Grossman's comments as a breach of parental faith, Dylan began to pull back from his manager, even as Grossman pressed MGM to come to terms. MGM, however, was having second thoughts about signing the increasingly reclusive singer after persistent rumors swept through its corporate halls that Dylan had joined the rock generation in more ways than one. Dylan, they believed, was living in self-imposed exile at Grossman's estate in Woodstock because he was hooked on heroin.

The label wanted to personally audition him, to make sure he was still, as they put it, "viable." Four months before the negotiating deadline, Richard Farina, one of Dylan's Village pals and a talented writer with the promise of a brilliant career ahead of him, died in a motorcycle accident, stunning the literary as well as the musical Village scene. It's said that Farina's death caused Dylan to get even deeper into heroin.

As MGM pressed Grossman for a personal look at his star, Grossman confronted Dylan, telling him if he didn't clean up his act he'd blow the MGM deal. Realizing how gone Dylan was, Grossman made arrangements to have him kept inside the house under heavy physical security, concocting the story of the motorcycle accident as a cover while Dylan detoxed. Grossman had many friends in Woodstock with enough influence who could have made Dylan's appearance at the emergency room of the local hospital for a minor spill on his bike appear on paper as if a major accident had actually taken place.

Grossman, meanwhile, had a contract in his pocket which MGM refused to sign. The latest rumors about Dylan were that he'd broken his neck and was a helpless quadraplegic. In desperation, Grossman brought MGM's contract to Clive Davis, the lawyer who'd prevented Dylan's first attempt at leaving the label and was now the head of Columbia Records. Grossman attempted to use the unsigned contract as a lever to negotiate a new contract for Dylan.

Grossman succeeded at Columbia, but it wasn't easy. At the time, Columbia's standard artist royalty was 5 percent, which Davis refused to negotiate, even though Grossman let it be known that MGM had offered 12 percent. Davis was feeling the pressure from Columbia, who wanted to keep Dylan, especially after losing the Righteous Brothers to MGM only weeks earlier, for an unmatchable $800,000 advance. The most Columbia had ever advanced a performer was $500,000 (for Doris Day, in the fifties, under the Mitch Miller regime).

Davis made Grossman one last offer of 7 percent royalties, plus 2 percent independent producing monies. The deal was unprecedented, the first time a label was willing to pay for production outside the house. It meant that Grossman and Dylan could hire their own producers and keep the difference of what they paid against the 2 percent. It was no secret in the industry that Dylan was, in effect, already his own producer, recording his albums "live" in the studio. Davis was aware of this and made the offer of 2 percent as a way for both sides to save face.

When Grossman took the new offer back to MGM, he was

met with a polite but firm turndown. Privately, Grossman attributed MGM's loss of interest to Dylan's drug problems, unaware a fourth player had emerged from these crucial negotiations: Allen Klein.

Klein, flush with his success handling Bobby Darin's finances, had acquired huge blocks of MGM stock and soon found himself caught in the middle of the boardroom battles MGM was having over the amount of money the record division wanted to invest in rock.

Davis, aware of the dissension within MGM, decided to shuffle the cards and deal Grossman from the bottom of the deck. He managed to "let" Klein see Dylan's royalty statements, something MGM had failed to get from Grossman, although not for lack of trying. Shortly thereafter, Grossman offered Dylan to Columbia for five years, no advance, for unprecedented 10 percent domestic royalties (7 foreign), with no minimum number of albums.

Davis accepted the offer, and the deal was made.

Dylan's fury at Grossman's having "imprisoned" him in Woodstock never eased, and eventually led to the collapse of their personal and business relationships. To make sure Grossman received nothing further from him, Dylan held back the best of his new songs until the final expiration of his Dwarf Music publishing contract. Only then did Dylan make his celebrated 1975 "comeback" album, *Blood on the Tracks*.

Like the industry in which he'd gained his fame and fortune, Dylan's priorities had irrevocably shifted.

Twelve

The folk-to-rock progression of the early sixties began in the coffeehouses and clubs located near the college campuses of Chicago, Boston and New York. At the same time, the inner city and outer 'burbs of these cities offered a different type of music in the bars where working-class teens hung out; eighteen- and nineteen-year-olds with day jobs and 409's not into acoustic attitudinizing. These were the joints where colored lightwheels rotated above sweating young strippers while live bands played in the corner where the jukebox used to be.

The bar bands of the early sixties had a circuit all their own, and produced some of the best rock of the transitional period after payola and before the Beatles. Unlike Bob Dylan, whose commercial audience was mainly to be found on the fringes of the college towns in the northeast, bar bands caught the attention of the nation's teens, hungry for rock and roll.

One of the best was the Jersey-based Four Seasons. Bob Gaudio, one of its founding members, had gotten into rock and roll early, helping out with some vocal backup for a Bronx band, the Three Friends, before starting to write songs. His first hit single, "Short Shorts" by the newly formed Gaudio-led Royal Teens, reached number three on *Billboard*'s February '58 chart, the thirty-sixth most popular record that year. The group went on an extensive bus and truck tour to promote "Short Shorts" and did the Alan Freed/Dick Clark circuits.

"I got a real quick taste of the record business at a very early age," Gaudio relates. " 'Short Shorts' was released originally on a New York independent label called Power Records. In those days, selling the master to a major was the name of the game. In our case, ABC-Paramount bid for 'Short Shorts' and made a national hit out of it. The obvious question is, did any of the money come back to us, but the better question is, did any of the money ever come back to the kids who were making records in those days? The answer in both cases would be no. We saw nothing from Power once it sold the master, leaving us far behind. We had nothing to do with the advances; and my total royalties, performing and as one of the writers, amounted to about $1,600 total, which I used to buy my first car, for cash."

Gaudio used the car to get around the bar circuit, eventually auditioning to be the keyboard player for bar band singer Frankie Valli's new group. Valli knew Gaudio from the Royal Teens and asked him to become one of the members of the Four Lovers.

Gaudio joined the Lovers on the New Jersey bar circuit, for $75 a week. Gaudio was soon writing songs for the group, tailored to the sound of singer Valli's unusual falsetto lead. Like most bands at the time, they wound up in Tin Pan Alley in search of a publisher who could sell them to a record company. "The philosophy in those days was that anyone who was writing for Tin Pan Alley was writing for someone who had a deal," Gaudio says. "The publishers were usually going after the artists that were happening at the time. If you wanted to perform as well as write, Tin Pan Alley really wasn't the place to be. I was more interested in getting a recording deal with the group than in selling my songs for someone else. To give us a song, even our own songs, wouldn't be a good business move for a publisher. In a sense, we were locked out by our ambition."

Most of the bar groups put the singers up front and the musicians in the back, with a highly choreographed presentation of someone else's songs. The Four Lovers (later renamed The Four Seasons) were different, being musicians who sang while playing instruments. "There really wasn't any influence on us," Gaudio maintains. "I can't think of any band that was a vocal group and played, as well. It was a necessity for us, because the type of music we were doing made it difficult for a pickup band to be able to follow. We worked a lot in those days with Bob Crewe, one of the first independent producers. We became his studio band, playing behind a lot of his acts, although the original intent was for us to record ourselves. We did backup on some pretty good records, including Danny and the Juniors' 'Rock and Roll Is Here to Stay.' We did backup for almost two years, working the clubs at night and recording during the day. We were doing better financially, but it wasn't what we intended when we went with Bob. Especially when we started giving up the club dates out of sheer exhaustion. We didn't want to be like all the other bands we knew. We were after something different, something more. We finally told Bob he either had to record us or we were going to split."

Crewe asked Gaudio to put four songs together on a demo, on spec, to show what the group could do on its own. "I didn't have a tape recorder in those days and I didn't have the patience to write down music," Gaudio says. "I'd come up with this melody, and the way I remembered it was by putting a quick lyric to it. I kept singing 'Sherry' all the way down to the car so I wouldn't forget it. When Frankie finally heard it, he flipped, but the other guys weren't sure. We rehearsed it and decided to let Bob decide. We sang it for him over the phone. 'Boys,' he said to us over the phone, 'If I don't fuck up that song in the studio it sounds like a number one record.'" On the strength of the demo Crewe cut a deal with Vee-Jay Records, and "Sherry" became the third biggest selling single of 1962.

Started in the fifties, Vee-Jay was a black-owned Chicago-based independent, in direct competition with its across-the-street competition, Chess Records. Vee-Jay was one of the very few rock and roll independents that managed to stay in business after payola, in spite of the fact that their entire inventory was seized and links were established between their distribution system and organized crime. Somehow they managed to hang in, although after 1960 they were anxious to replace their catalog of rhythm and blues with a more contemporary, i.e., "white" sound. When they heard Bob Crewe's "Sherry" demo for the Four Seasons, they decided to put everything they had into the group. The Four Seasons' first string of hits—"Sherry," "Big Girls Don't Cry," "Walk Like a Man" and "Candy Girl"—put Vee-Jay back on the rock and roll map.

Bob Gaudio: "The problem was, they just refused to pay, us or anybody. At first they didn't, and later they couldn't pay us what they owed, which enabled us to get the ownership of our masters—'Sherry,' 'Big Girls Don't Cry,' 'Walk Like a Man.' After that, we left the label and moved over to Phillips, where Bob Crewe was already established.

"But the crucial fact here is that we were in a tough litigation for close to a year. And because of that we didn't have any product out on the market. Everything had been going so well and, then, bang, we got in the middle of this problem and we were forced to stop recording. Doing business meant you kept releasing songs, one on top of the other. You didn't sit around in those days like Michael Jackson does today and put out a follow-up album three years later; you kept the heat on. You were supposed to release the next single as soon the last one was beginning to come down from its peak position on the charts. Which is why we were number one on the charts twelve out of fourteen weeks after 'Sherry' broke because of the release pattern with 'Big Girls Don't Cry.' We had three number ones in a row, and a couple of near number ones, like 'Candy Girl,' and then suddenly, just like that, we had no more records. A lot of people thought it was over for us. They thought the group had faded, that we had shot our wad, so to speak. The kids who bought records had no idea about what was going on behind the scenes, and why should they? The radio stations just stopped getting Four Seasons records, and as far as they or anyone else cared, we were finished. Things might have been a lot different for us had we known what was about to happen, with the Beatles and the British Invasion. Had we known, maybe we would have settled a lot earlier and kept ourselves hot. But we didn't know; no one knew the Beatles were about to bury every group in America. And the funny thing is, 'Please Please Me,' originally released on Vee-Jay, came to them from us.

"We had gone on tour in England after 'Sherry,' which was a big record in England, in 1962, the same time that 'Please Please Me' was breaking wide open with the Beatles. In fact, they came backstage to meet us at one point. And then I heard this record on the radio and said to Frankie, this would be a smash for us to cover, particularly with the falsetto part that would suit his voice perfectly. I was seriously considering covering it. We would have, except we had 'Walk Like a Man' waiting to be released, and I knew I couldn't put both of them out at the same time. When we got back to the States, I told Jay Lasker, the head of the label, I'd heard this record in England, 'Please Please Me' by a group called the Beatles, and told him we were thinking of covering it. I asked him how strong he felt about 'Walk Like a Man,' and he said he thought it was a number one record. I told them if we didn't cover it they should at least try to get the American rights to the master because it's going to be a number one record in England, very similar to what we were doing with falsetto and four-part harmony, and it could be big here. Lasker didn't say anything, I didn't hear from anyone, and then the next thing I knew, Vee-Jay had picked up the rights and put it out, just about the time the Four Seasons realized we weren't getting paid. Had we handled the situation differently, we might have wound up with the assets to the company, which would have included not only our masters, but the entire label, including that first Beatle album."*

The Four Seasons were thrown over, first by Vee-Jay and then by the American record-buying public, for the unlikeliest of new acts: four young men from Liverpool, England, who were total unknowns in America. How their music first came to America reads like a comedy of errors. Through a seemingly unrelated series of events, they first appeared in the United States on Vee-Jay to almost universal commercial indifference, the bottom of the rock pile.

Ironically, the story of the Beatles' conquest of America began in Tin Pan Alley, the musical mecca about to be buried for good by the coming British Invasion.

In 1962, Irwin Pincus, the independent Tin Pan Alley publisher, sent his brother to open a branch of the office in London to look for new music, as the shortage of new, usable product in America caused by the payola scandal continued. Once in England, Pincus's brother became friendly with Dick James, a small-time British music publisher. James had begun his career as a singer, working for George Martin before he'd become involved with his new "discovery," the Beatles.

Brian Epstein, the Beatles' manager, was still searching for a music publisher for his boys' songs and asked Martin for any suggestions he might have. Martin recommended Hill and Range, Elvis's publishers, and Dick James.

In a move that would one day come back to haunt the Beatles, Epstein rejected Hill and Range in favor of James, with whom he set up an initial meeting. The two hit it off, and arrangements were made for the establishment of Northern Songs, whose ownership was split 50–50 between James and the Beatles. James received an additional 10 percent to ad-

*By 1967, the group was $2 million in debt, owing largely to their legal problems at Vee-Jay and their difficulty regaining that momentum. Eventually, the group rebounded in the seventies, pulling in hit after hit, with the share of profits split between Valli and Gaudio passing the $50 million level. In addition to record sales and public appearances—Valli still performs with the group, Gaudio doesn't—the two earn approximately $700,000 a year on airplay of Four Seasons records.

minister Northern Songs, which gave him a controlling 55 percent interest in the company, the remaining 45 percent for the Beatles and Epstein to share. It was the first Beatles deal conceived and executed by Brian Epstein, and one of the worst that could possibly have been made. By putting control of the group's music into the hands of Dick James, Epstein unwittingly fell into the same type of deal that destroyed the careers of so many of rock's pioneers. In blissful ignorance, the Beatles eagerly gave away what was, in effect, their future. Almost all the financial turmoil the Beatles experienced during the next twenty-five years began the day they signed with Dick James.

It wasn't long before the unique structure of the Dick James deal reached Irwin Pincus, who heard about it from his brother. Ever on the lookout for new music, and sensing the possibility of a good enough deal in the wind to make any effort worthwhile, Pincus suggested they might be able to pick up the subcopyrights (foreign rights) to some Beatles' songs for American and Canadian distribution. The idea was to buy the rights to Beatles records to get to the songs, in order to place them with American acts. At the time, rock and roll was strictly a one-way street, with American performers all over England and Europe, while British performers were considered commercially unsellable to American audiences. After all, the reasoning went, Americans originated rock and roll; the British merely copied it. Why would anyone pay to see a copy when they could just as easily see the real thing?

Pincus secured the foreign rights to six original Beatles recordings—"She Loves You," "I Saw Her Standing There," "There's a Place," "From Me to You," "I Want to Be Your Man" and "Misery"—for no advance, strictly on the basis of a 50–50 split of any and all profits. "And," according to Pincus, "we couldn't get arrested. Every label passed on the Beatles and their songs; they just weren't interested."

Pincus eventually got one song recorded by Del Shannon, "From Me to You," on Swan, which went nowhere. The only other label he had anything to do with was Vee-Jay, which agreed to release "Please Please Me" as a single. Vee-Jay was by now desperate for product, as their only other act of any consequence, the Four Seasons, refused to continue to record for the label. Lasker remembered Gaudio mentioning the Beatles and took a chance with Pincus.

As it happened, "Please Please Me" became the biggest-selling record in Vee-Jay's history, surpassing even the Four Seasons' "Sherry" and "Walk Like a Man." The initial 1962 agreement called for a one-year license with an option, during which time Vee-Jay released the first Beatles album in America. When it failed to catch on, Lasker let his option lapse. This was December '63, only weeks before the Beatles first appeared on "The Ed Sullivan Show" and Beatlemania invaded America.

As teen America went crazy over the four mop-tops, Capitol Records discovered it happened to own the North American rights (via its parent company, EMI, which controlled the British rights) to the entire Beatles catalog. This left Vee-Jay with only one suddenly very valuable Beatles album. Lasker quickly went back into production, churning out as many copies of the original album as he could manufacture, booking every available pressing plant in Los Angeles. He churned out ten million albums before Capitol tried to stop him. At once, Capitol slapped Vee-Jay with an immediate cease-and-desist order, which Lasker ignored as he continued to press and sell the *Please Please Me* album. When the end came, Lasker closed his company's doors without ever paying a cent in royalties on what is variously estimated to have been the sale of millions of Beatles albums.

Still, there were those who doubted the financial staying power of the Beatles, including many record executives at Capitol. Glenn Wallachs, cofounder of Capitol Records in 1942 with Buddy De Sylva and Johnny Mercer, was certainly less than enthusiastic about the prospect of having the rockers on his label. A devoted middle-of-the-roader who envisioned Capitol as the home for the likes of Frank Sinatra, and who hated rock and roll, sat in the Hollywood Brown Derby having lunch with a couple of his industry pals at the height of the first wave of Beatlemania. "Jesus," he said, as he threw his hands up in disgust, having been ordered by EMI to release the Beatles on Capitol. "And now we gotta put out these goddamn mop-haired little bastards from England. Jesus Christ, 'The Beatles'! What a name! And that hair! It's gonna ruin Capitol, I'm telling you! It's gonna ruin us!"

Thirteen

In 1961, as the result of a $10 million stock buyout, EMI took over America's Capitol Records. EMI had been looking for an American outlet, and Capitol seemed the most vulnerable of the majors.

EMI—Electrical and Mechanical Industries—was the British-based home of the original German Gramaphone Company, which had expanded into England shortly after the end of World War II. In addition to its home phonograph, EMI developed a series of subsidiary record labels, from the very esoteric HMV Records to its self-described "junk" label, Parlophone, which specialized in low-end recordings of "popular" music.

In 1954, the first head of Parlophone retired. Named to replace him was George Martin. At the tender business age of twenty-one years old, Martin found himself in charge of the entire Parlophone label.

Martin brought his taste for music-hall comedy to the financially meager label, where it was relatively inexpensive to record the humor of Peter Sellers, which he preferred anyway, to skiffle, the sound that had lately caught on in postwar England. Called "washboard music" by British teens, after the sound Lonnie Donegan produced on his hit "Rock Island Line," Martin looked upon skiffle as little more than a passing fad.

What made Martin reconsider his opinion of the music was the unexpected success of Cliff Richard and the Shadows. To compete, Martin wanted very much to sign Tommy Steele, a young skiffler who could give Richard a run. The problem was, Steele wanted a large advance, which Martin knew EMI would never approve. The average EMI royalty was a penny a record sold, with a very few "name" artists able to get more, and almost never were advances given. With great reluctance, Martin was forced to pass, for the moment, on his desire to bring skiffle to Parlophone.

By 1962, the Beatles had been through the slim British roster of available labels without being able to make a deal. They resigned themselves to playing noon concerts at the Liverpool Cavern, where they were first discovered by Brian Epstein. Although his father's retail record outlet, NEMS (North End Road Music Stores), was located only two blocks from the Cavern, Epstein, who managed the store and prided himself on his musical knowledge, had never heard of the group until a steady flow of young girls began asking for the new Beatles record. "My Bonnie" was a single the Beatles had played backup on while in Germany, to date their only recorded song.

Epstein wondered why he'd never heard of the record, why it hadn't come in with the new shipments. His father's chain of stores was among the finest in the country, and NEMS was usually the first to receive new records. Epstein had no way of knowing that "My Bonnie" was available only on special order, as an import. Liverpool's seaport proved an advantage to Epstein, whose access to American records was greatly enhanced by his ability to import them directly from New York. He serviced an extremely loyal audience for American R&B, unable to hear it over the BBC, which banned the music from its airwaves as unsuitable for British audiences. It was inconceivable to Epstein that he'd somehow overlooked a hot new release; even more so when he discovered from one of his clients that the Beatles were playing every day not three blocks from the store. Epstein personally went to check out the Beatles, and as a familiar story goes, convinced them he should be their manager.

Epstein's first priority was to get the Beatles signed to a label. There were four major record companies in England at the time, all operating out of London: EMI, Decca, Phillips and Pye. Epstein relentlessly pursued each of them while ordering reams of imported copies of "My Bonnie," hoping to create some industry interest in the record.

None of it helped very much, as one by one, the record companies turned down the Beatles. EMI's scheduled tryout for the group was their last shot; and they prepared themselves for the worst, not knowing that Martin was still looking for a skiffle band willing to work for what little money he could afford to pay.*

Martin offered the Beatles a one-year contract, with a guarantee to record four titles. The Beatles and Epstein shared a total royalty of the standard EMI one cent a record—a fifth of a penny apiece. This meant that a million-selling disk, of which there were very few in England's history, would net the entire group, including Brian, a total of $10,000 (in equivalent British currency), plus whatever publishing money they earned. With four built-in one-year options, if the Beatles

---

*At least one record publisher felt that parent company Polygram may have pressured Martin into signing the Beatles, after Epstein's father let the label know he was anxious for his son to get into personal management. Epstein's retail record outlet was crucial to distribution throughout Great Britain and carried a lot of weight with labels. For all the legend about the "chemistry" between Martin and the Beatles, he may have been forced to sign the group regardless of whatever musical abilities they demonstrated during the audition. In that light, Martin's "helping" the band by suggesting they replace their drummer, and his inordinate amount of time "sculpting" the group's sound, take on a different meaning from the standard version of his being unduly impressed with the group's music.

lasted that long, their royalties were scheduled to increase, in the fifth year, to a grand total of two cents per record.

The initial publishing deal Epstein set up wasn't much better. He cut a deal with Ardmore and Beechwood, an obscure British firm with no power in the industry. On the advice of George Martin, Epstein sought a release from the company, which they gave him along with their blessings. He then approached Dick James, the result of which was the creation of Northern Songs.

It wasn't until January 1967, as the Beatles entered the studio to begin working on *Sgt. Pepper,* that Brian Epstein was finally able to get the Beatles' original penny-per-record royalty amended. Until then, for all the money and notoriety the Beatles had brought to EMI, and the $500 million worth of Beatlemania that swept through America, the Beatles were still literally working for pennies.

The new agreement called for the Beatles to receive a 10 percent royalty on all British singles and albums, escalating to 12½ percent after 100,000 copies of singles sold, and to 15 percent after 30,000 albums. In America, the figures were adjusted to 10 percent and 17½. As for Brian Epstein, he considered these negotiations among his best yet and hoped the Beatles saw them that way as well.

They didn't. Paul McCartney, in particular, was outraged by what he felt was an embarrassment, compared to what Allen Klein had been able to get for the Rolling Stones.

Klein had come a long way since his days with Bobby Darin. His next big deal had been the negotiation of a million-dollar contract for Sam Cooke with RCA, completed weeks before the singer's untimely death in 1965. Even before that deal was completed, however, Klein had made up his mind to go after the Beatles, by now the biggest thing in show business on both sides of the Atlantic. Klein's interest in acquiring the Beatles had to do with his desire to sign them to MGM, where he had become a major stockholder. On his own label, whatever profits he accrued as the group's manager would be small potatoes to what he could make from record sales. Unable to get to the group directly, he devised a clever strategy to demonstrate his abilities in such a way as to make the Beatles sit up and take notice. He'd go after the Rolling Stones and use them to demonstrate to the Beatles just what he could do.

The Stones were the perfect choice, not yet having made it big in the States. Klein thoroughly researched the Stones and discovered that their original contract with London Records was about to expire, and there was talk it might not be renewed. Arranging to meet with the group, Klein dazzled them with a presentation climaxed by the bold promise to guarantee not only that they wouldn't be dropped by their label, but that he'd deliver a hefty bonus from London to get them to renew.

The Stones gave Klein the green light to negotiate with Decca, London's parent company, the results of which were the personal deliverance by Klein to the Stones of a cashier's check for $1.25 million as an advance against their new royalty structure of 24 percent of the wholesale price of each record sold, approximately 75 cents an album; a far better deal than the pennies for which they'd originally signed. Disposed of in the wake of Klein's successful negotiation was the Stone's personal manager, Loog Oldham, who reportedly received a million-dollar out-of-court settlement to step out of the picture.

On the strength of his Stones deal with Decca, Klein took on every British act that came to him, and there were plenty, including Herman's Hermits, the Animals, Donovan and the Dave Clark Five. However, there was only one act he felt he had to have, and that was the Beatles.

Once McCartney heard of Klein's ability, he urged Epstein to renegotiate the group's deal with Capitol, which was how the revised Beatles contract came about. Still unsatisfied with Epstein, McCartney wanted the Beatles to merge with the Stones, under the financial umbrella of NEMS. It was an idea the others considered, as they were all envious of the kind of money the Stones were making. Epstein, however, was totally against it, and with good reason. He knew that any merger with the Stones meant taking in Klein, and he, Epstein, didn't want to be the Beatles' Loog Oldham.

When the rumors of a Beatles/Stones merger reached Klein, he could hardly contain himself. He envisioned a musical empire even greater than the one he had already built. Already, the pieces were in place for him to make the necessary moves, having just pulled off his latest coup, the acquisition of Philadelphia-based Cameo Records. Cameo had seen better days, when Dick Clark had been in charge. When Clark decided to move his entire operation to Los Angeles, late in 1964, he severed all remaining ties to Cameo, leaving the label in total chaos, on the brink of bankruptcy.

When Klein became aware of the situation, he "leaked" information of a possible merger between Cameo and Chappell's, a British music publishing firm. The rumor caused Cameo's stock to surge, and a merger did indeed take place, but not the one everyone anticipated. Klein merged his own accounting company with Cameo and created ABKCO Industries, rock's first corporate management conglomerate. Klein intended it exclusively for the financial management of his ever-growing pool of talent. In spite of an extensive investigation conducted by the Securities and Exchange Commission into rumors that Klein had falsely inflated the value of Cameo's stock to make the company cash-rich before the merger, no charges were filed and Klein walked away with all of Cameo's assets, including its back masters.

All of which made the idea of a merger between the Stones and the Beatles even more attractive. Nor did it hurt matters any that the Stones broke wide open in the United States in the first months after Klein had renegotiated their contract, and were now making millions under his financial guidance, while the Beatles continued to flounder under the hopelessly confused management of Brian Epstein. When John Lennon cried to the press that he was losing millions and on the road to bankruptcy, Klein cried for joy. It was only a matter of time, he believed, before he would own them.

. . .

If the Beatles were in financial trouble, it wasn't because they weren't selling records. Capitol was riding the crest of a profit wave the likes of which the industry hadn't seen since RCA and Elvis in '56. In the first five years Capitol had the Beatles, the label's annual earnings jumped from $30 million to $120 million, allowing Capitol to be competitive for the first time among the majors, all now chasing after every rock act still available, in the hopes of snagging the next Beatles.

The Jefferson Airplane/RCA deal was the first to break the one-dollar-per-album royalty barrier. Once that fell, competition increased among the majors for talent. In an era that produced some of the most socially conscious music in the history of commercial American entertainment, the groups were stampeding over each other in what one record executive of the time described as the "Kentucky Derby of Greed."

Among RCA's major acquisitions was "Mama" Cass Elliot, for whom RCA was willing to pay almost any price, as her defection effectively ended the Mamas and the Papas, the chief competition to RCA's own Jefferson Airplane.

At Columbia, the newly seated Clive Davis administration went on a signing binge, nabbing Janis Joplin, Donovan, Blood, Sweat and Tears, Paul Revere and the Raiders, the Chambers Brothers, and Santana, among others. Spending had become so uncontrollable that, upon acquiring Bonnie and Delaney from Atlantic for major money a week before they broke up, someone at CBS commented that only Clive Davis could sign "two groups for the price of four and wind up with none."

Many of the acts signed by Columbia had more in common than big-dollar contracts. They also shared a relationship with two of the decade's premiere American rock entrepreneurs. The first was Albert Grossman, whose role in the corporate expansion of the majors into rock became a prime factor in the rise of another of the decade's key players, a German-born immigrant on the financial periphery of the music business until he crossed paths with Dylan's manager at the 1967 Monterey Pop Festival. His name was Wolfgang Wolodia Grajanka, better known as Bill Graham.

After fifteen years of trying to make a living as a professional actor, a time of his life, in his own words, that he spent "not tearing the world apart," Graham left New York to start life over in San Francisco, where he became involved with the San Francisco Mime Troupe, a politically oriented street theater group. To Graham, the troupe's noncommercial activities were a welcome alternative to the disillusioning commercial theater from which he'd just retired.

To support their activities and presentations, the troupe regularly held fund-raisers, one of which Graham volunteered to produce, shifting his priorities from performing to fund-raising. His three-day "Trips Festival," held at the Longshoreman's Hall in January 1968, turned into a psychedelic free-for-all which attracted local "happening" San Francisco counter-culture notables, from Ken Kesey's Merry Pranksters and the Hell's Angels, to the celebrated Lawrence Ferlinghetti. The best part of the festival, everyone agreed, was the nonstop music played by the Bay Area's best bands. It was Graham's introduction to San Francisco's hip music community and a type of rock never heard on commercial radio; too loud, too long, too politically oriented.

Buoyed by the success of his festival, Graham was convinced there had to be a commercial audience for the music, if presented in an environment free of the restrictive boundaries of traditional "sit-down" concerts. He began to look for some kind of venue, a vacant supermarket or abandoned movie house, in which to create an atmosphere of musical and social freedom. After searching the city's neighborhoods for weeks, he discovered the vacant Fillmore movie theater. Scraping together enough money for a six-month lease, he borrowed a dance hall permit from a friend and went into the business of promoting rock and roll, Bill Graham style.

When he first opened the doors of the Fillmore in February of 1966, his entire staff consisted of his wife, Bonnie, and one assistant, Marushka Greene. From that modest beginning, Graham produced more than three hundred shows in the next two and a half years. Besides the Grateful Dead, the Fillmore became the home court for the Jefferson Airplane, Quicksilver Messenger Service, Janis Joplin and Big Brother and the Holding Company, and the Mothers of Invention. By September 1967, the demand for tickets to the powerhouse weekend shows was so great that Graham made arrangements to move them to a larger, abandoned ballroom, the nearby Winterland. Graham's theaters became the hip place to be, causing him to move to the larger Carousel Ballroom, rechristening it Fillmore West.

Graham's musical showplaces became the prime venues for the music of San Francisco's '67 Summer of Love. As the fall drew near, there was a sense that something special had taken place, and a couple of amateur rock promoters, Ben Shapiro and Alan Pariser, decided to put on an outdoor musical gathering, a West Coast version of the Newport Folk Festival, to acknowledge what everybody in the industry now called the "California Sound." The idea was to hold a noncommercial outdoor "happening," a celebration of all that was different and special about San Francisco's brand of rock music. It would be a gift to the people who'd supported the Bay Area bands.

Albert Grossman heard about Monterey and decided to check it out. A veteran of nearly fifteen years of folk festivals, he knew better than most how to spot new talent, and what to do about it when he did.

The idea was a good one, but proved too difficult for the two fledgling producers to pull off. They were unable to raise the necessary funds, and in a final gesture to seeing the festival continue, sold it outright to professional record producers Lou Adler and Abe Somer. Adler and Somer were less interested in the aesthetics of West Coast rock than the profits it was capable of producing. They continued to promote the festival's noncommercial attitude while privately canvassing the majors for financial underwriting. Several record companies cooperated, and the festival quickly became a giant supermarket of unsigned talent. As a result, the real action of Monterey took place backstage, in the makeshift green rooms and private bar areas where record companies made their deals. Adler hired a film crew to shoot the festival, and by the time the last act took the stage, had sold the film rights for $400,000.

Clive Davis also came to Monterey. After watching Janis Joplin perform, he offered her a contract, only to discover that she and her backup band, Big Brother and the Holding Company, had just signed with one of the new West Coast independents, Mainstream Records.

Over drinks, Grossman commiserated with Davis on the lost opportunity. "Let me see what I can do," Grossman said. Leaving Davis, Grossman found Joplin backstage and asked to see her copy of the contract. Going over it he found a half-dozen loopholes that could be used to nullify the deal. He urged Joplin to do just that, promising he'd get her a better one with Columbia if she let him represent her, an arrangement to which she immediately agreed. Before going back to Davis, Grossman signed Steve Miller, as well as the Quicksilver Messenger Service, added them to his roster of Joplin and the Electric Flag, the group he'd brought to the festival, and approached Davis for a $100,000 advance for the entire package. However, before the deal was completed, Capitol offered Quicksilver and Miller six figures each, and got them. Davis then quickly came to terms with Grossman over Joplin and the Electric Flag, fearing he might lose them as well. Davis agreed to $50,000 up front for the Electric Flag, a bargain, Grossman insisted; while Janis's deal escalated to $200,000, half of which went to Mainstream as the settlement Grossman had agreed to before going back to Davis.

The signing frenzy continued throughout the festival. Davis went on to sign Moby Grape, Laura Nyro, the Association, and Tom Rush, while Warners snagged what many felt was the class act to come out of Monterey, Jimi Hendrix (after he'd signed with Grossman). The label was more than happy to pay the $100,000 Grossman asked, hoping this was the rock acquisition that would finally make them competitive with Columbia.

Before the festival ended, Grossman was introduced to Bill Graham. Wasting no time, Grossman made a deal to promote his bands at Bill Graham's venues, as long as Graham agreed to expand his operation to the East Coast, where Grossman was located. Graham had doubts about his ability to compete in New York. Having failed there as an actor, he was reluctant to return.

He overcame his reluctance when Grossman offered to bankroll the purchase of the vacant Second Avenue Village Theatre as the future locale of the Fillmore East. The first official Albert Grossman/Bill Graham Fillmore East show was presented on March 9, 1968, starring Albert Grossman's Janis Joplin and Big Brother and the Holding Company, Albert King and Tim Buckley. To Graham, his arrival in New York represented the culmination of superb musicianship combined with the new idealism he'd discovered in San Francisco; surely the future of American rock and roll.

To Grossman, Graham's "new idealism" was the latest package for an old product. Monterey had proved that to him. Between sets of social relevance and political protest, musicians eagerly signed six-figure deals with recording industry reps as they sipped the finest champagne and smoked as much dope as was available.

Which was why, at Grossman's first meeting with the staff of the new Fillmore team, held without Graham's knowledge, he stated in no uncertain terms what the Grossman ground rules were: "This place is about money, not music. I don't care about the prestige of the place; if you want to book belly dancers, okay. We have a very high operating 'nut' and I want the place filled up. That's all that matters."

Fourteen

The Fillmore East came to dominate the New York rock scene, eclipsing the traditional Village circuit as the primary route of exposure for talent. Tom Paxton, on those early Village days: "New York was unbelievable in the '60s. In 1963 there were over thirty clubs on MacDougal Street alone. Greenwich Village was known the world over as the music scene. It permeated every college, the streets, and dives and even uptown social circles."

Among the most popular of the Village clubs had been Fred Weintraub's Bitter End, at one time the premier showcase for dozens of topflight musicians and comedians. By 1968, the Bitter End passed on to Paul Colby, the former record plugger. In the shadow of the Fillmore, the Bitter End launched the careers of Bill Withers, John Prine, Carly Simon, Arlo Guthrie and others whose sound didn't quite fit the progressive rock audiences at the Fillmore paid to hear.

"We kind of floundered that first year I was there," Paul Colby remembers. "I arrived in October '67 to manage the club, and there was already a lot of competition in the Village for talent, and the age of basket-passing had all but come to an end. There was the Gaslight right around the corner, the Cafe-A-Go-Go, Folk City, and we were all competing for the same pool of available talent. But I could see that the days of folkie clubs were fading. The really big rock acts were going over to the Fillmore and places like that. We were a small club, all the clubs were really nothing more than holes in the wall, and we just couldn't compete. Not just physically, but the money was getting totally out of hand.

"I remember taking a chance in January 1969 and booking the Everly Brothers for $3,500 for six days, after they'd switched to Warner Brothers and were having trouble breaking a new hit. Today that doesn't sound like so much money, but for me, I went sleepless that whole week. The most I'd ever paid an act before that was Joni Mitchell, who I gave $1,000 to, and previous to that I think I paid $400 to Kenny Rankin, and that was it. As for the Everlys, I knew I was taking a chance. They were more country than anything else, and had never played the Village; they hadn't played anywhere in New York in a lot of years.

"What can I say, they were a smash, and I knew I'd found the formula to keep going. Pay big bucks and get name acts. We charged six bucks admission, which was a lot for a small club in those days, and sold out every show. Eventually, we had to depend more and more on the record companies to showcase new acts. The record companies controlled the club scene, there's no doubt about it. They called the shots. Without their support, the Bitter End was dead.

"The business changed so much in those days. I remember going to a trade convention, and all the talk was about agents and managers and prices for acts, and who was returning the advance and who wasn't. Almost overnight, they began to dictate what kind of money they had to have to cover an act's expenses, regardless of whether the club made money or not.

"I remember exactly when the club scene really died. There was this big party happening for one of the superstars who happened to have started at the club, who always talked about being loyal to the club. I called to put my name on the list, and a little later I got a call back from his secretary telling me I couldn't come to the party, there were too many people going to be there. I hung up the phone and said to myself, it's over. They don't need the clubs anymore."

In 1969, the new Madison Square Garden opened in New York City. Although boasting to the trade of its intent to become the premier East Coast showcase, the architectural design of the Garden rendered it acoustically useless for live rock presentations, as their first ventures so aptly demonstrated. However, the lack of production value meant little to the acts attracted to the $50,000 guarantee the Garden offered for a single performance in its 20,000 seat arena. By contrast, the Fillmore's top pay scale, reserved for what Graham considered his best acts, was $20,000, and that was for four performances over a two-night period. As one observer on the scene recalls: "Bill had a kind of S&M relationship with all of his groups, acting the tyrant, paying what he decided was fair and working them hard for their money. As a result, a lot of the acts got a great deal of pleasure out of the opportunity to work the competition's side of the street, driving up their fees and working a hell of a lot easier in the process, as well as sticking it to Bill."

Graham's A bands began to desert the Fillmore for the the Garden, leaving a void filled by the steady stream of B acts, mostly British newcomers and unsigned American bar bands. Taking advantage of the new competition, talent management began taking a much tougher stand with Graham. If the Fillmore wanted a certain A band, it had to take two, sometimes three B bands on the same bill. It was a policy Graham found intolerable.

Kip Cohen, then Fillmore's business manager, recalls those times: "The Fillmore was a microcosm of all that was happening in rock, both onstage and off. Onstage, the music coalesced beautifully. There were blues-based bands like the original Blood, Sweat and Tears; classic British rock like the Who and Procol Harum; boogie bands like the Dead; folk-rock, brass bands like Chicago; and solo stars like Richie Havens. It all happened so fast, the international attention to 'the scene,' the major labels fighting each other to sign acts, management offices opening on every other block, agencies opening and growing into conglomerates overnight, rock agents springing out of nowhere, and major agencies like William Morris suddenly spawning rock divisions. Rock agents were a different breed; guys like Frank Barsalona, who'd been a powerhouse at the time at Creative Artists Management, left to start his own agency and changed the nature of the business."

Barsalona was considered by many to be the innovator of a more progressive representation, better suited to the needs of bands in the age of corporate rock. A product of the era of "meat market" talent, when record companies bypassed musicians in favor of formal relationships with packages like Alan Freed and Dick Clark, Barsalona, through his newly formed Premier Talent sought to put some of the power and a lot more of the money into artists' hands. For the Who, Barsalona was able to break the mid-sixties $10,000 live-appearance barrier, and as a result went on to represent Cream, Herman's Hermits, Jethro Tull and Peter Frampton. Premier became known as the agency that handled the best bands in the business, bands who were paid accordingly. Barsalona worked the rapidly expanding ballroom and arena circuit across the country. New markets were developing in every major city, and he often dovetailed his stable with the rapidly developing FM "progressive" radio stations.

Along with the growth of "progressive" rock and roll, FM became an integral part of the nation's entertainment network. FM successfully combined the business of music with the ideals of a generation looking for a more socially acceptable form of expression. A new set of "hip" jocks eagerly demonstrated their political awareness, while balancing their power within the industry. Often, stations participated with campus-based political groups, offering sanctuaries for draft resisters, to be harbored either at the station or at the college. During the marathons built around the sanctuaries, performers were likely to show up with test pressings of their new albums.

Where only a few years earlier it was extremely unlikely that any "star" rock and roll act could play anywhere but New York City, Los Angeles or Chicago, the ballroom circuit and FM radio made it possible for almost anyone near a big city to see Jimi Hendrix, Janis Joplin or Jim Morrison play.

"The economics of the Fillmore East, a 2,800-seat hall, set the 'ballroom' standard," Kip Cohen says. "The typical booking for an act with strength, a headline or A act, a fairly strong second act, and a possibly unknown opening act, with two shows each Friday and Saturday night, 8 and 11:30, grossed approximately $50,000 total for the four shows. A strong act would take half of that, 50 percent off the top for the gig. Compared to what they could get at the Garden, that was very low money. By comparison, lesser known acts doing shows in similar venues today—and in most cases they would only be doing shows there if they were lesser known, otherwise they'd be on the arena circuit—get that for one show. Also, no one toured with their own sound and lights the way they do today, which is one of the heaviest costs a band carries. We provided all of that.

"The reason Graham decided to close the Fillmore East and then the original Fillmore in San Francisco was, plainly and simply, greed. Not on his part, mainly the agents. They insisted on packaging, as agents always do, and Bill was just opposed to that. He saw packaging as a creative thing, his thing. Today, one 'buys' a package that originates with the agencies and management and that's it; there's two acts, never a third, and no one has any say about who it's going to be except the label and/or the agency and management teams. But in Bill's Fillmore days, he just wouldn't go for it, and I think rightly so. Once in a while a package was offered that was appealing. A manager would put his 'baby' band in front of his major act, and the show had some built-in integrity and sensitivity that was appropriate to the bill and our needs; but not often, not nearly often enough.

"I think what's really remarkable is that the Fillmore lasted as long as it did. In the midst of the increasing pressures from the industry, the ever more outrageous demands from the acts, not only money but food, women, whatever, Bill's having to constantly fly back and forth from coast to coast, the encroaching competition from the Garden, and new promoters like Ron Delsener and John Scher carving up New York really right from under his feet, it's a wonder he hung on at all.

"By 1971 the scene had grown ugly . . . uglier, as the loss of innocence on both the bands' and the audiences' part. New York went first, and in many ways it had to. New York never quite bought into the West Coast hippie thing, not really. In the East, those who pulled the strings weighed their every decision primarily from an economic standpoint, from the record companies down to the talent."

The scene that Graham had envisioned as the culmination of a generation's idealism had dissipated into an extended mean greed that came knocking at his front door. In 1970, the East Village neighborhood residents demanded more of a filtering down of the enormous profits it assumed Graham was taking out of his venues to finance his West Coast operations. The Hell's Angels, the East Village Motherfuckers, police surveillance and harassment, all protested the presence of Graham and the Fillmore. On one occasion, Graham gave the theater over to a number of local groups to voice their objections, an evening which quickly deteriorated into anarchy, with Graham being labeled a "capitalist pig" and demands that the theater be kept permanently open to the public with no charge for admission. A second occasion, which began as an ad hoc meeting outside the theater, ended in violence, with a forced entry that resulted in Graham's being hit across the face with a thick chain.

"After that attack on Bill," Kip Cohen says, "things went rapidly downhill, in spite of the fact that acts still wanted to

Al Jolson in minstrel blackface. *(author's collection)*

Bing Crosby—America's first pop crooner—is the second highest selling recording artist of all time. *(author's collection)*

Art Laboe hosting an early rock and roll show. Many would find the social mix and its implications disturbing. *(courtesy of Art Laboe)*

Ahmet Ertegan (with goatee), Ben E. King (with hat), and The Drapers at the New York offices of Atlantic Records, 1959. *(courtesy of Ben E. King)*

February 23, 1957, Times Square, New York: Alan Freed's rush to rock and roll glory. *(courtesy of Lance Freed)*

The Crowns: the beginning of rhythm and blues' crossover into the mainstream. *(courtesy of Ben E. King)*

Alan Freed as a young disk jockey in Akron, Ohio, in the early 50s. *(courtesy of Lance Freed)*

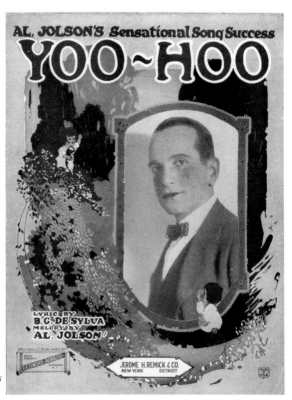

A Jolson "collaboration." *(author's collection)*

MOST OF ALL

WORDS & MUSIC BY **HARVEY FUQUA** AND **ALAN FREED**

REGENT MUSIC CORPORATION

One of Freed's "co-authored" songs.
(author's collection)

Rock and roll in the 50s. *(courtesy of Art Laboe)*

Rock and roll in the 50s. *(courtesy of Lance Freed)*

Bob Keane with Ritchie Valens—the height of 50s independent rock and roll. *(courtesy of Bob Keane)*

Bobby Darin, under Allen Klein's guidance, became rock and roll's first songwriter/singer/millionaire. *(author's collection)*

Art Laboe (left) and Dick Clark in 1959, prior to the payola hearings. *(courtesy of Art Laboe)*

Alan Freed and his third wife, Inga, during the payola investigation. *(courtesy of Lance Freed)*

Ricky Nelson: the all-white face of post-payola rock. *(courtesy of Art Laboe)*

Tin Pan Alley's 60s location: the Brill Building, 1619 Broadway, New York. *(courtesy of Artie Butler)*

Irwin Pincus with one of his five gold Beatle records. *(author's collection)*

Artie Butler (glasses) with Jay & the Americans (top row) and Lieber and Stoller (bottom row). *(courtesy of Artie Butler)*

The Four Seasons, 1964. The "American Beatles" at the height of their Vee-Jay period. Bob Gaudio (second from right), Frankie Valli (right). *(courtesy of Bob Gaudio)*

Mike Porco and Paul Colby, two legendary village club owners of the 60s.
(courtesy of Paul Colby)

Morris Levy (right) "sharing" a gold record with Tommy James and the Shondells. *(courtesy of Michael Ochs Archives)*

Elvis Presley with Ben Weisman in 1965. The plaque shows the names of some of the tunes Weisman penned for Elvis. *(courtesy of Ben Weisman)*

The Folk City Singers at the White House, 1965—a long way from the days of the Weavers. *(courtesy of Mike Porco)*

Dylan at Newport in 1965, a year before the "accident." *(author's collection)*

The legendary Fillmore East. *(courtesy of Josh White)*

Kip Cohen and Bill Graham at the Fillmore East in 1969. *(courtesy of Josh White)*

Danny Goldberg: one of the 80s breed of independent record label operators. *(courtesy of Danny Goldberg)*

Beatles' attorney Leonard Marks (center) with clients Eddie Murphy and Joe Piscopo. *(courtesy of Leonard Marks)*

Rockonomics. *(author's collection)*

play the Fillmore TV shows were being shot there, and Bill was getting all kinds of big money offers. Sol Hurok, the legendary uptown impresario, came to Bill with a plan to have the crème de la crème of British and American rock perform for a month at the Metropolitan Opera, in May of 1971, following the success of the Who's presentation there of *Tommy,* which Graham had produced. Bill got on the phone and started contacting all these groups, realizing what an opportunity this was. Rock was still an underground phenomenon, and here was the very fancy Lincoln Center people coming to him! They were willing to pay the headline act $50,000 for the week. However, the level of greed had reached such heights that the groups we approached, every one of them, poohpoohed the idea and turned down $50,000 as not being enough money to bother with. Bill couldn't believe what he was hearing, and really, that was the breaking point for him. He just said screw it, that was the last straw, and decided to close the Fillmore East."

Like the Fillmore, the Woodstock festival that took place in White Lake, New York, in August 1969 was supposed to represent everything the music of the sixties stood for. However, to those directly involved in its presentation it represented only the culmination of the type of corporate greed begun at Monterey and continued at the Isle of Wight (England), where Dylan, who'd worked for expenses at his early Newport appearances, played a single performance for a record $84,000. Woodstock became the symbol of peace, love and understanding to an eager public fed on the PR machine that backed the festival. To those more directly involved, those three days in the Catskills symbolized what to them sixties rock had become: the selling of progressive idealism for corporate profit.

The festival was conceived by John Roberts, a millionaire investment counselor with no previous show business experience. His intention was to use the festival as a way of establishing himself in the music industry. Taking his cue from Monterey, he figured to make a killing from the rights to a Woodstock feature film and record album.

As the three-day extravaganza continued, through the mud and rain, and the whole world listened and watched, Roberts stayed backstage, claiming that the weather and open-gate policy was causing his financial ruin, the festival already costing him three and a half million dollars.

Albert Grossman, who'd found a gold mine on the festival circuit, went to Woodstock to see to it that his pool of talent was paid—Jimi Hendrix ($18,000), Blood, Sweat and Tears ($15,000), the Band ($7,500), Janis Joplin ($7,500), Richie Havens ($6,000). A veteran of festival failures that often left his talent without enough carfare to get home, Grossman was suspicious of Roberts's financial backing. When Roberts began to complain about the high cost of continuing the festival, once the gates had been thrown open and everyone was admitted for free, Grossman offered him a million dollars in cash, on the spot, for the film and record rights, an offer that Roberts flatly turned down. Grossman knew for certain then, that despite his crying and cost cutting, Roberts was sitting on something big. Although the financial mismanagement of the festival wound up in several court cases that lasted for years (with some cases still in litigation), the movie went on to gross over $50 million, is in continual rerelease and available on video, and yielded two gold sound track albums.

Financially, the festival was an even greater success than Roberts could have imagined. As a rock event, however, it left a lot to be desired. One person who worked the festival recalls it from a performer's perspective: "I was pissed. It was supposed to be a music and art festival, but all it really was was the highest-priced talent available, flown in and flown out, without any positive interaction at all, the way it had been years before at Newport. There was supposed to be a revolving stage for the performers, making it easier for all those around to see. I think it revolved once and never turned again. They couldn't get the fences up to control the flow of the crowd and collect admission fees because they were too stoned. They couldn't provide for the crowd. Amateur time every step of the way. If you ever saw a scale model of Woodstock, you'd be shocked at just how tiny the stage actually was, both in front and backstage. The visibility factor had to be no more than twenty rows directly in front, and that was it. The film tends to romanticize it, but it was a total disaster if you were there. A lot of acts refused to play because they'd heard there was money trouble, and bags of cash were being produced to get them to go on, for fear of a riot breaking out in front if they didn't. For me, it was the end. I stood on the stage and looked out, and I realized most of what was happening was totally irrelevant.

"The reason it never happened again was purely a question of economics and had nothing to do with the so-called 'magic' that took place. After Woodstock, all anyone could afford was a single superstar act, like Altamont with the Stones, and maybe one more act to open. Jimi Hendrix went from his $18,000 Woodstock appearance to a $75,000 payday at New York's Randall's Island. A lot of people involved with the festival, even in the most minor ways, made careers out of going around the world and advising on how to promote rock festivals. Japan wanted to do one at Mt. Fuji, and sure enough, all the Woodstock 'experts' came out of the woodwork, charging mega-fees based on their having 'put on' Woodstock.

"The other big, big problem at the festival was drugs. Everyone had been using grass for years, it was just part of the scene; but at Woodstock, for the first time that I can remember, cocaine was being used openly backstage. The festival marked the push up to higher drugs, no question. It was inexpensive, it made everyone tolerate a lot more, and it was everywhere. Altamont, just seven months later, was a perfect example of where the festival scene, and drugs, were headed. Whatever the sixties were, they ended at Woodstock."

Jac Holzman, founder of Elektra Records, says: "By 1968, I began to think about getting out. To that end I began to clean up the company, meaning I began to make sure that every dollar was well applied. Nobody got to fly first class anymore, and I took a lot of chiding from other record executives for it. But I knew I'd get the money out in a multiple of profits from the sale of the company later on. At the time of Elektra's sale, you could still legitimately write up the assets. If you could document the value of an artist over a period of time, if you could document the worth of his masters, for example, you could use that to effectively evaluate what you were selling. In 1970 Warner Brothers bought Elektra, which I'd started for $600, for $9.8 million. The deal was handled by Steve Ross, one of the first "leveraged buyout" experts in the industry. He was extremely astute as to how to handle acquired assets in terms of getting the most tax advantage. He showed Warner how it was possible to write the inventory assets up to $20 million. With a tax rate of just under 50 percent, by legitimately writing the assets up to at least twice their present value and amortizing them over a sufficient period of time, they paid virtually nothing for the company."

Warner Brothers had formed its separate record division in 1958. Without sufficient experience or leadership, the company soon found itself over its head and lost approximately $3 million a year during its first four years. By 1962, Warner's executive board was close to throwing in the towel on the record division when a New York promoter convinced them that his folk trio could outsell Capitol's biggest act at the time, the Kingston Trio. The promoter was Albert Grossman, his trio Peter, Paul and Mary, whose 15 million album sales succeeded in saving the label.

Warner Records eventually became so profitable that it was able to lure Sinatra from Capitol by giving Sinatra his own label, Reprise, part of a multiple film/recording deal worth $22 million to the singer.

During this period, Warner Records survived a number of takeover attempts, until Seven Arts, a minor film distribution house, managed to gain control of the company's stock. The major achievement of the Warner and Seven Arts merger was the 1967 buyout of Ahmet Ertegun's Atlantic Records, one of the few surviving independents. The price was reportedly in the $20 million range. One of the reasons Warner wanted Atlantic was for its distribution arrangement with Polydor Records in England, and access to the catalogs of Eric Clapton, Led Zeppelin, and the Bee Gees. The acquisition of Atlantic made Frank Sinatra, one of rock's severest critics, a one-third partner in the largest rock label in America.

Seven Arts then sold Warner to the Kinney Corporation, in order to take the tax advantage of the capital gain. Kinney's purchase price of Warner-Atlantic was reported to be in the quarter-billion-dollar range. The head of the new conglomerate was Steve Ross, son-in-law of the family that had started Kinney. In 1967, Ross acquired Ted Ashley's talent agency for $10 million, to give Warner access to an even larger pool of available talent. Then, in 1970, he worked out the deal for the acquisition of Holzman's Elektra Records.

"I could see what was happening," Holzman says. "Distribution was going to come into the hands of fewer and fewer people. One of the main motivating facts for my selling Elektra, besides the money, was that I knew the label had to be connected to a larger distribution network, or we were in trouble. I had previously approached Warner about the possibility of forming some type of joint distribution operation in which I'd retain a 20 percent ownership, but the deal didn't work. Warner-Atlantic was heading in that direction on their own, and without a sufficient power base, I couldn't do it. In the end, it would come down to acquiring talent, and I wouldn't be able to compete with their promotion and distribution guarantees. Without being able to say that we had access to the same distribution strength, I'm out of business. The days of independent distribution, like the days of the independent labels, were coming to an end. I was in a somewhat unique position to be able to sell out for big money, or retain the company and maybe lose everything."

By 1971, the Fillmore, the Greenwich Village club scene, rock festivals and the independent record movement were mostly memories. Rock's social statements turned into financial ones, as big-name performers eagerly traded their self-worth for net worth.

Fifteen

B̲y 1970, the year the Beatles broke up, they'd sold 330 million records, albums and singles, and were the world's most popular rock group. When the end came, it wasn't over girlfriends, wives or "creative differences." The stories of conflicts over John and Paul's wives were so much industrial smoke blown by the rock and gossip press to assure the romantic faithful that the breakup had nothing to do with the one thing that actually caused it. The Beatles pulled themselves down a chasm to hell in a tug of war over the enormous profits of their records. The simple truth was, the Beatles broke up over money.

As early as *Sgt. Pepper,* dissension had been brewing among the four Beatles over whose music should be included on their albums. The value of the publishing, rather than the quality of material, was the problem. George Harrison, the first Beatle to record solo, in 1968, did so for a very simple reason. In order for him to make the kind of money that Lennon and McCartney earned, the way the Beatles publishing was set up, he had to record an album's worth of his own songs, rather than having one squeezed in between eleven Lennon-McCartneys.

In 1968 the Beatles set up Apple Corps Ltd., a London-based nonprofit combination retail outlet and arts institute. Its open-door policy was dedicated to the discovery of walk-in talent, with recording, filming and performing time to be paid for out of the profits of the storefront sales of Beatles-related items. John Lennon's utopian vision of artistic freedom was a venture that Paul McCartney described as an experiment in "Western Communism." It proved to be a painful experience that made them a laughing stock in both the financial and music communities.

The quick and utter failure of the operation resulted in huge losses for the Beatles. The final "event" of the retail establishment was the giving away of its inventory on a first-come-first-served basis to anyone who could get through the door.

Even the success of the first Apple single, "Hey Jude," backed by "Revolution," a double-sided hit that sold three million copies that first year, failed to restore the myth of the Midas touch to the legend of the Beatles. Apple Records was the only division of the "vision" that showed any kind of profit, and even there the Beatles seemed bent on snatching defeat from the jaws of victory.

The Beatles' accountants had, from the beginning, been the highly conservative London-based Bryce Hammer Ltd., headed by Harry Pinsker. When Lennon and Yoko Ono appeared nude on the cover of Apple's 1968 *Two Virgins* release, Pinsker and his associates removed themselves from all further contact with the Beatles, and assigned two junior accountants to extricate the company from the group's finances. Five weeks later, Apple was in chaos.

It couldn't have happened at a worse time. In the single year of Apple's existence, its retail policies had drained the £1 million (approximately $4 million) liquid assets the Beatles had invested in it. Approximately £800,000 went to Apple's setup, with the corporation's acquisition of 80 percent ownership in the Beatles, in return for 5 percent of the new corporation's stock for each Beatle. Because of this structure, the individual Beatles were personally liable for the hundreds of thousands of dollars' worth of debt that Apple quickly built, with the outflow increasing daily. At the height of their musical success, financial disaster seemed imminent, as John Lennon announced to the press that Apple was losing $80,000 a week.

Allen Klein took Lennon's comments as a signal that the time had come to make his move. He managed to arrange a personal meeting with Lennon, even as McCartney's new father-in-law, Lee Eastman, was putting the finishing touches on his proposal to handle the group's troubled finances. Lennon, razzle-dazzled by Klein's description of the ever-growing fortune he'd created for the Rolling Stones, directed EMI that from that moment on, all his financial matters were the responsibility of Allen Klein.

By 1968, NEMS, the company set up by Brian Epstein to formalize his management of the Beatles, was only technically still in existence. Epstein's sudden death had severed the last bonds between the group and their manager's company. Epstein's share of NEMS went to his brother, Clive, who was unable to extricate it from the avalanche of estate taxes which threatened to consume his entire inheritance. In 1967, only weeks after his brother's funeral, Clive Epstein received a million-pound offer for his share of NEMS, from Triumph, the British film corporation.

Eastman suggested to McCartney that the Beatles make Epstein an offer to buy back NEMS for themselves, salvaging the enormous profit potential in the corporation's share of Beatles publishing and masters. EMI, to insure a long-term commitment by the Beatles, offered to advance the group the entire purchase price, to be reimbursed out of future royalties.

Three Beatles—John, George and Ringo—wanted control of the Beatles to be divided between ABKCO and Eastman. McCartney, however, rejected Klein after a single meeting, insisting that only Eastman was truly capable of handling the job. Further, McCartney informed the others, Klein was having problems with the American IRS (a situation McCartney found out about through Eastman), which didn't seem right for someone supposed to be an expert in the handling of large sums of money. No, McCartney insisted, the only logical choice was to let Eastman turn around the Beatles' troubled financial empire.

The problem was, Lennon's attraction to Klein was almost purely emotional. Mick Jagger's constant gloating over how Klein had made the individual Stones wealthy men made Lennon furious with envy. Pressuring the other two Beatles to back him up, he formalized their association with Klein. In May 1969, in return for Klein's taking over the management of their finances, the three Beatles gave Klein access to 20 percent of their gross income from any new deals he made, including anything the group earned in the event of his eventual departure, 10 percent of Apple Records, 25 percent of all Beatles-related merchandising, 10 percent of any and all publishing by Ringo and/or George, a fully paid staff, plus personal expenses to be paid by Apple.

It was this deal that pushed McCartney to sue the other Beatles for control of the corporation's fortunes. Unfortunately, the timing of the lawsuit cost the Beatles their opportunity to buy NEMS, as Clive Epstein, impatient with the way negotiations were dragging on between himself and the two Beatles factions, now realized that the deal would have to be put off until the lawsuit was resolved. He therefore sold his share in NEMS to Triumph.

Klein lost no time in legally challenging Epstein's sale and pressured EMI to freeze all royalties that would otherwise be paid to the new shareholders of NEMS. His intention was to nullify the nine years remaining on the EMI-NEMS contract on the grounds that the sale of NEMS effectively ended the management clause of the agreement. EMI felt that it had no other choice and put all Beatles royalties in escrow, pending settlement.

Klein took the escrow account as a major victory, the first step in the renegotiation of a settlement. His motives in extricating the Beatles from NEMS, however, had little to do with the welfare of the Beatles, who stood to collect their money no matter who controlled NEMS. The way Klein's deal was structured with the Beatles was that, should the NEMS contract remain in force, he'd receive no share of the rich catalog of existing Beatles' publishing.

Klein's gamble paid off when Triumph agreed to relinquish its claim to all future shares of the Beatles' income, including Brian Epstein's original share of the Beatles' publishing from Northern Songs, for a one-time flat payment of £800,000 ($3 million), plus 20 percent of whatever was being held in escrow. In addition, Klein agreed to sell the Beatles' remaining shares of NEMS to Triumph for a half-million pounds of the company's stock. By doing this, Klein, according to the terms the three Beatles had agreed to, became immediately eligible to participate in all past Beatles publishing, in addition to $150,000 of the $750,000 the Beatles received.

Klein then turned his attention to Northern Songs, the Lennon-McCartney publishing firm still administered by Dick James. The Beatles had become so successful that in 1967 alone, Northern Songs put a million pounds into the pockets of Lennon and McCartney (which they promptly funneled into Apple), royalties on 159 songs. James was ecstatic, as the Beatles were legally obligated to write for Northern Songs until 1973. The way they were selling records, there seemed no limit to how much they were going to earn. The details of the revised Northern Songs publishing agreement that Brian Epstein had completed just before his death called for seventy original Lennon-McCartney songs to be released by EMI over the next nine years, the real reason the Beatles stopped touring and limited their work to the studio.

In the meantime, Klein, as a signal to Northern Songs, won major concessions from EMI, which agreed to increase the Beatles' U.S. royalties to an unprecedented 25 percent of the *retail* price of their records, to be paid directly from Capitol to Apple, eliminating EMI's double-dip—a royalty no group had ever bettered, not even the Stones. This deal entitled Klein to a piece of the Beatles' share of their existing publishing.

James became increasingly uneasy about Klein's expanding

influence and control of the Beatles. When Klein came after him to revise the Beatles' piece of the Northern share of the group's publishing, as he figured they would, he decided to avoid the confrontation completely and sold his interest in Northern Songs to the notorious Sir Lew Grade, known in the film industry as Sir Low Grade.

Both John and Paul were furious over the sale and united behind Allen Klein's promise to do something about it. Klein was furious also, but for a different reason. The Beatles' catalog was worth an additional publishing fortune to him, but only if renegotiated. An outright sale left Klein without a penny from Northern Songs' share of pre-1967 Beatles' publishing.

Klein devised a retaliatory plan that was brilliant in its simplicity. He'd simply buy up to 20 percent of the remaining at-large shares of Northern Songs stock for the Beatles, a move that would result in their gaining a 51 percent majority and the power to veto the sale. In order to effect the purchase, Lennon and Klein combined their resources, with John putting up his entire remaining stock in Northern Songs and Klein his MGM stock. In deference to Eastman, Paul refused to financially participate.

In order to convince the at-large stockholders to sell them a controlling interest, Klein agreed to extend the Lennon-McCartney songwriting commitment beyond the 1973 cutoff. At this point, John exploded, and complained to the press that his songwriting talents were being taken away from him and put into the hands of "suits" who didn't know or care anything about him or his music. Lennon's tamper tantrum, as Grade described it, put enough stockholders on his side to deny the Beatles controlling interest. The sale went through, just as Allen Klein assumed total control of the Beatles' finances, over the fierce objections of Paul. In May 1969, Klein convinced John, Ringo and George to sign a three-year contract, formalizing their relationship for the first time.

Having failed to nullify the sale of Northern Songs to Grade, Klein now attempted to renegotiate Northern's royalties directly with EMI and Capitol. If successful, he would still be eligible to share in the profits of the existing Lennon-McCartney catalog. EMI all but threw him out of their executive offices; but Capitol, aware that the Beatles were their only major act in light of the Beach Boys' recent defection, agreed to listen. Klein pressed for a hefty increase for the group. Capitol eventually agreed to a revised royalty of sixty-nine cents for each Beatles album, including repackages and "best of" compilations. Having completed the Capitol deal, Klein went back to Lew Grade. A deal was struck for the Beatles to sell their publishing interest in Northern Music to Grade, to avoid what promised to be a long and expensive series of suits and countersuits. Lennon and McCartney each made approximately $5 million in cash from the sale of their share of Northern Songs, and in doing so forfeited any future claims to their share of the company's royalties for the Lennon-McCartney catalog.

With the sale of their share of Northern Songs, all further obligations to write and publish as Lennon-McCartney ceased to exist. At that point, the Beatles slipped into history.

All that remained was the long and bitter court struggle by Paul McCartney to extricate himself legally from the clutches of Allen Klein, a battle so costly that two years after it began Apple was forced into receivership, in spite of an aggregate income from 1962 through 1970 of $38 million.

And that still wasn't the end of it. In 1971, the McCartney camp accused, and went on to prove that Klein had decided to ignore his contractual agreements with the group and had simply helped himself to 20 percent of all Beatles royalties, even though he was legally entitled to only 10 percent. Klein's defense was that he was actually underpaid, because he'd figured his percentages from Apple's cut, rather than Capitol's, at the point of sale origination. This argument was totally in conflict with the specified Apple-based profit tier that he himself had devised, and was summarily thrown out of court. Additionally, various audits taken during the initial phase of the trial returned highly conflicting amounts of monies owed and monies due, plus extreme confusion as to how what albums, in which remix, belonged to whom and for how much. Upon appointment of a receiver, it was hoped by all that a quick settlement could be reached. What was at first predicted by the presiding judge to be a case that would run into several months pressed on for years. It took six years just to separate the Beatles from Klein and another two for George, Ringo and John's individual contracts to be settled. In December 1983, Klein lodged complaints in U.S. courts against all the Beatles and Yoko Ono, for $42 million in commissions he claimed were still owed him by the Beatles, plus an additional $10 million in damages.

In 1977, ABKCO accepted a $4.2 million settlement from Apple, with separate settlements worked out later in the cases involving individual Beatles. However, various tax and related legal problems of cases involving Apple, the Beatles, and Lennon versus McCartney were far from settled, and pushed into the eighties and beyond. No final settlement is yet in sight.

Klein continued to maintain control over the Rolling Stones, even after serving a two-month sentence in 1979 for income tax fraud on unreported income he had received from the unauthorized sale of more than $200,000 worth of bootlegged *Concert for Bangladesh* Apple albums, whose profits had been specifically designated by George Harrison to help feed that country's starving children.

Sixteen

The Beatles' escalating fortunes approached the exotically unreal, as the financial stakes reached into the billions. Their story was one side of the business of rock in the sixties. The flip side, not nearly as fabulously fortuned, nevertheless represented the vast majority of sixties rockers coming off the artificial high of making music, without a financial parachute to cushion their fall. Barry Goldberg's story represents a different day in the life, the professional musician who fell between the lines of rock's incorporation papers.

A member of Dylan's band at the historic Newport '65 festival, Goldberg went on to become one of the founding members of the Electric Flag, the blues-based band Albert Grossman brought to Monterey and subsequently signed to Columbia in the bungled deal that gave Janis Joplin to Clive Davis.

Of all the bands that emerged from Monterey, the Electric Flag may have offered the most potential for superstar status. However, a year after signing with Columbia, the group had disintegrated into total confusion. One band member described it as the result of an unresolvable clash, not over musical directions, but the choice of drugs; a classic heroin/acid dichotomy that ultimately proved unresolvable.

Barry Goldberg recalls the events this way: "We got a contract from Columbia after playing at Monterey. Clive

Davis signed us on the spot, thanks to Albert Grossman, and the band members all moved into nice houses in Mill Valley. It was a strange, wild, bizarre time. Money would come via per diems, we'd get what we needed for expenses and we could draw from our substantial advance from Columbia, although I have no idea what the amount of that advance actually was. Albert took care of things like that for us. Anyway, we had a lot of potential, and a lot of problems. Egos, for one thing. If we'd stayed together there's no question we would have been a supergroup. Drugs, for another. It became a disoriented and depressing situation, something that I had to personally get out of, as did Michael [Bloomfield] a little later. The life of the band was really less than a year. I was there eight months, then Buddy Miles took over. We had a couple of albums that didn't really do anything, and that was it.

"After that, in order to keep myself going, I started writing songs with Gerry Goffin. We had a couple of big songs. 'Gotta Use My Imagination' was a number one song for Gladys Knight and the Pips. Unfortunately, I was caught in the publishing game and didn't make a cent off my music. I think I did that song for Screen Gems, which was a huge publishing firm. When any of them knew they could take advantage of you, they did. You'd go up to their offices and say, hey, I've got a great song here I've just written, and if they liked it they'd say, okay, we'll take it and give you seventy-five dollars for it. And that was for 100 percent of the publishing. Once my song hit number one, they signed me to a publishing contract for a little more money, but I still had to relinquish 100 percent of my end; in other words, no royalty, just salary. I worked there for a year and wrote songs that sold five, maybe six million copies and wound up with ten, maybe fifteen thousand dollars total, and part of that for playing on the records. A lot of the songs I wrote are still selling, still making money. I still receive maybe five thousand dollars a year for performance, but nothing for the publishing. It would have been nice, but I knew what I had to do in order to make whatever money I could to keep me going, to feed my family. I had no choice because there was no choice offered. That's the way the companies operated."

Even those companies that began as the alternative to the very same exploitation they'd later be accused of. One of the saddest examples was Motown, the major "black" independent rock label.

Motown was the brainchild of Berry Gordy, Jr., a former amateur prizefighter who'd hooked up with another boxer, Jackie Wilson, to help launch Wilson's musical career. Gordy wrote "Reet Petite" for Wilson, which became a minor local Detroit hit in the summer of 1958. When Wilson failed to have a follow-up, Gordy's career in music seemed to have come to a dead end. He then took a job as a $90-a-week chrome trimmer at a Ford assembly plant. Always a song noodler, he occasionally wrote tunes for the groups that played the local after-hours clubs near the plants.

Borrowing $700 from his sister, he recorded one of the lounge groups he'd done some writing for, a group that called themselves the Miracles. Taking a handful of demos with him to End Records, then one of New York's "race" indies, he managed to get a deal, with the Miracles' recording of "Got a Job," a gimmicky sequel to the Silhouettes' smash "Get a Job." The royalties he received from End for "Got a Job" came to a grand total of $3.19, in spite of the song's reaching number one on the R&B charts.

Gordy's experience with End led him to start his own company. His only real business experience was at the Ford factory, which he used as a model for the structure of Motown, to be run on the principles of mass production and salaried workers to build a musical empire. He developed talent through Smokey Robinson's Artist Development Department, out of which emerged Mary Wells, Motown's first successful performer. Wells succeeded in placing three top 10 records on the R&B charts, and then helped Motown to break into crossover pop, with the Supremes, Martha Reeves and the Vandellas, and the Temptations.

A year later, Smokey Robinson and the Miracles broke through on the Tamla subsidiary with "Shop Around." A year after that Tamla went gold with the Marvelettes' "Please Mr. Postman." Gordy then produced the Contours' classic "Do You Love Me" and followed up with a release of the first album by one of his personal "prodigies," "Little" Stevie Wonder.

Throughout the sixties, Motown became the primary outlet for black rock and roll, melding what was left of rhythm and blues into a softer, less sexually threatening sound. It substituted the point of view of a middle-class high school teen for R&B's aging, sexual bluesers, to make an across-the-board appeal to the lucrative teen market.

Still, major problems were brewing at "Hitsville," as Gordy called his company. At its heart was the all-too-familiar scenario of artist exploitation. Behind the successful image of the all-black independent, Motown was controlled almost exclusively at the nonperforming management level by a group of hand-selected white accountants and investors who reported directly to Gordy. This team ran the finances of the corporation, while Smokey Robinson assumed control of the development of talent. Gordy put together the best of the black Detroit performers to fill the slot left vacant by the abolition of fifties R&B, making certain the music they sang was acceptable for the white-dominated airwaves of the early sixties. The difference between classic fifties R&B and sixties Motown was the lowered age of those who sang the songs. In the fifties, R&B had the aroma of whiskey and women soaked through it. Motown's music was high school–level courtship material. In effect, Gordy had integrated his business and his music, using white management to develop his financial empire, while absorbing the sound of white pop into the urban street music of Detroit's working-class blacks. The success of Motown proved the crucial link to the survival of rock's black musical roots.

By 1971, the label's major hit-writing team, Holland-Dozier-Holland sued the label for what they claimed were more than $22 million in back royalties they were owed. Several acts followed HDH's lead and challenged the sales figures on which Gordy based their royalties, and were fired. More than one Motown act wondered how it could draw upwards of ten thousand people at nightly personal appearances and still be earning a couple of hundred dollars a week.

Martha Reeves, lead singer of the Vandellas, has admitted she never made more than $200 a week at Motown, while her records ("Dancing in the Street," "Jimmy Mack") sold into the millions. When she finally made the break from Motown, it cost her new label (MCA) more than $200,000 to settle what Gordy claimed were "advance debits" still outstanding against her account. As there were against Paul Williams, the original lead singer of the Temptations, who ultimately committed suicide when his career failed to recover after his confrontation with Gordy led to his being put on "permanent suspension."

Gordy maintained the rights to all the names of Motown groups and insisted on lifelong performance contracts with his artists, which prevented most of his acts from being able to leave the label. Stevie Wonder was one of the few who were successful in attempts to negotiate with Motown. His age became the prime factor in what might have been a successful challenge to the invalidation of his contract, on the same basis Dylan once claimed, that he'd signed it while still a minor.

After auditing Motown's books in 1971, the year he turned twenty-one, Wonder found his royalties in order, with about a quarter million dollars in trust for him. That figure would undoubtedly have been much higher if Gordy hadn't negotiated Wonder's publishing deal to be the lowest artist percentage in the industry, down from the standard 50–50 split to 2 percent for Wonder, 98 percent for Motown. Wonder, feeling he'd been dealt with unfairly, refused to renew his contract. Gordy offered Wonder a full 50–50 split on all future recordings, which Wonder agreed to for a five-year period. In 1975, Wonder's contract was once again renegotiated, with a guarantee of $13 million over a seven-year period in return for one album a year.

In 1971, Gordy moved to Hollywood, hoping to diversify Motown into film and television, and in the process suffered the loss of Michael Jackson, to Columbia. With many of his acts hopelessly deadlocked in legal challenges, and all of Gordy's attention shifted toward the movies, Motown ceased to be a major influence in the record industry. During its glory days, Motown grossed an estimated $40 million annually, successfully placing 70 percent of its product in *Billboard*'s top 100, with the vast majority of the profits remaining out of the hands of the performers.

Stax was the Memphis-based record company owned by Estelle Axton and Jim Stewart. They started Satellite Records in 1959, and started over with Stax (*St*ewart and *Ax*ton) in 1960 after Satellite went belly-up in the wake of payola. Axton and Stewart christened the company "Soulsville, USA." Stax and Stax-Volt, the independent subsidiary formed under the distribution auspices of Atlantic, went through three highly successful phases, latching on to the soul/rock boom of the sixties. The initial burst was the Carla Thomas era of bluesy vocals; followed by the Booker T. and the MGs period, highlighted by "Green Onions"; and climaxed by the emergence of Otis Redding, heir apparent to Sam Cooke, whose explosive performance at the Monterey festival seemed to assure a long and successful place in American mainstream rock. His untimely death in a plane crash in 1967 effectively ended the Stax-Volt era. Like so many independents, there was neither enough money nor talent to overcome the loss of even one key act. With the decline of Motown and the demise of Stax, rock and roll was once more almost completely in the hands of the majors.

The decade of the sixties had begun with the singer/songwriter's liberation from the exploitation of Tin Pan Alley, only to end with most rock and rollers still hooked to the same financial plow they continued to drag across Maggie's corporate farm.

Seventeen

From an economic point of view, 1971 was a terrific year for rock, ushering in a decade of nearly uninterrupted profits. The widespread acceptance of prerecorded tape became a reality with the introduction of the Muntz eight-track cartridge and later that year, cassettes, breathing a second sales life into record company backlists.

General Recording Tape was the first of several companies to license the catalogs of record companies. GRT struck a deal with RCA for exclusive duplication rights to its entire catalog for a five-year period, beginning in 1972, for $7.5 million. With the combined sales of tapes and albums a factor for the first time, the U.S. recording industry racked up sales totaling $1.2 billion, twice the gross of 1960.

The greatest concentration of sales was by a relatively few acts. One method initiated by the industry to expose the audience to as much new product as possible was rack jobbing, which resulted in the demise of one of the last remaining independent operations in the business of music: independent distribution.

The average rack capacity in a department store was about a hundred albums and the top forty singles. To get on the racks, it was necessary to be on the charts. In order to be on the charts, it was necessary to have rack space. The only way onto this ever-revolving carousel was radio, which became an increasingly critical factor in the manufacture of hits. In the Fillmore era, a hit record could still be broken without benefit of major exposure on the airwaves. In the seventies, radio once again became the definitive make-it-or-break-it route to the charts. The one-time "enemy" had become its most vital promoter.

Independent program directors became the newest power brokers within the industry, replacing the independent record distributors of the early sixties. Bill Drake, one of the first to develop the radio network concept for rock, converted independent stations to "Drake" stations, supplying identical format and preprogrammed music; mixing oldies, album cuts, hits, and new up-and-coming singles; eliminating the local deejays. Becoming a Drake station was a very attractive package for station owners, reducing what was their major expense, the salary packages of in-house "personalities."

The advantage to the record industry was the opportunity the Drake system offered to instantly expose new product to a national audience. So effective was radio's ability to capture its target audience, that the combined revenues of American radio reached approximately $1.4 billion in 1971, a figure that more than doubled itself by the end of the decade.

Another way record companies sought to increase sales was through the support of tours. Although festivals had died with Altamont, and the Fillmore ballroom circuit was moribund, there was still a market for live rock. While tours could not, by themselves, create hit records, the combined radio support and label promotions created an "event" out of new releases, which helped to launch them into the commercial arena. Live concerts became the best way to maintain audience interest in a successful act and a key factor in breaking a new one. Virtually every rock group eagerly toured behind the release of a new album, with record companies assuming all expenses, paying the acts nothing more than per diems.

Touring reverted to what it had been before the days of the ballrooms, less a function of performance than promotion. Rock stars were subjected to the demands of tour managers and record company executives who booked them onto radio shows, personal appearances at record stores and whatever other promotions they could come up with to generate sales. In many ways, the company system of tours had reverted to the same system originally devised by Alan Freed, an exchange of talent services for exposure of product.

Tour expenses were always picked up by the record company, managed by an in-house promoter whose job it was to deal directly with each city's venue. Tours worked on tightly controlled budgets, down to the last foreseeable detail. Under the general heading of "Talent," a promoter had to consider the following: the headline act's guarantee (if any, usually applicable only to the biggest acts) against a percentage plus bonus if the concert sold out; the expenses involved in ticketing, including the cost of printing and distribution, plus the percentage due to Ticketron and other computerized outlets; the rental fee for each venue, usually a percentage against a guarantee, whichever was greater; a house manager's fee; a general manager's fee; the cost of ushers, security, air conditioning and other unit-based costs. Each tour needed a treasurer to keep track of all cash transactions, including the supervision of ticket sellers and the handling of box office receipts. Road crews had to be assembled with a production manager to supervise the construction and breakdown of the stages, lighting, video projection systems, sound, curtains, additional seats, and spotlight operation. Local union laws varied, but there was always a minimum requirement for several Teamsters to be present and paid, whether or not they did any work.

Additional tour expenses included limos; the rental and/or transport of pianos and organs; instrument tuners; dressing room refreshments and hostesses; trucks, buses, vans, trailers, drivers, and private telephones. Insurance premiums had to include personal liability riders for property damage, fire and theft. Lawyers were needed for the coordination of all contracts. Accountants had to figure all due payments for hotels, advertising, promotion, public relations, posters, flyers, in-house doctors, overtime, Sunday union premiums, and tips.

In the end, the headline act usually wound up paying for everything out of the sales of records, before the dispersion of royalties. Because of this, several groups unable to break hit singles relied even more heavily than others on tours to sell their wares, often coming out on the deficit end of the profit scale. The Grateful Dead, one such group that toured almost constantly in the early seventies without "hits," fell into heavy debt to its label, Warner Brothers, and was forced to stay on the road for five years before earning a penny in royalties. At the same time, Crosby, Stills, Nash and Young, on the strength of the group's hit single "Suite: Judy Blue Eyes," grossed $9.3 million in twenty-four stops, their bottom-line profit in the millions after tour expenses were deducted from record sales.

The breakdown on the sale of an $8.00 album, ($7.98 being the average retail cost in the early to middle seventies) gave the record company approximately a dollar in profit, the remaining seven going to manufacturing, distribution, production costs, producer royalties, publishing, advertising, and finally, talent. If a group sold 200,000 units, the record company's profit might reach as high as $200,000, while the performer's take might be nothing, after reimbursement of tour expenses against royalties. A typical royalty, figured at 7 percent of the same 200,000 units sold at $8 each is about $112,000. Because the expenses of a tour usually exceeded the sales that resulted from it, only the biggest acts, such as the Rolling Stones, ever saw any money off touring. The Stones demanded and received 90 percent of tours' grosses, a figure Atlantic was happy to give because of the huge sales of the entire catalog of albums whenever the group toured. The Stones were, however, the exception rather than the rule.

Into the seventies, the majors continued to consolidate and gain power through buyouts and takeovers that allowed them to dictate terms to their stable of performers. In most cases, rock stars had no choice but to go along with the parameters laid out by the majors, as they were now the only game in town.

The general realignment of the majors' control of subsidiary and affiliate label distribution evolved into six major networks:

CBS owned and/or controlled Columbia Records, Epic, Portrait, Blue Sky, Caribou, Jet Kirschner, Life-song, Nemperor, Philadelphia International, T-Neck, Tabu, Unlimited Gold and City Lights.

RCA had RCA Records, Bluebird, Rocket, Different Drummer, Windsong, Grunt and Arista.

MCA had MCA, Motown and Source.

Capitol had Capitol, United Artists, Blue Note, EMI (American), Harvest, Angel and Seraphim.

Warner-Elektra-Atlantic (WEA) had Atlantic, Atco, Big Tree, Cotillion, Rolling Stone Records, Swan Song, Nonesuch, Elektra/Asylum, Elektra/Curb, Warner Records, Warner-Curb, Warner-Spector, Bearsville, Dark Horse, Island and Sire.

Polygram had Capricorn, Casablanca, Phonogram, MGM, RSO, Deutsche Grammophon, Phillips, and Privilege.

In addition, every major had counterinvaded England and Europe, most with branch operations in London.

Sales and profits in 1973 reflected rock's incorporated state of affairs. CBS led all companies with sales totaling $362.5 million, yielding a net profit of $25 million. WEA did $235.9 million with a net of $22.2 million; Capitol, $142.3 million with a net of $5.2 million.

With that kind of money, companies weren't afraid to spend on those acts which made the most. Excess became the status symbol of the seventies, as each label encouraged their lead acts to extravagance as a prestigious display of success. One publicity manager recalls the glory days at Atlantic this way: "I was working with [Led] Zeppelin, Bad Company, the Rolling Stones. It was incredibly exciting to tour with the Rolling Stones for a couple of weeks, or work with Zeppelin for ten nights straight. It was the heyday of rock excess, when everybody was rolling in money and there were limousines to take you to the bathroom. The company rule was 'Whatever it takes, you do it to keep everyone happy.' One night we had three different acts appearing in different L.A. venues the same night, and as part of the job you had to show up in person for each act to show that you cared. We had Bad Company at the Forum, Manhattan Transfer at the Roxy, and another act somewhere else. Everyone involved was told to get a limo and make at least the beginning, middle break or ending of a show, and not let on that you weren't there for the whole thing. The idea was to make each act feel they were the most important. To a lot of them, that was a higher priority than making money, and the company was happy to oblige.

"Zeppelin was a major act on Atlantic, signed just after the Warner's buyout, and when they hit they all but paid for the label's acquisition. They were awarded their own label, a practice begun by the Beatles with Apple and the Stones with Rolling Stones Records, distributed through the parent company. It was like starting an independent label, without the problems of finance or distribution. The major advantage to a group getting its own label, and only the very top got them, was the cutting of a better deal via the sharing in some of the distribution profits and the ability to sign up acts, with the opportunity to own masters. That was the whole idea behind Zeppelin's signing Bad Company to its subsidiary [Swan Song]. It was a beautiful shelter for their enormous profits.

"Anyway, Zeppelin signed a group called Pretty Thing and were debuting them at the Shrine Auditorium. It was my job to find a place for the reception to be held for the band's label debut. The downtown Hyatt House had just opened, with a very large banquet room available for parties. Which was what I needed, since a Zeppelin 'A' list invitation meant that everyone and their uncle was going to be showing up. I went down to the hotel and discussed the arrangements with them, and everything went fine until I said, by the way, we'll be bringing in Thai food, because the band had just gotten into Thai food. They had a favorite restaurant in L.A. and wanted only their food to be served. The restaurant said they were sorry, but no food could be brought in from the outside. I asked them what the cost would be for them to cater the party, and they said $10,000. Fine, I said. Here's the $10,000. Make the food, don't make the food, donate the food, eat it yourself, do whatever you want with it, but don't allow the food to show up because we're bringing in our own food. No problem, he assured me, with a smile and a wink. No problem at all.

"Another time we were at the Edgewater Hyatt in Seattle. The key rooms of the hotel face Puget Sound. After being there for a couple days, around checkout time, Zeppelin's manager went to check the group out and the hotel informed him of an additional bill for room trashing, a favorite group sport in those days. Seems the boys had tossed a few TV sets and pieces of furniture into the Puget. The manager said no problem, what's the damage, the hotel asked for $3,000 and was paid. The official of the hotel, upon receiving the money, smiled and said, you know, that's something I really admire about you guys. You don't know how many times I wish I could do that, just go in and trash a place and not have to worry about it afterwards. No problem, the manager said, have a room on us. With that, he paid him an extra couple of bills and went with him to a room, which the guy then proceeded to trash, while the boys watched.

"Alice Cooper was the first rocker to play Lake Tahoe. The label threw an enormous junket for the occasion, flying press and celebrities in from all over the country. We hired Ward Sylvester's rock jet, the one that everyone had to have as a prestige item, even if it was a hop no farther than L.A. to Tahoe, or Tahoe to Vegas. It became a prestige thing, to see which group could 'outtour' the other. Elton John's [tours] were probably the most extravagant, because he was able to sell the kind of records that made it possible for MCA to absorb the up-front expenses.

"In the seventies, everyone got a billboard on Sunset [Boulevard]. That was the thing, that's what you had to have. What most acts didn't realize in those days or just didn't care about was that they were paying for that billboard. Everything came off the act's cut of profits. Everything and more. That's the way the majors worked."

The one independent label that continued to thrive into the seventies was A&M Records. A&M was the brainchild of Herb Alpert, a then obscure studio musician and would-be recording mogul, and Jerry Moss, a hustling record promoter from the Bronx. They came together as a team after Alpert and his new partner, Lou Adler, an insurance salesman with a desire to write pop songs, made a successful cover version of the Hollywood Argyles' 1960 "Alley Oop." "Oop" was a regional West Coast hit record. Alpert threw together a hastily gathered so-called band consisting of out-of-work studio singers and redid the record for the East Coast, recording it in one day, pressing it the next, and getting it into the stores and on Dick Clark's "American Bandstand" the day after that.

Jerry Moss was hired to help with promotion, and within weeks the Dante and the Evergreens version of the song was national at number 15, at the same time the original Argyles version was number one. Released on Madison Records, the hit proved to be the label's high point and endgame, as the independent label folded in 1960's postpayola shakeout, ending the team of Alpert and Adler. The following year, Alpert and Moss teamed up as the Diddley Oohs, and recorded "Hooray for the Big Slow Train," a hoped-for follow-up to "Alley Oop." In the year between "Oop" and "Train," Moss had relocated to the West Coast to start his own publishing firm, Irving Music. Although "Train" went nowhere, it served as the seed for the partnership that eventually became A&M Records.

Alpert and Moss placed their first song, "Circle Rock" (the Salmas Brothers), with Bob Keen's label. Keen, coming off the loss of Ritchie Valens, signed Alpert and Adler as staff songwriters, for $35 a week, and put them to work with Sam Cooke. The result was Cooke's hit recording of "Wonderful World," just as Keen Records fell into disarray and Cooke left the label for RCA, the result of an Allen Klein negotiation.

Having had enough of the hit-or-miss world of independent rock and roll, Alpert turned his garage into the offices of A&M, and together with Moss, began in earnest to develop their own label. In 1966, Tijuana Brass, fronted by Alpert on trumpet, placed five albums in the top twenty *simultaneously*. With this, A&M entered the lucrative bidding wars for new talent and found itself in competition with, among others, Lou Adler, who'd also formed his own label, Dunhill Records. Adler, armed with the Mamas and the Papas, then took off for Monterey.

A&M stayed away from the festival, sensing a corporate grab bag, and instead developed their own unique roster of talent. It was their desire to remain independent with integrity, to present a musical dynamic somewhere between the British Invasion and MOR, with a roster that included Cat Stevens, Carole King, the Carpenters, Cheech and Chong, Procol Harum, Phil Ochs and Rick Wakeman.

Gil Friesen, president of A&M Records, whose initial introduction to the then independent record promotor Jerry Moss came via Alan Freed and who rose through the industry via the major-label record promotion circuit, says: "The beginnings of A&M were a combination of Jerry Moss's entrepreneurial spirit [and] Herb Alpert's desire to do it a different way. Initially, it was to release the records Herb had made, which was the genesis for A&M becoming known as an artist-oriented label. After all, half of the partnership was an artist, and so the artists' viewpoints were always going to be respected and incorporated into the operation."

A&M's importance to the record industry went beyond catalog and sales. It epitomized the alternative to everything corporate rock had come to represent. Alone among the majors, A&M became a role model for those who still believed in the art and message of rock and roll.

In 1975, record and tape sales reached a new annual high of $2.36 billion, with the major grossing acts being holdovers from the sixties. The Rolling Stones sold $13 million worth of tickets on their U.S. tour, with tours by the Who and Bob Dylan taking in nearly as much. While these acts helped to keep the corporate economy healthy, the fact remained that rock's prime corporate earners were aging, while the estimated cost of breaking a new act, according to one record executive at the time, was in excess of a half-million dollars in recording, touring and promotional costs.

Nevertheless, the industry poured millions into the development of new acts. However, when the Next Big Thing did arrive, it wasn't the result of calculated corporate manipulation, or independent integrity. Just one more hopeful unknown come knocking at the company door.

Bruce Springsteen's arrival at Columbia has been well documented, the now familiar story of how ex-Marine Mike Appel got Springsteen an audition with John Hammond, who in turn convinced Clive Davis to sign Springsteen after Davis had passed on seventeen previous acts Hammond had wanted to bring on board.

Springsteen's first two albums did poorly, as he struggled to find an audience for his music. *The Wild . . .,* album number two, did less than 50,000 copies in its initial go-around, resulting in Columbia's demand for an audition tape before giving the go-ahead to the next one. It wasn't until Springsteen's third album and first hit single, the 1975 "Born to Run," that Springsteen officially arrived, his star status celebrated by simultaneous *Time* and *Newsweek* cover stories. The *Born to Run* album sold 1.2 million copies in its initial release period, at which point Springsteen decided to sever all ties with Appel.

Under his arrangement with Appel, there was a 50–50 split on all performance and publishing royalties, although Springsteen received only about nine cents an album, to Appel's thirty-six cents.

Appel felt entitled to his cut for the five years he'd spent trying to "break" Springsteen, having to take a second and third mortgage on his home to keep the band afloat. Unable to agree on an amiable severance, Springsteen sued Appel in federal court for fraud, breach of trust, undue influence and recovery, while Appel countersued. During the lawsuit, Springsteen refused to record any new material, or was prevented from doing so by Appel's lawsuit; in either case, losing the momentum he'd built up with *Born to Run.*

One of the factors that finally led to the out-of-court settlement with Appel was Springsteen's behavior during the pretrial hearings. One observer of those hearings recalled the performer's severe temper tantrums and abusive language whenever any mention was made of a possible resolution in regard to Appel's claims. The performance continued until the judge informed Springsteen that everything he was doing and saying could be read into the trial record. Realizing the importance of his image to his songs, Springsteen thought better of going to court and, after three years, settled with Appel. Sources close to both parties revealed that Appel received a seven-figure settlement, plus a percentage of all existing Springsteen records and a piece of all subsequent releases. Springsteen then bought back Appel's interest and regained total control of his publishing.

Springsteen managed to come back from his self-imposed exile, releasing *Darkness on the Edge of Town* in 1978. It sold as well as *Born to Run,* doing the same 1.2 million copies in its initial run, breaking 2 million a year later.

It was a good sign that 1978 was going to be another financial record breaker. By the end of the year, the record industry had grossed more than $4 billion, yet another record-breaking figure. The reemergence of Springsteen provided the basis of CBS's billion-dollar year, while Warner came in second with a gross of $600 million. Polygram did $1.6 billion off the strength of a single album, the Bee Gees' sound track for *Saturday Night Fever,* which sold an astonishing 28 million copies. The Stones toured the U.S. again, pulling in more than $6 million and creating yet another upsurge in their backlist sales, and there was even talk that the Beatles might get back together. As the seventies drew to a close, the economic health of corporate rock seemed better than ever.

One observer described the euphoria that suffused the record industry as a kind of reckless arrogance, a privileged flight without seat belts on the most luxurious of corporate excursions.

Which may explain the high number of casualties when the company jet crashed headfirst into the mountainside of reality.

PART THREE

Comin' Back for More

Eighteen

Rock and roll had done a 360° turn to become the leading voice of the commercial mainstream. All that rock had originally represented—social integration, teenage rebellion, the voice of the working class—had been transmogrified by the calculated manipulation of the corporate machine. Rock stars no longer symbolized the rock counterculture. They were, instead, the very icons of material extravagance; their self-indulgent music, dress and style of living in marked contrast to the mass audience they no longer cared to represent. Lyrics preached passivity and conformity rather than assertive individuality. The romantic ideal reverted to the courtly syrup of prerock pop.

In 1974, *Variety* projected a financial downturn in the dollar gross of the music industry, with only the biggest names—Dylan, the Stones, the Who, Crosby, Stills and Nash, Elvis Presley, and Jethro Tull—continuing to sell out concerts. The average age of the American teen, *Variety* pointed out, was rising, as the median age of Americans crept upward into the high twenties and out of the major record-buying age range.

The complacency of the music business combined with its naturally shrinking constituency were the two major components that led to the "Crash of '79," the first rumblings of which could be heard in England's 1976 punk movement.

Working-class teens had become fed up with Mick Jagger's

endless ego, the pomp displayed by the likes of Led Zeppelin, Emerson, Lake & Palmer, Yes, and Pink Floyd, and John Lennon's recondite devotion to Yoko Ono. Rock's neo-elite no longer spoke to this new generation too young to remember Beatlemania. To them, all long hair meant was not being able to afford a haircut and rock superstars were overindulged rich men who lived in foreign countries to avoid paying taxes that helped to service the working class. As a form of protest against the rock establishment, punkers adopted the attitude of rebellion and dressed themselves in the leathers of the original teen rebels of the American fifties, a bizarre commentary on the twisted values of establishment rock.

The Sex Pistols, the first punk rockers exploding out of the British working class, came and went in a rock flash. Their arrival at commercial stardom effectively marked the end of their social relevance.

The Pistols were the brainchild of Malcolm McLaren, an unctuous cash-and-carry philosopher whose blatant, if calculated greed shocked the British stiff upper lip even as it caused the record companies' mouths to salivate. Every major label lunged after the Pistols, believing they could clean up their act and make a killing.

After a year of almosts and near misses, McClaren signed the group to a two-year contract with EMI. The Pistols received a $100,000 advance upon signing, only to be released two days later after a wave of protests from shareholders outraged by the group's use of foul language on the BBC and their open mockery of the Royal Family with their performance of "God Save the Queen."

McClaren let it be known that EMI had paid the band a "kill" fee of $125,000, bringing the band's take to $225,000 without so much as having recorded a single note. He played the events for all they were worth, and the message wasn't lost on the band's following. The Sex Pistols had ripped off the rock establishment and gotten away with it in a cynical blaze of glory.

A blaze that grew even more heated. CBS, WEA and A&M

all expressed interest in the "hot" new British band. A&M came in with the highest bid, nearly $400,000, and signed the group, only to dismiss them a week later over what the label called "artistic differences," for a kill fee of $200,000. Once again, the band collected without having released so much as a single note of music.*

The end for the band came when they finally released their first music. "God Save the Queen" shot to number two, and the group disbanded. Success killed the message; a familiar rock scenario.

The Sex Pistols had sent a message to corporate rock and roll. Beneath the satirical mockery of the band lay a widespread rejection of what rock had become, a message a lot of young people in England got into. In America, that message was lost in the nagging drone of corporate rock's latest revelation: disco.

The distance between the majors' corporate sell mentality and what was happening on the musical street was such that the small gang of punk-influenced bands that started to maraud the bars of urban America, playing the most original, authentic rock-based music in the country, couldn't get themselves signed to any major labels. As a result, they received little or no exposure on the radio, on concert tours as openers for established acts, or in the *Rolling Stone*-dominated rock press. The Ramones, for example, were considered noncommercial by every major label: too risky, too far-out, too unmusical, and according to one scouting report, too young! That they still managed to gain a reputation should have signaled to the corporate powers the shifting of musical tastes, away from the congealing modulation of seventies pop-rock to the majority of the next generation's prime re-

---

*These artistic differences were understood by some within the industry to be A&M's suddenly cold feet at the thought of alienating their British audience, combined with the label's awareness of its American reputation for the level of integrity involved with their choice of music. Others felt that A&M may have bowed to pressure from RCA to drop the group, as negotiations had been continuing for some time about the prospect of RCA's taking over A&M distribution. A&M label head Derek Green's only public statement at the time concerning the Pistols was, "[I] changed my mind."

cord-buying constituency. Instead, the majors put their money on the relatively safe disco, the preferred music of those who spent bucks rather than time on rock and roll.

Originating in the new dance clubs of the mid-seventies, disco was a corporate dream. Constructed on musical anonymity, disco was the aural equivalent of the one-night stand. With its slick, coke-intensive soft-core promise, disco depended less on star quality than on studio production, making individual performers easily expendable.

The first American group to successfully blend disco with the distant sound of punk was Blondie, a downtown New York avant-garde act lost in the morning-after that came to be known in the rock press as "postpunk." Stagnating within the club circuit limbo of New York's East Village, Blondie shifted its musical attitude with the release of "Heart of Glass," a disco-flavored tune that went top 10 and pointed the way for the type of music needed for John Travolta's new film vehicle, *Saturday Night Fever.*

The Bee Gees were commissioned to provide the sound track. From the moment it was released, *Saturday Night Fever*'s double album of disco-flavored tunes buried the competition. As *Fever*'s sales skyrocketed, "super groups" such as Emerson, Lake and Palmer and Santana lost fortunes touring to half-filled arenas while "fuck music," as record executives called it, packed the dance floors of Studio 54.

On the strength of disco, the annual gross of record sales nearly doubled to an all-time high in 1977 of $3.5 billion, eclipsed by a $4 billion take in 1978, as the *Fever* sound track sold 28 million copies, the best-selling album of all time. So heavy was the demand, that empty covers were shipped with coupons inserted where the record was supposed to be, redeemable on a first-come basis. On the heels of the *Fever* phenomenon came *Grease,* another John Travolta movie, another "rock" sound track good for 15 million units.

And 1979 looked to be even bigger, until the industry suddenly deflated in the winter of '79. By the end of the year, the sale of platinum albums (1 million units sold) dropped from

112 to 42. Gold albums (500,000 units) experienced a similar drop, from 193 to 112. In dollars, the drop marked the first year since 1970 that gross sales had failed to increase. Record (and tape) sales dropped to $3.6 billion, down from an all-time high of $4.2 billion just one year before. And no one in the industry could figure out why. The same record executives who looked like financial geniuses the year before now shook their heads and raised their palms to the sky, insisting the problem couldn't be with the music.

Shipments of *Saturday Night Fever, Grease,* and the unfortunate sound track to the revisionist film of *Sgt. Pepper (RSO),* the three most popular albums of the year, started to come back in unprecedented numbers. MCA, the label that had produced two of the three sound tracks, laid off 300 record personnel and pared away those acts whose margin of profit was insufficient in the double-digit inflation marketplace. MCA's actions signalled the arrival of a new era of austerity in the record industry.

A&M Records, one of the few remaining independents, decided to end its independent distribution and entered into a pressing/distribution deal with RCA.

Gil Friesen, president of A&M Records: "We went to branch distribution with RCA on February 15, 1979, and I'd have to say it was a genius move. The timing was perfect because the record industry, there's no other way to put it, went into the toilet. All the records we had out with independent distributors began to come back. We really didn't know how many we had out there; we had no specific inventory control, no computers the way we have them today. We would ship records to Detroit, or we'd ship them to New Jersey, and they'd ship them to Florida or St. Louis, all over the place, with no exclusive territories and everything on consignment. Collecting our own money was not an easy thing to do. I'd have to credit Jerry Moss with saying, enough, we don't know where our records are, and deciding to make the move to RCA, just as the industry was starting to crash. The situation with *Saturday Night Fever* and *Grease,* well, those companies shipped so many copies, and when they started coming back, everything the industry had out there started coming back. In some ways, it might have been the best thing that happened to the business because it finally made them pay attention to the record business. It was no longer a free-for-all expanding market. It was, going into the eighties, an industry where there was going to be tough competition for market share, with business principles that governed."

Touring, which had been the single most important arm of record promotion after radio, was either drastically cut back or eliminated. Perks connected with touring, everything from gourmet meals backstage to gourmet drugs delivered by a paid employee of a record company, vanished overnight. Regardless of how big an act was, all tour costs were now to be paid against royalties. Those rock stars whose albums hadn't sold to the expectations of their labels were the first to feel the effects of the new economics. Tom Petty, whose sales figures fell below the expense of his tours, was forced into bankruptcy, with $600,000 worth of personal debts.

The industry slump continued into 1980, with disco's dramatic collapse now complete. The dance-oriented music accounted for less than one percent of all record sales. Hardest hit was CBS, off 46 percent in annual profits. Warner, A&M and MCA felt the impact as well and further reduced their in-house staffs, and thousands of industry careerists found themselves without jobs. RCA imposed a ceiling return policy of 20 percent, a practice that was immediately echoed by Polygram. Warner offered an incentive program for retailers with greater profits on reduced returns, as well as increased cooperation in regional advertising. All the major record companies increased the price of albums by one dollar, the result, they claimed, of the enormous increase in the cost of oil-based vinyl. The industry then turned its focus to home taping, blaming the new technology for the continuing depression.

The disappointing sales of Fleetwood Mac's *Tusk* ($15.98), at two million units, one-sixth what the group's previous release, *Rumours,* had done, was blamed by Warner on the growing trend toward home taping. *Tusk,* the label claimed, was by far the most requested "play-through" album.

The late seventies saw recordable cassettes emerge as the primary tape format for the home and car, a trend that many FM radio stations capitalized on by playing complete albums, presumably for its audience to tape. There was nothing gray, vague or indistinct about home taping. The only option the record industry believed it had was the imposition of a tax on cassettes and recorders. At the same time, stations were threatened with the loss of record advertising if they refused to discontinue album play-throughs. CBS projected an $800 million loss in record sales, citing home taping as the reason. Even sales of the venerable 45 single, the backbone of the industry, slumped, accounting for less than 10 percent of all record sales. As if things weren't bad enough, video games became the new teen rage, and the hottest selling item of 1980 was the Sony Walkman, which sold 5 million units its first year.

In two years, the record industry had fallen into total disarray, and no one could say for sure what had gone wrong. No one, that is, except the public, which seemed to echo through its actions what the Sex Pistols had screamed five years earlier. Corporate rock and roll had become overpriced, self-indulgent, boring and banal, something no tape tax could fix.

In the end, those who'd devoured rock and roll were in turn devoured by it. For the Crash of '79 began a chain of events that resulted in the eventual sale of Columbia Records to the Sony Corporation, a move that signaled the ultimate incorporation of what had become the industry of rock and roll.

Nineteen

On a cold November morning in 1987, the battle ended for control of the billion-dollar record division of the Columbia Broadcasting System. On that day the professional home of Billie Holiday, Bob Dylan and Bruce Springsteen became a wholly owned Japanese corporation.

The takeover was the result of the unresolved turmoil at CBS that began during the Crash of '79. Early into the new decade, a series of boardroom shuffles resulted in the unexpected ouster of then chairman of the board and founder of CBS, William S. Paley. Paley's ironclad hands-on style of doing business was often cited as the primary reason for CBS's fifty-year run as the premier entertainment conglomerate. Paley prided himself on a personal involvement at all levels of corporate involvement, from crucial boardroom votes to the approval of which advertisements ran over his airwaves.

In 1978, the death of his wife, the celebrated "Babe" Paley, marked the beginning of the chairman's recession from total involvement with his company's operations. The TV network dropped from the top of the TV ratings for the first time in nearly twenty years, and the record division experienced a disastrous loss of profits. As a result, Paley seemed vulnerable.

Many within the company expressed disbelief at the noticeable change in the direction of the corporation and the series of deals that eventually made it susceptible to takeover. One such deal was the signing of Paul McCartney for a reported $20 million, a deal the company wanted so badly that it threw in the CBS-owned Frank Loesser catalog of music as an extra incentive. At least one executive at CBS during these negotiations remains convinced that had Paley been more directly involved with the company, the deal would never have been made. A study of record sales covering the thirty-year history of rock revealed that a performer's peak sales period averaged two years. Postpeak, repackaged backlists account for the ever-increasing percentage of those sales. CBS's deal with McCartney made no provision for the bulk of the artist's catalog, which was mostly Lennon-McCartney songs.

The subsequent failure of McCartney's initial CBS album to go platinum marked the deal as an unqualified disaster. Paley's multimillion-dollar failed investment into cable, what he referred to as "tuxedo television," further weakened the aging chairman's position. Finally, Ronald Reagan's requisite criticism of the networks' coverage of the White House seemed particularly directed at CBS's traditionally liberal news bureau. Paley's position at CBS had weakened to the point where his position as chairman of the board was seriously threatened. He relinquished his seat of power to Thomas Wyman, a further signal to the corporate world that the once-mighty entertainment conglomerate was ripe for takeover.

In 1984, the network was formally attacked by two factions of the conservative right: Ted Turner, whose Turner Broadcasting had succeeded in cable where Paley had failed, and Senator Jesse Helms of North Carolina. Both men led organized attempts at acquiring controlling stock interest in the corporation. CBS was forced to sell off huge chunks of its substantial assets and stocks in order to survive.

Laurence Tisch, then the major stockholder of Loew's Corporation, was invited in as a "white knight" and began to buy up huge blocks of the newly available CBS. By 1986, he was the corporation's chief stockholder, with 24.9 percent of all available stock, at an average price of $120 a share. In buying onto the board of CBS, Tisch made no secret of his support for Paley, which appeared to revitalize the founder's active interest in his company.

All during his acquisition period, Tisch maintained that he had no intention to take over the company. His investment represented just the opposite, he insisted: a commitment to keep CBS from those who wanted to do just that.

After Turner and Helms failed in their attempts, Coca-Cola was believed to have made a backdoor offer of $160 per share for CBS' stock. Marvin Davis (who eventually took over Twentieth Century Fox studios) was said to have offered as much as $170. With each failed takeover, Tisch increased his influence with the board as the symbol of CBS's ability to withstand all comers. Then, in September 1986, Tisch and Paley joined forces to formally oust Wyman from his chairmanship in a deal that included a $4.3 million cash buyout and $400,000 annual retirement salary to ease his fall from grace. Wyman's ouster set up Paley's anticipated return to the coveted chairmanship of his beloved company.

However, Paley failed to receive a vote of confidence from the board, and was forced to take a corporate backseat to Tisch, who now began to surgically dissect the corporation. In the two years that followed Wyman's ouster, Tisch engineered CBS's divestiture of its book publishing division for $500 million, its music publishing division for $125 million, and its magazine publishing division for $650 million. CBS was left with four flagship television stations, the TV network, eighteen radio stations and CBS Records. As CBS's chief stockholder, Tisch made what one insider estimated to be a billion dollars in windfall profits. And still he wasn't satisfied, for in December 1986, word swept through Wall Street that CBS Records was about to be put up for sale.

For a long time CBS Records had been the most profitable division of the corporation. In 1986, the Columbia Records division of CBS Inc. earned operating profits of $192.1 million from a gross sales income of $1.49 billion, 45 percent of CBS Inc.'s operating profit. According to Al Teller of CBS Records, this figure is a reflection of the corporate policy of releasing about 150 albums per year from a roster of 200 artists. Teller, in an interview with the *New York Times,* said: "The superstar is the giant bonanza. The big hit is to develop superstar careers. That is the biggest win you can have." Columbia releases approximately forty albums a year by newcomers, at least a third of whom are never heard from again. According to the label, the benchmark for minimal success is the sale of at least 100,000 copies of an album. Four years after the record industry's crash and CBS's disastrous McCartney deal, Columbia Records was the first of the majors to significantly rebound, showing a profit on the strength of two acts: Michael Jackson and Bruce Springsteen.

The rest of the industry struggled to hold the line in an extremely fluctuating marketplace. Forty-nine albums went platinum in 1983, down 11 percent from the fifty-five albums of the previous year and a full 25 percent from the sixty-six that had made it in 1980, the last year before industry figures reflected the post-*Fever* fallout. Only two singles went double platinum in '83, while gold albums were down a full 31 percent from 1980. There was a further industry decline in the production and release of new albums, down to approximately 2,600, as compared with a 1978 high of 4,200.

Groups were signed and developed on a very short leash, with most of the initial profit reverting to the label. The Hooters, for example, sold approximately 450,000 units of their debut Columbia album. CBS signed the Hooters in 1984, after the band's ten-year struggle to sign with a major, and advanced $200,000 to make their first album. In addition, the label spent $300,000 promoting it, including $75,000 for the making of a video. The Hooters received about 85 percent of the $5 wholesale price of their album. According to the group's management, the album barely made enough to recoup the advance, the recording costs, touring expenses, management fees, and other start-up and living expenses.

While the Hooters broke even, the label grossed approximately $3 million. In order for them to keep their momentum, the label estimated that the follow-up album had to sell at least a million and a half copies.

Columbia's major resurgence, however, came on the strength of Michael Jackson's 1984 *Thriller,* which sold more than 25 million copies worldwide and outdistanced even *Saturday Night Fever* as the all-time best-selling album. In spite of an escalating royalty rate that paid Jackson $2.10 on every album sold, totaling more than $35 million in domestic royalties and another $20 million worldwide (not counting hit single sales and publishing), for a total of more than $150 million, Columbia's total worldwide profits from the *Thriller* album and its record seven hit singles came to an estimated half-billion dollars.

The Jackson album revitalized the record-buying public. On the solid-gold heels of Jackson's *Thriller,* Springsteen's *Born in the USA* sold more than 20 million copies worldwide, yielded six hit singles and became the highest selling Columbia Records album of all time (Michael Jackson's *Thriller* was released on a Columbia subsidiary—Epic), causing an upsurge in Springsteen's backlist. Hit albums from U2 on Island, Lionel Ritchie on Motown, Phil Collins on Atlantic, Dire Straits, Prince and Madonna (Sire) on Warner Brothers, helped pull the industry out of its five-year slump.

Technology, the enemy of the record industry in the early eighties, became its best friend with the introduction of the compact disc. Introduced in 1983, by the end of the following year 7 million CDs had been sold in the United States, accounting for an infusion of cash into the record industry of approximately $100 million. By 1986, that figure reached a billion dollars, a figure that doubled a year later, with about 50 percent of the sales off the disc reissue of label backlists. CDs became the prime force behind the much-heralded sixties "revival," as records that had long since dropped out of the sales arena made surprising resurgences. Groups such as

Blind Faith, Cream, Love, and the Doors were discovered on CD by a generation too young to have known them on vinyl the first time around.

And this time, the technicians got it right. CDs had no recording capabilities.

All of which added to CBS Records' good fortune, making it once again the most profitable record company in the world, with a 1987 gross that totaled nearly $1.5 billion and yielded a profit of $162 million. Its nearest competitor, the giant Warner Communication entertainment complex, grossed $1.1 billion for a profit of $150 million.

Precisely because CBS Records was so profitable rumors persisted that it was up for sale. Media consultants continued to warn the industry that its prosperity was "soft," due to the uncertain nature of yet another new format about to come onto the scene. DAT—Digital Audio Tape—was rumored to be able to match, if not surpass, the sound quality of CDs, with the added ability to record from any other format with absolute fidelity. The implications of DAT technology application to bootlegging and piracy threatened to do far more damage than whatever had been inflicted by the arrival of recordable cassettes a decade earlier.

CBS was well aware of the economic threat that DAT offered to the stability of the corporation. Industry observers felt that Tisch was likely to make some kind of move while profits were up. Tisch had three options for the record division. He could keep it intact and ride out the DAT situation, hoping that profits continued to rise. One advantage to this option was the possibility of across-the-board taxation, allowing the record company's profits to be offset by whatever losses the company incurred in its other divisions.

Another option would spin the record division off into a separate subsidiary, to protect its profits from the losses of other divisions. A third would sell it to the highest bidder and reap the benefits of yet another windfall profit.

Nelson Peltz, chairman of Triangle Industries, was ru-

mored to be interested in acquiring Columbia Records, as was
Stephen Swid, who'd already purchased the publishing division. Some observers felt that those rumors were being
spread by none other than Tisch, in the hope of driving up
what was presumed to be by far the highest bid: the Sony
Corporation of Japan's cash offer of $2 billion. Sony obvi-
ously wanted Columbia for its backlist to eliminate the costly
battle for the right to market its potential gold mine, the DAT
home recorder. In the time-honored tradition of Western
capitalism, Sony sought to financially absorb the competition
and turn the problem into the solution.

In early October 1987, a bill was introduced in Washington
to require all DAT hardware sold in the United States to be
adjusted to prevent copying; and Tisch, to the surprise of
many, turned down Sony's offer, citing tax disadvantages.
With an annual operating income of approximately $160 mil-
lion, a $2 billion buyout would result in an immediate profit
tax to CBS Inc. of more than $600 million, in addition to
individual taxes on shareholder dividends. In addition, 1987
was the so-called "swing year" of the Reagan Tax Reform
Bill. Accordingly, a one-year postponement of the sale meant
a 9 percent reduction in corporate taxes. A spin-off, on the
other hand, eliminated the profit tax for '87, allowing the
company to sell a year later for the reduced '88 rate, with the
additional benefit to stockholders of proportional dividend
taxation. This allowed a shareholder to pay tax only on the
increase of the stock's net value, provided the IRS didn't
challenge the spin-off as part of a delayed agreed-in-principle
sale.

In September, CBS Inc.'s stock sold at $190.25 a share. As
rumors of an anticipated sale or spin-off persisted, the stock
climbed to a high of $225.70 before leveling off at $220 a
share. It was thought by some Wall Street observers that
Tisch had already struck a deal with Sony for the company,
in the form of a long-term note buyout, allowing CBS to
borrow against the sale and avoid corporate taxes.

October 19, 1987: Wall Street had a heart attack and all

bets were off in the wake of Black Monday. Almost immediately, Tisch reactivated negotiations with Sony, as CBS found itself suddenly in need of immediate capital. The fifty-point drop in CBS's stock aggravated what was already bad news from another source. Anti-DAT technology had proved futile; there was no effective way to prevent recording without impairing the quality of playback. Already, "gray-market" hardware had begun to enter the U.S. via Canada. In addition, Michael Jackson's *Bad* and Bruce Springsteen's *Tunnel of Love* failed to approach the sales figures of *Thriller* and *Born in the USA,* respectively. Paul McCartney continued to show dismal returns with his latest album, and Mick Jagger's initial solo album was a bust.

All of these factors contributed to the final sale of CBS Records to Sony on November 19, 1987, for the now very acceptable $2 billion in cash. CBS's stock rose to $176 a share from its postcrash low of $152. The deal had gone down in the early predawn hours. William S. Paley provided the swing vote necessary to close the deal, in a move some took to be the ultimate revenge. Shortly after dawn, Laurence Tisch emerged from the closed doors of the boardroom at CBS headquarters in New York, to issue the following statement: "After long discussion and very careful review, our board concluded that this is a very attractive offer in terms of value to the shareholders, while it also provides an important source of capital and allows us to focus all of our energy and resources on our core business of broadcasting."

Michael P. Schulhof, director of Sony of America, issued that company's only comment: "Sony very much looks forward to working with the talented people at CBS Records."

Walter Yetnikoff, the president of CBS Records for thirteen years at an annual salary that had reached $900,000, was offered a $20 million multi-year contract by Sony. The contract ran for an estimated ten-year period and included the promise to keep Yetnikoff's twenty-person team of top management intact.

Sony knew what it was doing in keeping Yetnikoff. His reign

at Columbia had begun in the turmoil and confusion that followed the forced resignation of Clive Davis. It was Davis's bad luck (or worse) to get caught in the maelstrom of drugs, payola and alleged organized crime activities that hit Columbia Records in the spring of 1973, as the Federal Strike Force Against Organized Crime focused on Columbia. Pop singer O. C. Smith accused the label of having colluded with organized crime members to cheat him out of his royalties from his recording of "Little Green Apples." Smith named names for the strike force, beginning with Pasquale Falcone, alleged go-between for the mob and the record company. The investigation that followed turned up a number of questionable practices under the Davis regime and at least one drug-related in-house arrest.

By the time Smith's charges failed to hold up in court, Davis was long gone, replaced by Yetnikoff. Davis considered an offer to head up the newly organized American division of Sony, Inc. He turned down the opportunity in favor of starting his own record company, Arista, although what might have occurred if Davis had been involved with the negotiations between Sony and Columbia invites interesting speculation.

Yetnikoff inherited a label caught in the middle of a major federal crime commission investigation; the sudden death of one of its major performers, Janis Joplin; and the departure, dissolution and/or failure of such big money acts as Simon and Garfunkel, and Miles Davis. Clearly, Clive Davis's departure was the end of one era and the start of another, with John Hammond providing the continuity. Hammond, who'd bridged the Mitch Miller/Clive Davis transfer of power by bringing Dylan to the label, this time got behind Bruce Springsteen, whose career had floundered under the previous regime.

In spite of his spectacular success with Michael Jackson and Springsteen, Yetnikoff's position at Columbia remained tenuous. His relationship with Laurence Tisch deteriorated in the months prior to the sale of the company. The two had battled over the budgets ever since Tisch's arrival, and it was clear to close observers at Columbia that the only reason Tisch retained Yetnikoff was to provide a semblance of order and continuity at the record division for the sake of its pending sale. Had Tisch ultimately declined Sony's offer, Yetnikoff's services would almost certainly no longer have been required.

Sony, on the other hand, had no apparent knowledge or interest in the daily operation of Columbia Records and was willing to pay to keep Yetnikoff aboard, no matter what the price. As if to compensate for the privilege of retaining Yetnikoff, hundreds of middle-level staff were eliminated.

Changes were felt throughout the new company. Mick Jagger, who hadn't toured with the Rolling Stones in years, quickly agreed to tour Japan in 1988 for a reported eight-figure profit. Michael Jackson's *Bad* tour debuted in Japan, where he grossed what was reported to be in the "high seven figures."

In the year after Sony's acquisition of Columbia, Japan emerged as the premier showcase for rock's superstars, where the very strong yen made going to Japanese an extremely profitable venture. A single performance before 50,000 Japanese packed into a single stadium meant a gross of two and a half million dollars. Top-line Western rock stars could demand and get as much as 95 percent of the house gross, as compared to an average 60 percent top stateside. The net profit for an American rock star's ten show/two week tour of Japan, including the obligatory million-dollar sponsorship deal and live TV special, averaged between fifteen and twenty million dollars in 1987 and 1988.

Stateside, rock hit a new low in crassness. Madison Avenue blazed new trails in rock's social iconography by the simple act of turning Marvin Gaye into a California raisin. Revolution? That was a new hairstyle, a different brand of cooking oil, or a pair of blue suede Nike's.

Twenty

O nce classified as "commercial," the success of America's popular entertainment, its music, film, theater, literature, becomes a function of profit, rather than performance, further defined by its functional environment. Commercial programming is received "free" on TV, while artistic film and theater are purchased with the price of admission; a significant class distinction in a consumer-oriented society where art becomes the privilege of those who can afford the entry fee.

The distinction between the elitist pursuit of art and the consumer purchase of goods has defined the structure of the America corporate media for nearly sixty years. As the distinction between the presentation of entertainment and the selling of product becomes less clearly defined, the difference between an artistic statement and commercial product becomes increasingly difficult to recognize.

With rock and roll's entrance into the mainstream, its social importance diminished as its potential to sell products increased. By providing "free" music as advertising for a product, the distinction between the records being played and the regular commercial pitches blurs. Ultimately it becomes difficult to distinguish between the record and the commercial, or to decide which to buy.

In the fifties, the harmonies of rock and roll were its best metaphor for teenage America's uncorrupted vision of romantic perfection. And from the moment rock first came over the airwaves, it was that idealism that sold everything from pimple cream to pop soda. Until adolescent rebellion evolved into product conformity. The first time Elvis slung a guitar over his shoulder, he might have been a rebel. The millions of kids who slung guitars over their shoulder to be like him were rock's first product consumers.

Those who still find in rock and roll some veiled social threat are in a way more subversive than the professionals who make records. The time-capsule morals of Tipper Gore and Allan Bloom mark them as only the latest but certainly not the last to raise an eyebrow over young America's "obsession" with rock music. In light of the music industry's profitable involvement in all facets of the commercial mainstream, the story of rock and roll should be used by the Harvard School of Business as one of its case studies. Far from the threat that political and social critics would have it seem, rock and roll has become the corporate spine of American entertainment.

One of the depressing truths of rock's getting into bed with Madison Avenue is that often those who control the publishing of some of rock's greatest music aren't the artists associated with the song. The artists have no say in whether or not the music they're identified with in the public's mind becomes part of a commercial campaign. "Whole Lotta Shakin' Goin' On," Jerry Lee Lewis's fifties rocker, has been sold to seven different companies without Lewis's ever having given his direct consent. Agencies who strike deals with publishers often actively seek to place their music with advertising agencies, sending out complete lists of what's available, and for how much.

On the other hand, many rockers who've been in the business for the long haul and never quite saw the kind of money their music earned for record companies, managers and agents, now see advertising (and movie sound tracks) as a way to balance the ledgers. The price for using a rock song in a commercial is often the most expensive component in that ad's budget. A sponsor may pay anywhere from $20,000 to millions. ZZ Top sold the rights to their 1984 regional hit, "Legs," as part of a multimillion-dollar arrangement with the manufacturers of panty hose who planned to put the songs into twenty separate commercials. The average, according to industry sources, is about $100,000 for a one-year license; about four runs of the usual thirteen-week commercial cycle.

Some sell for reasons other than the need for extra cash. Pepsi was able to buy into the Michael Jackson phenomenon for a record $15 million because it was said that Jackson genuinely liked the way Pepsi tasted. Jerry Garcia claims commercials are okay because they put musicians to work. Paul Kantner defended the Airplane's Levi's commercial because he felt that jeans symbolized the counterculture. Phil Alvin sang one for Budweiser so he wouldn't have to go on the road. Laurie Anderson did a Reeboks in order to fund the building of a studio. The Long Ryders agreed to a beer commercial because they said they were broke, the same excuse Woody Guthrie used in the forties when he allowed Lucky Strike to use "So Long It's Been Good to Know You" in their cigarette ads.

Even the Rolling Stones played the game, letting Jovan sponsor one of their tours. The door opened for the marriage of product with performers on the concert stage. Genesis, David Bowie and Eric Clapton, among many others, allowed their music to become intertwined forever in the minds of their fans with the corporate logo of a brand of soft drink, beer, or perfume, all but obliterating the original intention of the song, the singers and the music that put them in a position to do the hustle in the first place.

Rock's self-appointed integrity savior, Neil Young, decided to make the scuffle sanctimonious by recording "This Song's for You." MTV promptly banned it for its inclusion of the actual sponsor products it then proceeded to attack. Young's attack on the commercialization of rock for profit ignored the larger issue of his own usurpation of American rhythm and blues, only the latest in his long history of "borrowed" styles.

It puzzled many why Young was outraged at the song's exclu-
sion from the MTV playlist. He was at least twenty years older
than the average rock video performer (thirty years older than
the average viewer). He rejected everything the station stood
for. MTV's acknowledgment underscored that what they and
their audience were buying wasn't what he was selling. Logi-
cally, Young should have celebrated this rejection as further
proof of his own musical integrity. Instead, his selective ideal-
istics and chameleon stylistics proved only that he had no
musical style, other than his neo-populist stand; his outrage
at rock's commercialization flying in the face of the T-shirts
he sold at his own concerts. Young's attack on corporate rock
was the equivalent cross-signal to David Crosby's anti-drug
raps. Along with Steve Winwood and Boz Scaggs, Young's
calculated image, down to the obligatory leathers and torn
jeans, made them all indistinguishably foolish; more Malcolm
Forbes than Marlon Brando.

None of which is any worse, some may argue, than Warner
Entertainment's MTV, the eighties TV version of top 40
radio, where it has become all but impossible to distinguish
between the commercials for products and the videos for
songs. MTV's greatest "triumph" has been to lower the age
when adolescent idealism shifts to active consumerism: the
average MTViewer is between eleven and twelve years old.

To be fair, there has been at least one positive result of the
mass commercialization of rock in the eighties. The use of
Percy Sledge's "When a Man Loves a Woman" introduced
rhythm and blues to a new generation of British teens, leading
to a full-scale revival of American fifties R&B, and a return to
the charts for the first time in three decades of the music of
Jackie Wilson and Ben E. King. Like the ad for that dishwashing liquid claimed, it was enough to make the situation almost
nice.

Until the Beatles.

How their music wound up hawking sneakers and what they
tried to do about it became rock's worst case scenario, a
Pandora's box of corporate deception and cunning criminal-

ity so outrageous as to make John Lennon's personal breakdown and professional withdrawal seem by comparison acts
of heroic defiance.

To fully understand what happened, it's necessary to pick
up the ongoing saga of the Beatles with Paul McCartney's
1978 $20 million deal with CBS that included, as an induce-
ment to sign, the complete publishing catalog of the late
Broadway composer Frank Loesser.

It was this inclusion which began McCartney's serious consideration of the acquisition of music publishing as an excellent tax-shelter investment and ongoing source of income.

McCartney never had a better chance to gain total control
of the Lennon-McCartney catalog than when, in the late seventies, Northern Songs was once again put up for sale.*
McCartney found himself in a bidding war with Michael Jackson. McCartney offered $40 million, while Jackson offered
what some estimates suggest was as much as $100 million in
cash. Ironically, it was McCartney who first turned Michael
Jackson on to the financial advantages of accumulating musical catalogs. During the recording of "The Girl Is Mine," a
single that appeared simultaneously on Michael Jackson's
Thriller and Paul McCartney's *Tug of War,* McCartney advised
Jackson to look into publishing acquisition.

Losing the opportunity to reacquire his own music,
McCartney nevertheless continued to collect the music of
other rock stars, including, upon the death of Norman Petty,
the complete Buddy Holly catalog. He allowed Holly songs to
be used for commercials, claiming that Holly's death permitted the commercial use of his music to find a new generation
of listeners, while Beatles music was off-limits because three
members of the original group were still alive.

When the Nike "Revolution" ad first appeared in the fall of
1985, it reunited those survivors in a combined effort to stop
what they considered in principle to be against everything

*Northern Songs, which held a valid contract for all Lennon-McCartney songs
through most of the seventies, unsuccessfully sued McCartney for the rights to
continue to publish and control his post-Beatles material.

they'd stood for as the Beatles. It wasn't the first time the Beatles had brought legal action against the unauthorized use of their name, image and/or music. Twenty-plus years of such ongoing litigation has been augmented by a series of costly and not always successful challenges, including suits against the promoters of various unauthorized "Beatlefests," flea-market souvenir extravaganzas that have so far produced an estimated $100 million in sales of bootleg records and cassettes, unlicensed souvenirs, publications, videos and recordings, not a penny of which reverts to the Beatles.

Probably the best-known "Beatles case," prior to Nike, was the suit they brought against the producers of *Beatlemania,* an hour and a half Broadway show conceived and produced by the partnership of Lieber and Krebs. *Beatlemania* offered four musicians impersonating the Beatles in various stages of their career performing "in concert." After years of court battles, Apple Corps Ltd. was able to win an infringement suit against the producers that prevented the further representation of the Beatles' physical images, plus a high seven-figure fine. The case was appealed, during which time the producers offered to settle. The agreement included the discontinuation of the presentation of the show, the withdrawal of the film version and all record albums, plus an undisclosed amount of money which an informed source has revealed to be upwards of $5 million.

Another case took place in England, in the early eighties. Heineken Beer, in conjunction with EMI, decided to run a promotion in which five beer bottle caps or can tops entitled the holder to a discount of the purchase price of Beatles cassettes. The campaign used the image of the Beatles in the print, TV and radio ads, and so outraged Ringo Starr that he urged the other two Beatles and Yoko Ono to join him in suing the beer company. The case has not yet gone to trial.

When the Nike commercial appeared in 1985, it was George Harrison and Paul McCartney who decided to sue. They prevailed upon Leonard Marks, of Gold, Farrell and Marks to handle the case. Marks was already involved with the

Beatles, handling their lawsuit against Capitol/EMI for alleged misappropriation of huge amounts of royalties by the
record company. That litigation, begun in 1979, was crawling
through the due process of the American court system when
the Nike ad appeared.

The commercial showed off a series of yuppie-types
doing their physical workout thing interspersed with a sports
superstar—John McEnroe, among others—the common
bond between all parties being their choice of Nikes, with
"Revolution" playing underneath the thirty-second spot.
Nike claimed only two hundred letters of complaint and a
significant upsurge in sales. The spot was nevertheless considered by the surviving Beatles so distasteful that in spite of
Yoko Ono's initial position of passive endorsement of the
commercial as a way to help "demythify" the life of John
Lennon, she eventually joined Apple Corps Ltd. (the Beatles)
in their joint 1987 lawsuit against Nike, Inc., Capitol Records,
Inc., EMI Records Limited and Wieden and Kennedy Advertising (the makers of the ad), over the alleged illegal use of the
actual Beatles recording of "Revolution" in a campaign to sell
Nike sneakers.

Marks focused the thrust of the lawsuit so as to reflect in no
uncertain terms that the Beatles never intended to write and
sing rock music to peddle beer, hawk panty hose, shill for
hotels, or push running shoes. It was a simple, affirmative
stance that quickly and effectively laid out the thrust of the
Beatles' case, as well as articulating what so many others,
musicians and the public alike, felt about the use of rock music
to sell products. Yet, even as the Beatles sought to extricate
their music from the commercial, there were many who felt
they'd voluntarily allowed the song to be used. A full-page
article in the "Show Business" section of *Time* magazine (May
18, 1987) titled "Wanna Buy a Revolution? The Beatles Shill
for Sneaks as Madison Avenue Rocks Out," implied that the
Beatles were part and parcel of the campaign to sell Nikes,
and were in it only for the money.

The truth of the matter was, like many artists whose music

found its way into commercials, the Beatles never saw a penny for the use of "Revolution." All payments for the right to use "Revolution" went to Capitol Records and Michael Jackson.

In its defense, Nike believed it had legally acquired the rights to "Revolution" and sought to reaffirm that right after the Beatles brought suit. Nike had originally approached Capitol/EMI to lease the rights to the song. All agreed on a license fee of $500,000, half of which went to Capitol for the master recording, the other half to Michael Jackson as publisher of the Beatles' catalog.

The Beatles argued that Capitol/EMI had no right to license "Revolution" or any other *actual Beatles recording* for any use whatsoever; that the master rights to any and all originally performed Beatles songs were specifically limited to the sale of Beatles records, tapes and compact discs. The master rights, according to Marks, were separate and equal from the mechanical rights. (According to the Copyright Act of 1909, amended in 1976, mechanical rights are those granted for the reproduction and distribution of a copyrighted composition on phonograph records, tapes or discs to the public. The mechanical rights are exclusive to the copyright owners.)

The right to reproduce original recordings for the purposes of "synchronization" in films or videos is known as "synchronization rights" and requires "synchronization licenses" for recorded music. The distinction is made between the right to record a new version of a famous song and the use of the original "master" recorded version. In the Nike case, the Beatles charged that Capitol/EMI had exceeded their legal rights to use the masters of Beatles music, which, according to law, were specifically limited to recordings. No synchronization rights had been granted by the Beatles to Capitol/EMI for the use of their original recording by Nike. The legality of Capitol's leasing the mechanical and synchronization rights to the Beatles' original recording of "Revolution" by Capitol Records became the issue. The Beatles' position was simply that Capitol/EMI had licensed the original master recording of "Revolution" for commercial endorsements without the group's expressed, formal permission.

Capitol/EMI clearly intended to test the extent to which they could profit from the exploitation of mechanical rights of its extensive library of master recordings. They took the position that having manufactured and distributed or licensed the manufacture and distribution of the original recordings of the Beatles in the United States (and EMI in England) since 1962, they were entitled to all mechanical and synchronization rights to the group's catalog. A victory in the courts for Capitol could result in the acknowledgment of the total, exclusive rights to any composer's original material, in return for recording and distributing it.

In August, Nike took out a full-page ad in the *Los Angeles Times* that sought to gain public favor for what had become its controversial use of the song. The ad included the following statement by Nike:

> You may have heard that Nike is being sued by the Beatles. That's not exactly true. Nike, along with our ad agency and Capitol/EMI Records, is being sued by Apple Records. We negotiated and paid for all the legal rights to use "Revolution" in our ads . . . with the active support of Yoko Ono Lennon. We also believe we've shown a good deal of sensitivity and respect in our use of "Revolution."

The company showed so much "sensitivity" that, with the first anniversary of the original commercial's broadcast, Nike announced that a second version had been made and was set for release in March 1988.

Less than a week before the new commercial was set to air, in a move that shocked Madison Avenue and the major record companies, Capitol/EMI announced its willingness to settle out of court with the Beatles. It was a stunning, unqualified victory for the Beatles. Capitol/EMI had capitulated, agreeing to discontinue the licensing of the master recording of "Revolution" to Nike, who in turn announced its immediate intention to pursue other avenues of promotion.

Why did Capitol/EMI and Nike reverse its position? The reasons were purely economic. The Beatles were probably one of perhaps half a dozen rock acts with the financial resources to pursue a lawsuit against a major record company to its conclusion. Had it been almost any other group, capitulation by the record company would have been highly unlikely.

The final negotiated agreement assured the Beatles that Capitol/EMI would not issue any license agreements in the future for Beatles recordings. It seemed the end of the year-long nightmare. Then word reached the Beatles that Michael Jackson, through his financial management team of Swit, Bandeer, and Koppelman, might be actively peddling other Beatles songs in his catalog, eager to recoup on his investment. One reported deal with CBS was for a series of half-hour shows based on various Beatles songs. None of the Beatles had been consulted, which led to Paul McCartney's issuance of a public statement that he and John Lennon had always refused the numerous offers made to them over the years for the use of their music in commercials and other ventures, and, he, McCartney, always would.

The resolution of the Nike case allowed Marks to concentrate on the 1979 Beatle lawsuit against Capitol/EMI. According to Nike, it was this lawsuit which caused the Beatles to sue over "Revolution." "We feel we're a publicity pawn in a long-standing legal battle between two record companies," was how Nike interpreted its position; a victim caught between Capitol and Apple.

The issue at hand was the payment of royalties which the Beatles claimed Capitol Records owed them. The dispute had already resulted in the delayed issuance of Beatles CDs. In 1986, three full years after the introduction of the new format, not a single American CD of the Beatles was available for purchase.

How important were CDs to the backlist of the Beatles? When Columbia signed the Rolling Stones to their label for

$25 million in 1983, the deal included the rights to the back catalog of Stones albums (unlike the $20 million McCartney deal, which included no Lennon-McCartney material). By releasing the entire back catalog on CDs, Columbia recouped its investment in less than a year.

Considering that it costs about a dollar to manufacture a CD, with the retail price twice that of an album or cassette, the profit potential in CDs is huge, with backlists inventory offering the largest potential for profit.

But not for the Beatles, as Capitol/EMI continued to resist issuing Beatles CDs. According to Marks, the CD situation was just the latest in the ongoing battle between Capitol/EMI and the Beatles, a move to pressure the Beatles into settling their long-standing claim for unpaid royalties.

The Beatles claimed that Capitol owed them unpaid royalties on 19 million albums and singles. Capitol's position was that the records had been mostly post-Beatles "solo" albums, and as a result of their not having sold, were duly "scrapped." It was, according to Dan Murdock, of the New York law firm Donovan, Leisure, Newton & Irvine which represented Capitol, "all a huge misunderstanding." Most of the units in question, he insisted, weren't Beatles albums at all, but albums recorded by individual members of the group. When it became apparent to Capitol that their selling life had ended, they were "scrapped"; melted down or crushed for the recycling of the vinyl. Marks considered this explanation insulting. The real reason the albums were "missing," he insisted, was to avoid having to pay royalties on them.

At issue was the common industry practice of "scrapping." Legal scrapping occurs when albums are destroyed or physically marked, usually by puncture, to be properly identified as a return and charged back against royalties. As a standard industry practice, artists and their representatives never get to check the actual physical plant manufacture of records. It's almost impossible to conduct a completely accurate inventory audit. A company could conceivably report the manufacture of a million copies of a record, press two million, sell a hundred thousand, and report an inventory of nine hundred thousand physical units left over, when in fact the actual "inventory" contains a million salable records the artist never knows exists.

A series of charges and countercharges developed. Capitol asked the court to have the case thrown out for lack of specific evidence. The Beatles countered with a request for permission to continue the lawsuit, asking for a total of $80 million in damages. The court sided with the Beatles.

An audit was taken by Apple for the period 1969–1979 by the accounting firm of Satin, Tenenbaum, Eichler & Zimmerman. The audit found over twenty separate areas where Capitol/EMI had "wrongfully accounted" in the specific areas of promotion, manufacture and sales, with the result being about $19 million in unpaid royalties due the Beatles.

The 1980 audit revealed that according to Capitol's own records, the company continually scrapped and remanufactured the same Beatles albums. Further, in a deposition given later that same year by Bhaskar Menon, Capitol's chief executive officer, it was confirmed that although the Beatles had ceased recording in 1969, the sale of Beatles albums still amounted to nearly 30 percent of all Capitol's record sales. This led the Beatles to wonder just why Capitol would routinely destroy a significant number of their albums to regain the use of the vinyl, presumably to repress the same album.

In a deposition taken March 21, 1986, Dennis White, Capitol's executive vice-president for Record Group Services, testified he was aware of two separate instances in which records that Capitol had designated for scrap were in fact sold. According to White, Don Zimmerman (president of Capitol Records, at the time of the following allegation the senior vice-president of marketing) informed him (White) that "scrap" was being sold from Capitol's Jacksonville, Illinois, plant and "was not drilled [punching holes in records so they cannot be resold or returned for credit]." Private investigations followed up this testimony and uncovered the identity of a record wholesaler purportedly involved in the transaction of what were claimed by him to be "millions" of "scrapped" records to one John LaMonte, a convicted felon with a long history of underground activities, many of which directly involved the record industry.

John LaMonte had been arrested at his business, House of Sounds, Inc., located in Darby, Pennsylvania, by the FBI in February 1977. A search of the premises uncovered $7 million worth of counterfeit recording equipment. It was determined by the FBI that LaMonte was the head of one of the largest record and tape counterfeiting operations in the country. At his arraignment, LaMonte pleaded no contest to 16 counts of a 149-count indictment, each count representing a different counterfeit record title. He was sentenced to eighteen months in prison, fined $25,000 and placed on three years' probation. The court also ordered all records and equipment at the House of Sounds to be destroyed.

The operation LaMonte headed as the president and majority stockholder was a sophisticated buy/reproduce/sell scheme that employed more than fifty people operating out of a five-story warehouse LaMonte owned. House of Sounds was ostensibly a wholesale operation specializing in previously released recordings, manufacturers' overstocks, and "cut-outs"—records that have not sold well and been returned to the record company for credit. Cut-outs are usually sold to the public at bargain prices, from ninety-nine cents up to four dollars. LaMonte began in the cut-out business operating out of a storefront in Darby, Pennsylvania, before moving to his warehouse. In 1976, the third year of House of Sounds' operation, LaMonte grossed approximately $4.5 million.

In late 1972, LaMonte, along with James Kennedy, the owner of Arnold Kennedy Printing Company, Inc. of Philadelphia, set up an album cover copying operation under the name of James Enterprises. This operation was managed by John Gallagher and Harry Lasky, two employees of Bell Telephone, who later took a 10 percent interest each in James Enterprises.

The first album LaMonte and Kennedy counterfeited was *Introducing the Beatles (Please Please Me)*, the first American Beatles album originally released on Vee-Jay. Kennedy photographed both sides of the album cover and record label, while LaMonte employed Virtue Recording Studios of Philadelphia to produce a new set of master tapes from the record. The master tapes were then sent to Tracy Val Company of Summerdale, New Jersey, and Audio Matrix of the Bronx, New York, to produce the molds used in the final production process. LaMonte used several pressing plants—Clairion Record Manufacturing Co. and Paramount Record Manufacturing Co., both of Philadelphia, and Rite Record Productions, of Cincinnati, to press the records and affix the counterfeit labels. Clairion employed about twenty workers and operated twelve record presses from 1973 through 1977, with 90 percent of its business coming from House of Sounds.

From 1973 through 1971, James Enterprises produced approximately 1.7 million covers for House of Sounds. LaMonte sold his finished products, complete with cut edges to make them appear to be legitimate cut-outs, to retailers in the United States and Europe.

LaMonte and Kennedy then created a fictitious company, Amigo Records, to cover the purchases of tapes and recording equipment from several illegal sources.

According to the deposition given by Dennis White, LaMonte was the key figure involved in the purchase of "substantial quantities" of Beatles albums from Capitol Records, referred to by LaMonte as the "Apple deal." Capitol/EMI sold illegal Beatles "scrap" to LaMonte on an ongoing basis for eleven years, at least from the time of the amended and expanded Beatles contract, until White's sworn deposition before the U.S. Department of Justice's Organized Crime Strike Force, headed by Thomas P. Puccio. White asserted that during the eleven years, Capitol allegedly granted La-

Monte (and others in similar but not related "scrapping" operations) the right of return. All records LaMonte shipped back to the company were then deducted from Apple due royalties. The LaMonte operation allegedly included (but was not limited to) the shipment of records marked for "donation to charitable causes" by Capitol and therefore not eligible for royalties, most of which wound up in the general market competing with "legitimate" Beatles albums.

LaMonte purchased the "donated" recordings from wholesaler Richard Taxe, who obtained them directly from Capitol. One such operation involved the combined donation of 150,000 undrilled albums (significant quantities of which were Beatles albums) supposedly marked for donation to Boys Town of the Desert, albums which eventually found their way into the retail marketplace. As many as a half-million Beatles albums were "donated" from a single Capitol plant in Glendale, California, and eventually sold illegally over the retail counter.

In 1985, Sam Citro, then Capitol Records' vice-president of sales, was fired by the company after being cited by Capitol executive Walter Lee for alleged involvement in the scheme to sell records designated for charity.

Apparently, LaMonte wasn't the only "wholesaler" with whom Capitol and other record companies were allegedly doing business. Apple's audit revealed that as early as 1969, Capitol allegedly misclassified an enormous number of Beatles albums as "promotional," including 95,000 promotion (nonroyalty) copies of *Abbey Road,* about ten times the industry norm, even though the number of promotional albums usually decreases with an act as popular as the Beatles. Documents revealed that Beatles recordings designated for promotion were, in fact, improperly distributed for profit to record wholesalers. In their lawsuit, the Beatles claimed that these "promotional" classifications were the camouflage for the illegal sale and distribution of Beatles albums, for the purpose of avoiding the payment of royalties. Further, al-

though the Beatles' amended contract drew specific guidelines for the distribution of promotional albums, those
guidelines were ignored as Capitol freely used Beatles "promotional" albums as a form of payment to retailers in order
to gain window display space for other Capitol artists.

There was more. The 1969 contract between Apple Inc.
and Capitol/EMI was structured by Klein as a "buy/sell"
rather than the far more common "royalty" contract. The
arrangement called for Apple to buy Beatles albums manufactured from Capitol's masters and to sell them to the company
at a specified price higher than the "buy," the difference
being Apple's profit (the "buy/sell" spread). The contract
also contained a provision designed to have Capitol reward
Apple for the continued deliverance of "hit" records by increasing the profit margin up to 25 percent on certain albums
that achieved gold record status (500,000 units sold). According to the Beatles, Capitol reneged on its agreement to adjust
the spread, based on a method of "averaging" that included
what were in no way what could have been considered "Beatles" albums. "Sometime in New York City," for example, the
non-Beatles Lennon-Ono double album was included in Capitol's calculations of Beatles album sales and cited as just
cause for not paying what Apple felt was its just royalties.

Further, in April 1980, Capitol reported a number of thefts
of albums from its Los Angeles warehouse, including a large
quantity of Beatles records. Although the records were deducted from royalty consideration, upon their recovery, no
evidence was offered to show they hadn't been restored to the
inventory of sales.

And still more. As of January 1, 1969, Merco Enterprises
was a wholly owned subsidiary of Capitol. Merco received
what were termed "free goods" whenever it purchased records from Capitol, its parent company. Although the practice
of "free goods" was construed as a sales inducement for
wholesalers and retailers, by selling to Merco, Capitol was, in
effect, discounting to itself and then selling the same goods

at full price, thereby further reducing royalties to be paid to Apple, Inc. This practice, according to the Beatles, had been going on since 1969.

For all the above cited reasons, in June 1988, the Supreme Court of the State of New York, County of New York, Judge Elliot Lamby presiding, ruled that despite challenges by Capitol/EMI and a request that the lawsuit be dismissed, the Beatles could proceed with their $80 million suit against the record company. The ruling overturned a 1987 lower court decision which restricted the Beatles to pursue its case for $30 million in compensatory damages, but not the additional $50 million they sought in punitive damages. At the same time, the court found no connection between the delay of the release of Beatles CDs by Capitol and the royalty issue, and dismissed that $40 million lawsuit. Shortly thereafter, the first of the American Beatles CDs went on sale.

Ultimately, what's at stake for the Beatles is the ownership of their publishing rights and master recordings. They hope finally to regain control of their music as a result of what they claim in their suit to be twenty years of financial misdealings and commercial misuse of their music by Capitol/EMI.

The difficult and financially tangled history of the Beatles represents the ongoing exploitation of rock artists that has been a part of the business from the earliest days of rhythm and blues. Capitol is by no means the only label that has ever been involved in a dispute over payment of royalties. In April 1988, Salvatore Pisello was convicted of income tax evasion in a case involving money received from MCA, Inc., for the illegal sale of discontinued records. Pisello is believed by federal authorities to be a member of the New York Gambino family, a charge he denies. No charges have been brought against MCA.

Organized crime's involvement in the record business has involved jukeboxes, independent promotion, personal management and payola, including the supply and distribution of drugs, women and cash to buy influence and exposure on the airwaves. In 1986, a federal investigation into the ongoing practice of payola revealed that extensive bribery, in the form of cash and drugs, was an active part of record promotion responsible, according to one record source, for up to thirty new singles being added to FM playlists on any given week.

In retrospect, the biggest change in the promotion of music by the majors brought about by the 1959 payola hearings was the rise of the independent promoter, as record companies sought to separate themselves from the most vulnerable link in the manufacture of hit records. As late as the winter of 1988, Joe Isgro, William Craig and Ralph Tashjian, three highly successful independent record promoters, were investigated by a Los Angeles branch of the federal Strike Force of the U.S. Department of Justice, Division of Organized Crime and Racketeering, for their alleged connection to organized crime involvement in the promotion of certain acts and artists, many of whom were associated with at least one major record label. At the present time, the federal government is prosecuting Craig for an alleged payoff of $212,650 to a number of well-known deejays, and Tashjian for income tax evasion related to his having provided $58,000 worth of cocaine for the purpose of buying radio influence for certain records. Isgro, considered the biggest and most influential record promoter on the West Coast, has been cooperating with the Justice Department on the investigation into alleged illegal practices that are believed to involve the knowing, active participation of several major record companies. Isgro is strongly suspected of sending cash amounts of up to $5,000 through the mails or via Federal Express in order to get certain records played on the radio. The Justice Department suspects that Tashjian acted as a middleman, supplying cocaine, women and money to local program directors to play certain designated records and submit favorable reports to influential trade papers. All the allegations involving Isgro and Tashjian are denied by their attorneys, and Isgro has sued a dozen labels he'd worked with for monies he claims were never paid, one reason he may have voluntarily turned state's evidence.

Although no label was willing to discuss its relationship to any independent promoters, one highly placed industry source revealed that as standard practice upwards of $100,000 is normally factored into the budget of any potential hit record. In reality, this is payola designated under a variety of promotional headings. Often, the source continued, "independent" publicity offices have, on at least one occasion, been created by a company, fully staffed and put into business for the sole purpose of laundering payola funds. The company is then hired to promote a record, charges the record company a fee, and uses that money for payola.

Charges of outside influence go beyond the actual promotion of records. Michael Jackson's 1984 "Victory" tour became the target of the Reverend Al Sharpton, who, as the head of his own consulting firm, the Georgia-based Hit Bound Inc., threatened local Jackson promoters with racial boycotts if he, Sharpton, wasn't cut in for a portion of the box office. Sharpton had allegedly employed similar shakedown methods with the national tours of Lionel Ritchie, Whitney Houston, Prince, Marvin Gaye and Luther Vandross. Sharpton publicly warned the Jackson tour promoters that there was no way he'd "stay off the gravy train . . . no way I'll allow that money to stay totally in the white community." Sharpton was given the official title of "Tour Community Relations Director"; was put up, at the tour's expense, at the finest hotels in every city the tour played; and given up to 8,000 tickets to be distributed to poor black kids who otherwise wouldn't be able to afford to see the show, tickets whose distribution was never accounted for by Sharpton.*

---

*In August 1988, Internal Revenue Service agents contacted "Victory" tour promoter Chuck Sullivan for details of his financial dealings with Sharpton. Sullivan turned over more than fifty checks made out to Sharpton's "Jackson's Community Relations Group," totaling more than $519,510. New York promoter Ron Delsener stated that Sharpton was "lying if he said he was co-promoter . . . It's simply not true." Several spokespersons for the ongoing investigation into Sharpton's operation have suggested that the donated tickets to the Jackson shows were sold through mob-controlled outlets, and the money split between the mob and Sharpton. Sharpton contends that he is the victim of a racially motivated "political witch-hunt," and

In the summer of 1988, Roulette Records president Morris Levy—the same Morris Levy who first brought Alan Freed to New York City thirty-five years earlier—was found guilty on charges of conspiracy to commit extortion. The charges involved a deal between Levy's record company and "Out of the Past," a record distribution operation headed by John La-Monte, the same John LaMonte implicated in the Beatles "scrapping" lawsuit against Capitol/EMI. According to the government, LaMonte served as the middleman in the sale of 4.7 million MCA records supposed to be marked for cut-out. When LaMonte refused to pay Levy because of the inferior quality of the merchandise, Levy and two associates, alleged organized crime figure Dominick "Baldy Dom" Canterino and Roulette Records comptroller Howard Fisher, attempted to extort the money from him. Late in 1988, Levy announced the sale of Roulette Records to KB Communications of New York for $4.5 million. The sale included 1400 master recordings on Roulette and its twenty subsidiary labels. Levy announced plans to retire to Australia pending the successful appeal of his conviction and ten year sentence for extortion and conspiracy. Levy, upon posting $3 million bail, publicly acknowledged for the first time his formal connections to the Genovese family, a "confession" that came on the heels of FBI documents revealed by the prosecution that confirmed Levy's ongoing relations with Genovese family boss Vincent (the Chin) Gigante.

In February 1979, John LaMonte became a fully cooperating witness for the U.S. Department of Justice and remains free, living under an assumed name as part of the Federal Witness Protection Program. [See Appendix A]

Leonard Marks's history of successful rock litigation had begun long before his involvement with the Beatles. Marks

---

insists he personally distributed the tickets to poor kids through unnamed "prestigious people on a national level." He is currently under investigation for income tax evasion, having failed to file returns for at least the past five years.

had previously handled suits for Diana Ross, the Bee Gees, Madonna, Grace Jones, Paul Anka, Jimmy Webb, Burt Bacharach, Hal David, Jerry Leiber and Mike Stoller. Cases involved either copyright infringement, challenges to authorship or unfair company practices and policies involving talent. With Leiber and Stoller, for example, Marks successfully handled the songwriters' lawsuit against music publishers Hill and Range, for alleged royalty improprieties stemming from the firm's "offshore" banking practices that had made it all but impossible for the duo to audit the company's books.

Marks cut his teeth in rock litigation by successfully defending Mike Appel's interests against Bruce Springsteen. Although this initial foray into rock litigation had been on the side of management, it resulted in a number of cases in which Marks found himself in a position to represent performers unable to free themselves from what were essentially illegal contracts that shifted the balance of power and the bulk of their finances into the hands of record companies. One almost always mandatory inclusion in artists' contracts requires that unless specific objections in writing are submitted within a period of six to eighteen months regarding suspected financial irregularities, all rights to future claims shall be waived. Most recording contracts are drawn in New York City, the corporate headquarters for the majors, where state law specifically allows for a six-year period of challenge, unless that period is contractually waived by the artist.

The long roster of rock stars who've spent years and fortunes trying to extricate themselves from prohibitive contracts includes Pete Townshend and his group, The Who, which, after two false starts under Helmut Gordon and Pete Meadow, signed a management deal (which gave away 40% of their income) with ex-film producer and bon-vivant Kit Lambert and tough Eastender Chris Stamp, the result of which was years of complex negotiations (including an unsuccessful takeover bid by Allen Klein) between the band and its management to correct what were initially among the lowest royalties ever paid to a sixties British supergroup. The

Who's finances were further eroded by a lawsuit involving early producer Shel Talmy who was awarded a royalty on all their LPs up to and including Who's Next in 1971, including their magnum opus and best seller Tommy. It wasn't until 1973 that Townshend, Daltrey and the rest began to see a more reasonably scaled share of publishing and performance profits.

Ray Davies of the Kinks signed away a full 50 percent share of all his U.S. earnings before his percentage of publishing is configured; Fleetwood Mac, whose royalty structure resulted in founding member Mick Fleetwood's going bankrupt; Sting's signing away of up to 75 percent of his Police profits, the real reason for the group's dissolution, rather than the "creative differences" cited by band members at the time; Elton John's fifteen-year legal dispute with Dick James over what John considers an unfair percentage of publishing profits reverting to the publisher.

In addition to the "names" whose cases receive some attention in the rock press, there are literally thousands of cases involving performers below the ladder rung of wide public recognition, where the cost of litigation becomes prohibitive and often projected to be more than whatever belated settlements it might yield. The position of the majority of record companies was expressed off the record by the defense in a dispute between Jimmy Webb and his record company over unpaid royalties: in allegations of royalty irregularities, the policy is to pay only if actually caught cheating, or if ordered to make restitution by the courts after long and very expensive litigation. In most cases, unless the sum of money in dispute is greater than $50,000, the reality of the cost of litigation makes the bringing of an action an unprofitable situation. Further, there is an almost universal fear by recording artists that any sort of challenge will result in an industry-wide blacklisting of their music.

All a part of what Leonard Marks refers to as "the industry's persistent course of conduct."

Twenty-one

In spite of Sony's promise to keep CBS Records intact, only the most naive or hopeful believed no operating changes were forthcoming. Within months, hundreds of positions were either phased out or consolidated, in the wake of what Sony claimed to be an unprofitable 1987 fourth quarter, the first period of its buyout.

Traditionally, the fourth quarter is the most profitable for record companies, due to the Christmas upsurge in sales. Yet, the company's year-end report showed that Columbia Records posted no profits for the quarter, prompting a flurry of lawsuits between various record executives working under an executive incentive program and a continuation of the bad blood between Laurence Tisch and Walter Yetnikoff. Tisch had Columbia file a lawsuit against Yetnikoff for mismanagement of CBS Records during the transitional fourth quarter. Yetnikoff responded with a statement to the press following a stockholder's meeting that "if he [Tisch] thinks Sony is afraid of him, he's wrong . . . if he wants a fight, he'll have a fight." No action on the suit has yet taken place.

Meanwhile, there was apparently no end to those attempting to take advantage of the Beatles, the Japanese being the latest to cue up for the dole. In the summer of 1988, the

Beatles filed charges against Teichiku Records of Japan to stop the distribution and sale of *The Silver Beatles,* an illegally distributed compact disc offering demos of pre-Ringo Beatles material; even as Yoko Ono was in Japan to promote long-distance calling for Kokusai Denshin Denwa, that country's telecommunications monopoly. Lennon's "Imagine" was the commercial's theme, leased from Yoko for a reported fee of approximately $70 million.

As the 1988 summer drew to a close, the record industry continued to be the target of takeovers and buyouts. Late in 1988, Motown Records was caught in a takeover bid by Boston Ventures, which then found itself in a struggle with MCA, Motown's distributor, for control of the company's stock. Motown had resisted an MCA takeover bid in 1986. Into the flurry of activity between Boston Ventures and MCA, came Virgin Records and Polygram with bids for Motown. Some industry observers felt that the label's sudden vulnerability was the result of rumors begun by Berry Gordy, who was anxious to shed his label. Since its inception, Motown had produced more than a hundred number one singles, a backlist of rock music worth millions. The 1987 resignation of Motown president and CEO Jay Lasker (former president of the defunct Vee-Jay) was considered by many to be the final blow to the label's ability to remain independently competitive. Lasker reportedly resigned in the wake of Berry's announced intention to add more non-American performers to the company's roster. When asked why he was willing to sell Motown, Berry Gordy replied that, in effect, he could no longer compete with the majors for the acquisition of talent.

Motown Records, one of the original rock independents, was formally taken over in August 1988 by MCA and Boston Ventures, for a combined buyout of more than $61 million. Gordy's only binding stipulation of the deal was a guarantee that at least 10 percent of the company would remain minority-owned.

Finally, late in 1988, rumors spread through the record industry that A&M Records was for sale at an asking price of between $400 and $500 million; the prospective buyer being Bertelsmann, the German conglomerate that owns RCA and distributes A&M. Another potential buyer was said to be Disney, one of the companies that failed to acquire CBS prior to Sony's takeover.

And still they come, young men and women from all across the country, wanting to be a part of rock and roll. To them, record companies represent their ticket to glory. Often, they have no realistic concept of corporate rock and roll. Their image of record companies is more often than not a place where the business of music is conducted in an atmosphere like the best video: energetic, exciting, glamorous, sexy, and always filled with very loud, endlessly playing music. Arthur Levy, Columbia Records' national coordinator of publicity, offered this more accurate view of what it's like, from the privileged position of being on the inside.

"I began like a lot of others, as a rock writer, which was an outgrowth of my college experiences, living the lifestyle of rock and roll in the sixties. My first real job was with Atlantic Records, in 1975, where I began as chief writer at Atlantic, replacing John Charles Costa, making $12,000 and sitting on top of the world because of it. Costa was one of the original group of rock writers to make the transition from the late sixties into the early seventies as a 'house hippie.' He was the first house hippie at Atlantic Records, that's for sure. I replaced him, writing liner notes for albums, bios of the artists, press releases, the house organ bulletin, new album release sales figures for the label, anything that required writing. If Ahmet Ergetun had to give a speech, I'd be called in to write it. If Atlantic signed a new act, I wrote it up as 'the signing story.' I do a lot more besides that today at Columbia, although I still essentially do all of that. Now I have to see that the story gets printed and shipped along with the albums."

Here, Levy offers a corporate evaluation of the relative success of various Columbia acts: "For all the money they

made on Epic during the *Thriller* run, Columbia probably
made as much, or more on the major label with a group like
Men at Work or Loverboy: steady, reliable, major acts that,
based on their budgets and promotion, returned what they
were expected to, with enormous profit differentials. An act
like Men at Work, which had two enormous albums, broke
chart records by having three number one records in a row
which no one since the Bee Gees had done, really ran their
expected course. That they faded badly on their third album
is as much a function of the business end as the music itself.

"A lot of people here feel they picked the wrong first single
for their third album. There's sort of an axiom in the music
business: if you pick the wrong first single out of the box, it's
very very difficult, it's virtually impossible for the second single to turn around and be a hit. When radio stations try a new
single from Columbia's promotion team which suggests this
is the cut we want you to play, and the station manager says
it doesn't sound like a hit to him, but goes along with it, and
it doesn't happen, it never happens that the second single
reverses it and turns into a monster hit. Radio is very reluctant
to give you a second chance. The first single doesn't have to
go to number one, it just has to be respectable. If it doesn't
do anything, if it doesn't get above, say, number forty-three
with a bullet, you can bet the second single is not going to
happen, no matter how big the group is. When that happens,
a group's career can be snuffed, just like that. Like Men at
Work, like all the new-wave bands you can name who had big
break-outs for their first singles and were never able to repeat
it. And that's not necessarily bad. As long as you know there's
room out there for the Billy Joels and the Bruce Springsteens,
artists who are going to put out two, three, four singles from
an album, and keep their presence. They're the meat and
potatoes of a major label."

One of the "heroes" of the postpunk movement was Elvis
Costello, considered by many to be the finest rock lyricist
since the Beatles. To many, he represented the best of what
seventies rock had to offer. Costello ultimately failed at Co-

lumbia and left the label, according to Levy, because "quite
simply, the record company started to take him for granted,
and that was the kiss of death for his type of act.

"An Elvis Costello record was no longer a special event.
Each of the first three or four Elvis albums was a special event.
My Aim Is True was gigantic; not in terms of sales, because
actually it was the third Elvis Costello album, *Armed Forces,*
that became his biggest seller of all time. It took him actually
to the third record to actually have an album go gold, I think
he sold 650,000. But what happened with him, he was just too
prolific. His records ceased to be events because they just
came too quickly. No one is supposed to put out more than
one record a year. No one is supposed to put out records
chock full of incredible songs ten months apart. People as
artistically gifted as Elvis should put out records, at the most,
once every year and a half and have those records just climbed
all over by the public. Instead, Elvis wrote just so fast and so
well that his records simply ceased to be something special at
the label. By the fourth album, he was putting out records so
fast—*Get Happy* and *Taking Liberties,* each with twenty songs
on them, within ten months of each other. If you totaled his
output to the label in a year-and-a-half period, he'd given the
label something like fifty-eight songs. Compare that to Bruce
Springsteen, who gives the label twelve songs every two and
a half years. With Costello, people here just couldn't deal with
the amount of music that he was giving the public.

"Rule number one at a record company: You have to turn
on the people who work at the label first, in order for them
to then go out and be missionaries for your product. The
Hooters are a perfect example. With *All You Zombies* they
turned everyone on at the label. As a result, we went out and
felt confident about turning the radio people and the press
on; they got excited and turned on the public, who bought the
records. That's the chain, and that's how it works.

"With Elvis, that all faded, from the point of sales initiation
inside the company. There was that and a very specific career
choice he made that essentially blew it for him at the label. In

the course of his touring, he discovered country music and decided he wanted to go to Nashville, to meet the music people there and record. They loved him and welcomed him with open arms. Especially George Jones. There was an affinity there, whatever it was based on. They were both sort of outcasts. George Jones was coming out of a very depressing period of his life; his career was starting to blossom again. Elvis Costello was new, happening, and represented a whole new audience for George, making all his attention very flattering. He took Elvis under his wing, and Elvis appeared as a guest on the George Jones cable TV special. In the space of a few months, he had this incredible exposure of being involved with all these country people and cut a country album, *Almost Blue.* Terrific album, except for one thing. Either Columbia, Elvis or his manager, Jake Riviera, sat on the album. For whatever reason, that record did not come out at the time Elvis was in the midst of having his country surge. Instead, Columbia and Elvis together put out these two albums, *Get Happy* and *Taking Liberties,* these two indigestible albums of twenty songs each; and a year and a half after the country thing, along come the powers that be, at Columbia, or with Elvis's own management and decide okay, now we're going to release *Almost Blue.* When it came out, everyone here said, what is this, why? God only knows what the reason was, but it was held back for a year and a half. When it finally came out, after the very disappointing sales of *Get Happy* and *Taking Liberties,* following his biggest album, *Armed Forces,* it was a disaster, barely selling 200,000 albums.

"At that point, Elvis became almost a total write-off at the label. The album that followed *Almost Blue, Imperial Bedroom,* which should have been an event, was treated by the record company as oh well, another Elvis Costello album that's not going to do anything. Then *Punch the Clock*—'Another Elvis album we have to deal with?' A year later, *Goodbye Cruel World;* it was almost a foregone conclusion it was going to fail miserably, and it did.

"Around the company, they were saying, almost as a joke,

Elvis, leave! Why did you re-sign in 1982? Around here he
was considered high and dry, but still could have commanded
for himself a huge deal. There were plenty of labels around
that would have killed to get him. So why did he sign? Maybe
because he owed Columbia a lot of money. There were probably a lot of outstanding advances, putting him in a position
where he couldn't afford to leave the label without having to
pay big bucks to buy out his contract. Even when the label
didn't care about him anymore. Sure, he could come to America and sell out concert halls, but that's just not where the big
money is, not with the expenses involved in touring. He was
once a gold record–selling artist at Columbia, he knew that,
and he knew he'd never be that again. Not at Columbia, anyway. I should say not at CBS Records in the United States.
Elvis was never signed to Columbia worldwide. He'd make
separate deals with the United States and Canada, and with
Europe. For awhile he was making separate deals country to
country, which was really a mess, under the advice, presumably, of his manager, Jake Riviera. There was a lot of money
to be made that way, but it puts the overall financial condition
of an artist in a mess. For Elvis, though, his days at Columbia
in America were numbered.

"Especially after some other, tangential events had taken
place. His A&R man, Greg Geller, who'd discovered Elvis, as
the legendary story goes (by the way, absolutely true), playing
on a soap box across the street from the record convention,
signed and nurtured him, left the label to return to Epic and
'help' it after a core group left to form Affinity. Geller's departure left Elvis without a champion at Columbia. Then his
product manager, or as they're now called, his marketing
director, Dick Wingate, left. Once that happened, there was
no base of support at the label, and that was it. Finally, Elvis'
sin was that he was too good. He didn't screw anybody, he
didn't burn anybody. Had he been a shade less geniuslike,
maybe he could have tapped in on a broader spectrum. But
Elvis, in the end, is cursed with being just another rock genius."

Levy's breakdown of Columbia's method in the making of a rock star: "A product manager's job is to work with an artist from the time of his signing, through conception of an album, to the realization of a finished product; to create the package, coordinating the art department with his personal management; formulating the marketing campaign, which includes everything from advertising, merchandising, pinups and posters, stand-ups, cut-outs, mobiles; in effect the liaison between the act and all the other departments of a record company, publicity and promotion.

"Obviously, the marriage of a marketing director and an artist is crucial, since so much of the artist's public image is shaped by the marketing director. Every idea has a price and a place, and the consequences of a campaign can be quite significant. For example, with Journey, when they did that 'radio' album, their marketing campaign included a store display that cost a hundred dollars for each model, of an actual radio station, with a lighted neon transmitter. They were sent out to accounts, and because they looked so good they stayed in the windows of stores for weeks.

"Inevitably, a manager will cut through and deal directly with an art director, with a publicist. For one thing, the artist almost always wants input. To that end, the manager develops relationships with people he's able to have a one on one with, and that's not frowned upon. The point is, if you had every manager on the label constantly barraging every department, you'd have chaos. Yes, that's why certain acts sign with an A&M or an Arista, because you can have that very situation and it's not even a traffic jam because their rosters are so limited. But when you're talking about the kind of rosters that a Columbia or an Epic has—well over a hundred highly active acts at any given time during the course of their product year, up to two hundred acts that are signed; of those highly active acts forty or fifty in the process of breaking a new album, touring, making a video—that's just not possible. The product manager or marketing director slows down the direct interference and makes all the connections work. Columbia

has been using this system since the early sixties, when it
crossed into rock. Al Teller and Clive Davis were primarily
responsible for the development of it, and it stuck. Today,
product managers are universally 'young' people, mostly
right out of college where they were involved with the promotion end of campus-related record company activities, with a
little bit of experience in some other area of the company,
maybe merchandising, so they have a little bit of experience
how the company works, but still where they can be molded
and not set in their ways.

"There's the industry above, which is corporation versus
corporation. WXRK-FM, in New York, for example, only has
so much room to add records per week, and each company
competes for that room. If they add too many of the other
guy's records, they can't add as many of ours, and so forth.
The industry below is another story. You have people that
staff these corporations, and they all go from company to
company. A week doesn't go by when you don't know someone who's switching labels. We all talk to each other; part of
our job is to know what our peers, our compadres are doing.
We'll know when our competition is coming out with a big
product, and maybe we'll hold back on ours to make sure we
get enough saturation. That kind of action goes on even in-
tracompany. We knew, for example, that Michael Jackson's
first single off *Bad* was going to go to number one on the R&B
chart, but we wanted L.L. Cool J to have his number one
record first, even if it was for only a week before Michael. So
we had to push up L.L.'s record to give him his shot.

"The bottom line is that the record company calls the shots
because the record company is the bank. Which is why all the
bands in the world want to sign with major labels, no matter
how free and independent their onstage image might be. Very
simply, if you make a record and it sells, the major record
company can and will write you out a check to reward you for
selling a lot of records. Why don't groups want to sign with
Marty Scott's Gem Records, for example? Because you can

sell a trillion copies of a record and you may never see a check. It sounds funny, but independent, small labels just can't afford to have hits. Look at George Thorogood on Rounder Records. He wasn't able to make a cent until he switched to Capitol/EMI. It's almost a catch-22. Small, independent record labels are not geared towards having massive hit records. They can barely handle the distribution, and they can never pay off the artists in a satisfactory manner; whereas major labels do it as a matter of course.

"To that end, the major record companies do not want to be patrons of the arts. A record company wants to sell product. They want to know there's a management situation behind an act that's pouring money into the act; that's supporting them on the road; that's paying the guys the per diems; that's taking care of bookings, getting them hooked up with the proper agencies and the right tour packages. None of which the record company pays for. If it's a promising group, and the record's doing well, and everyone likes the tour, the record company will participate financially by taking out advertisements to promote the tour along the way. If a group does a twenty-city tour, the record company product manager picks out ten, twelve, maybe fifteen cities in which to have advertising campaigns: print ads, smart FM radio ads, personal appearances on the progressive stations. All of that is paid for by the company. None of this money is kicked back to the group. It's written into the original contract what the advertising budget will be, with revisions if a record's sales pass a certain plateau. As long as a record company is making money, they'll likely throw more money after it. They'll pay additional man-hours for the local publicity man in each town to take the group around, meet the radio personalities, make an appearance at the record shop, sit for interviews, throw a little reception, have a small gathering backstage after the show, throw a joint someone's way, maybe do a little tootsky in the dressing room. You know you own a radio guy for the next three months if you introduce him to Clarence Clemons after a Bruce gig. That's where the record company is spending its money, not on the per diems of the group. Today, from the signing on, they want to know there are other, outside people involved. And that's why it gets harder and harder for unknown 'baby' acts to get 'discovered' off the street. Acts that get signed are acts that have solid management, mostly management you've previously done business with, or lawyers with acts that are well known on other labels. The record company knows that these are people it can deal with, and who are committed to the act, pouring money into it, so that by the time the act comes to the label they're not depending upon us to support them. They're depending upon us to help them sell records, and that's a very big difference.

"Ideally, a group makes a record for us, sells a lot of copies, gets a very big check from us and from their publishing company, and everyone's happy. Not ideal is when the company spends a lot of money, the record doesn't happen, the group takes more and more advance money to defray whatever expenses it has or to go back into the studio. All of a sudden, at the end of the campaign, the album is over, it went up the charts as high as it's going to get, the tour is finished, the singles have stopped, and the group is in their limbo phase. It's getting ready to write and record another album, figuring its next step, and they're $300,000 in the hole to the record company.

"The Clash spin-off, Big Audio Dynamite with Mick Jones, is a good example. Terrific group; they've put out two albums and the fact there's no more Clash makes them very important. They're a good band; they have high credibility among the critics, politicos and all that; great management from Gary Kurfirst's Overland Productions, one of the biggest and most important managers in rock and roll today—the Eurythmics, B-52s, Ramones, Talking Heads. CBS has poured in more than $650,000 into the group. That's how much the group owed CBS, and the company was still spending money on them. Because Al Teller believed in the group, because of

Gary Kurfirst's track record, and because everyone at the label agreed this was an important group. And that's money the label will probably never see, because the group just hasn't yet made it with the public.

"Which really isn't all that different from what was going on at the height of the idealistic sixties. Yes, Clive [Davis] was signing acts that had a certain aesthetic; but his bottom line was the same as it is today: he wanted to make money. In those days it may have been easier to tap into a vein of honesty and social commitment with the kind of acts you were signing, whereas today it's real hard to find that. Today, so much of what we do is still colored by the dance music syndrome. It's that pervasive; and unless you're a label completely willing to turn your back on pop you have to go with a lot of that, which was totally unheard of fifteen, twenty years ago, not part of the equation at all.

"Look at Bruce's first single off of *Born in the USA* or *Tunnel of Love.* Both instances—"Dancing in the Dark" and "Brilliant Disguise"—are essentially dance-flavored numbers, able to be programmed on CHR (contemporary hit radio), top 40 radio, and progressive FM. This gives Bruce exposure between Madonna and Jeffrey Osborne. The rest of the stuff on Bruce's albums, especially on *Tunnel of Love,* could never be played on top 40. The fact is, Bruce has to make this type of concession, or maybe compromise, for the sake of having that first big hit single off the album. He has to be in the groove.

"Or the Rolling Stones. When Columbia bought their label, they completely remixed all seventeen Stones albums from *Sticky Fingers* on—the London records weren't part of the deal—and released them simultaneously around the world. And they sold like crazy. It was a great move. The problem with the Decca/London CDs were that they were badly mastered. It was a shoddy job by Allen Klein done because everyone involved had it in their head they were going to make the Rolling Stones sound like people remembered them sounding. Well, fuck that, because that's not what digital sound is all about. It's about using the new technology to enhance the sound, and that's a concept that CBS has perfected.

"Music is the only American art form that has an industry built around it; an industry of demographics, technology, manufacture, distribution, merchandising. It's the curse and it's the blessing of rock and roll."

Twenty-two

Curses and blessings. Late in 1988, Japan sought to expand its hold on rock and roll, as JVC (Japanese Victor Corporation) made overtures into the possibility of buying out RCA, its American-based parent corporation; a move that would leave Warner-Elektra-Atlantic as the last wholly owned American record company.

Curses and blessings. Paul Rothchild, on the state of the music today: "I suppose things are very much the way they were in the fifties. Take payola, for instance, and the recent busts. I suppose, in a way, it's a healthy thing, because it creates the environment for the countermovement. The reason you have it happening now, is because the music's bad, which leads to the same environment. For example, along with payola, there's a reactionary return to the folk music movement. Suzanne Vega, Steve Forbert, Tracy Chapman. Look at Bob Dylan, bigger than ever. Folk clubs are opening up all over the place. There's a folk music ground swell at exactly the right place: the college level. The stuff that's on MTV and the radio just doesn't speak to that age anymore. It's either aimed too low, like MTV, or too old, like 'classic rock' formats. The other reaction to what's going on is New Age music, or as I like to refer to it, 'newage.' Garbage. It's the musical refuse of the culture.

"To my mind, the thing that's wrong with popular music today is that young people go into it for the wrong reason—to become rich, and that's not the eye you have to have on the ball. One of the reasons why Springsteen is so successful in the face of all that, without my trying to get into his soul, is that he tries to keep his focus purely on the truth of his youth. That's what rock and roll is all about."

In the hands of a roster of music executives who are the moguls rests today's very big business of rock and roll. The following represent the modern power elite:

Jeff Ayeroff and Jordan Harris: Having made their mark at Warner and A&M, respectively, they both left their labels to join Richard Branson for the start-up of the U.S. division of Virgin Records. Their fast-expanding roster of talent includes Keith Richards, Steve Winwood, Roy Orbison and Ziggy Marley.

Irving Azoff: The former personal manager for the Eagles, Stevie Nicks, Boz Scaggs, Dan Fogelberg and the Go-Gos, Azoff is now the head of MCA Records.

John Branca: A partner in the firm of Ziffren, Brittenham & Gullen. The mastermind behind the purchase of the Lennon-McCartney catalog for Michael Jackson. Branca represents Peter Gabriel, Don Johnson, Mick Jagger, David Lee Roth and the Beach Boys.

Jheryl Busby: President of MCA Records division of black music. Introduced black music to the previously "all-white" label. Acts include Jody Watley, the Jets, New Edition and Ready for the World.

Clive Davis: The former head of Columbia survived his 1974 ouster to form Arista Records, the home of Whitney Houston and the Grateful Dead.

Tom Freston: President of MTV. Freston rose from the marketing division of the Music Television Network to assume control of the Viacom-owned cable conglomerate. Conceived by Warner-Amex as an outgrowth of their 1980 two-way interactive cable experiment QUBE, MTV began broadcasting in August, 1981. MTV's original pilot was a thirteen and a half hour broadcast called "Pop Clips," hosted by ex-Monkee Mike Nesmith. Bob Pittman and Sue Steinberg crafted the 24 hour music concept based on radio's AOR (Album-Oriented Rock), aimed at a college-age audience. In 1985, Pittman attempted an unsuccessful leveraged buyout of the MTV Network (MTV, Nickelodeon, VH-1) which resulted in his departure. The company was taken over by movie theatre owner Summer Redstone. Redstone has expanded the reach of MTV to affiliates in Europe, Australia, and in the near future, Japan. Although MTV doesn't disclose its ratings, one insider reports there Neilsen to be under 1. Poor ratings led to MTV's radical shift in musical selection from AOR to CHR and heavy metal, late in 1986.

Gil Friesen: President of A&M Records. As head of the only independent "power" label, his supervision of such acts as Janet Jackson, Suzanne Vega, Squeeze, Sting and others has kept him on top of the personal vision the label came into existence to realize: the offer of original talent, regardless of its immediate commercial potential.

Dell Furano: President of Winterland Productions, the largest American rock merchandising company. Responsible for the ancillary merchandising at rock concerts. Winterland grosses upwards of $125 million dollars on the sale of rock tee shirts and programs, with prices for a high-demand item—a two dollar wholesale shirt with a Dylan or Springsteen logo—fetching as much as thirty-five dollars. Major performers often make more from the sale of merchandise than ticket sales. It's not unusual for a high-demand act to gross upwards of one hundred thousand dollars a night from the sale of related paraphernalia bearing its logo.

David Geffen: Founder and head of Geffen Records, Geffen has brought "rock" back to Broadway, reviving the uneasy relationship begun in the early fifties when *West Side Story* redefined rock in its own image. The producer of rock-oriented films—*Risky Business* and *Little Shop of Horrors,* as well as Broadway shows that include *Cats* and *Dreamgirls*—Geffen's label offers heavy metal, pop and ballad rock. His roster includes Whitesnake, Aerosmith, Sammy Hagar, Cher, and Robbie Robertson.

Trudy Green: The leading female manager in rock and roll. With her partner, Howard Kaufman, Green manages Heart, Whitesnake, John Waite, Stephen Bishop and the Jacksons (minus Michael).

Bill Graham: A survivor of sixties rock, Graham is one of the few of that era to remain relevant into the eighties. With the death of Albert Grossman, Graham becomes the last power link to the halcyon days of the New York to San Francisco connection. At fifty-eight years of age, Graham continues to produce rock shows at the international level, including benefits in El Salvador, Live Aid and Amnesty International. Bill Graham Productions has handled the Soviet tours of Carlos Santana and Bonnie Raitt, as well as all of Dylan's and the Grateful Dead's recent (individual) tours.

Jimmy Iovine: The Phil Spector of the eighties, Iovine's production carries the sound of postpunk, postdisco, and postmetal between the grooves of contemporary record producing. One of the two most sought-after record producers in the business.

Quincy Jones: The other one. Jones began his producing career twenty-five years ago with Lesley Gore's "It's My Party." He is one of the first black executives in the record business and is now the head of his own label, Qwest Records. Michael Jackson's producer for *Thriller* and *Bad,* Jones is credited with crafting those albums into the crossover sound that made them the huge sellers they were.

Leonard Marks: The entertainment lawyer defending the Beatles and by extension, all performers, in their fight to keep the corporations honest.

Brian Murphy: The premier concert promoter of Southern California. As head of Avalan Attractions, he controls who plays what venues in L.A.

Mo Ostin: Chairman of the board of Warner-Elektra-Atlantic.

Anne Robinson: Co-founder, president and chief executive officer of Windham Hill Records, the $30 million-a-year showcase label for New Age music.

Joe Smith: A veteran of corporate rock boardrooms, Smith learned his craft at Warner/Reprise and Elektra/Asylum/Nonesuch. Now the head of Capitol Records, Smith has been brought in to salvage the downward fortunes of Capitol/EMI.

Walter Yetnikoff: The head of Columbia Records, Yetnikoff has thus far been able to retain the label's essential roster of superstars, and the American personality of a corporate rock and roll giant.

Many performers who no longer cash out at their labels and are subsequently dropped have found new life heading their own independent operations. Patrick Sky's New Jersey–based Shanachie Label exists for the purpose of releasing new recordings for his small but loyal following. Similarly, John Prine's L.A.–based Oh-Boy Records functions as his outlet. By keeping recording costs down and personally supervising distribution (including strategically placed mail-order ads), both have been able to turn a profit by selling as few as 40,000 albums, a figure considered below the disaster level by the corporates.

A growing number of independent careerists have succeeded in carving out an alternative approach to doing business in today's world of corporate-dominated rock. One such person is Danny Goldberg, founder of Gold Castle Records. Goldberg's career began at *Billboard,* during the height of the first rush of sixties FM rock, as a concert reviewer. From there, Goldberg wrote for *Record World, Rolling Stone, Village Voice* and *Circus,* before being hired by Led Zeppelin to do promotion for its own Atlantic subsidiary, Swan Song. Zeppelin made Goldberg vice-president in charge of publicity and artist relations, serving as the press liaison for the band and the label's owner, Peter Grant.

It was while at Swan Song that Goldberg first thought about starting his own label. After splitting from Zeppelin in 1976, he started his own public relations company. He became involved with the promotion of Albert Grossman's Bearsville Records before going into partnership with Stevie Nicks and Paul Fishkind, Grossman's partner, to create Modern Records. After securing a distribution deal with Atlantic, Modern released Stevie Nicks's first solo album, which sold three million copies. After Atlantic vetoed several projects, Goldberg sold his interests in the label and looked to start again. He created Gold Mountain Records (distributed by A&M), which failed, then Gold Castle Records. For Goldberg and others like him, the struggle to produce good music in a business dominated by the majors remains the basis of the ongoing struggle.

"Distribution in the record business will always have a tendency to be centralized," Goldberg says. "The dilemma for the independent is that if he only has ten records a year, and two of them are huge hits, he's chasing to collect his money from the retailers. In this business, because of returns and other factors, you don't get paid up front. The lag time is a minimum of ninety days, and that's if you're paid on time. Warner's, on the other hand, is going to get paid immediately for last quarter's Madonna's sales because the buyer wants the new David Lee Roth, and they won't get the Roth product if their accounts aren't up to date. That was really the economic force behind centralization in the music industry: to build up enough volume so that retailers would have an incentive to pay on time. The financial vulnerability for an independent can result in your losing more with a hit than with a moderately selling album. If you ship a million copies of an album and you've been paid for 800,000 of them, you're in big trouble. To that end I see distribution remaining centralized, with a further shakeout of the industry to where instead of six majors, only three or four remain. What's happening more and more are what's called P and D deals. A P and D is a pressing and distribution deal. For a percentage of the wholesale price, the major will distribute the records and collect the money from the stores, in some instances do the physical pressing, but will have nothing to do with any of the advertising, promotion or actual recording. The independent pays his own manufacturing costs, shipping, virtually all costs, with his profit potential as high as a dollar fifty to two dollars per unit.

"The biggest nondistributor label is A&M, which is distributed by RCA but remains a completely independent entity. RCA's biggest advantage for A&M is that it allows the company to relieve itself of the burden of having to try and collect money. The same thing with Virgin and Island, which are distributed by Atlantic but remain completely creatively independent in terms of their marketing and promotion; and Chrysalis, which goes through CBS. Polygram now distributes me, but I haven't got a permanent deal with them.

"Another independent is Larry Welk, son of the famous TV bandleader Lawrence Welk, whose Welk Music has successfully targeted the 'baby boomer' audience. Almost none of their recordings are ever on the air, surely not top 40 radio and never MTV; yet for those aging first-generation rockers and folkies, his catalog remains essential. Welk Music is an amalgam of Vanguard Records, which they purchased outright, plus a selection of big band music, some classical, along with a TV packaging operation that sells records under a subdivision known as Heartland, all operating independently through their own distribution network.

"Another independent, Ira Moss, has focused his records on the literate upscale boomer audience. His sales come mostly from displays in bookstores, where among the stacks of literature his racks of cassettes and midline albums offer a cross-section of popular and classical music; again, all independently owned and distributed.

" 'New Age' music has helped these small, independent companies mine an entrepreneurial niche, to target and reach the upscale postrock audience; helping to extend the record-buying demographics of the core pop/rock audience; helping to keep the independent music business alive in such diverse outlets as bookstores, the Nieman-Marcus catalog, the Literary Guild, health-food stores, supermarkets, Woolworth's, 'new-age' rackjobs. There's plenty of room for independents today but no room for another WEA, CBS, EMI, or MCA. It's just the focus of what an independent does that's changed. He's no longer the guy who gets the records manufactured, picks them up from the plant, puts them in the back of the car and drives them to the stores, like Ahmet Ertegun did in the fifties. Today an independent is someone who puts out music because, basically, he likes it; the music as well as the freedom to do whatever the hell he wants."

"If it's not in the grooves, it ain't gonna happen," says Harold Bronson, cofounder of Rhino Records, another of the new independents. Rhino began as a small L.A. record store specializing in independent recordings and sixties music. Today, it stands as a showcase of the marriage of music and marketing, catering to a small but growing audience of rock aficionados. Rhino's roster of sixties-revival and eighties garage band music, is a testament to the between-the-cracks survivability of the small record company in the eighties arena of corporate giants.

"I think there's a growing awareness of independent labels like Rhino where it's not all just numbers, both within the industry and with the public," Bronson says. "We've always seen ourselves as mavericks in the record industry. Basically, our label grew out of the backroom of our record store. We were experimenting in putting out records, getting distribution in a very minimal fashion, and we kind of grew from that. I think every rock and roll fan probably fantasizes at one time or another about owning a record company. We wanted to do it, we liked it, but we didn't have any specific goals in mind. In our early stages, if we put out an album that sold between five and ten thousand copies, we'd be pretty content with that. You can be when you have five or ten employees. Today we have over fifty employees, and if our records sold ten thousand copies apiece we'd be out of business. Overall, though, we can afford to sell considerably fewer records than a major would have to, in order to show a profit. Because of that, we can put out different types of records. Rhino's main thrust is 'oldies,' a genre the majors look at in a real minimal way, as a sort of tribute; their main source of income comes from new, hot artists, getting new artists onto the radio to make them hot. In the wake of Monterey and Woodstock, the record business changed, with albums selling more than singles, making rock a big-bucks industry, a more 'serious industry,' rather than an entrepreneurial eccentricity. And the key to rock in America is radio airplay. In the sixties, radio was the key to progressive rock music; in the eighties, it's the main reason rock isn't progressive. If *Sgt. Pepper* came out today, radio wouldn't play it. That's the difference. At Rhino, we don't really depend on radio play. We deal mostly with the music that was made when, no matter how creative it might have been, it was never considered a serious art form; music that came before Led Zeppelin, a group that took itself very seriously and was probably the biggest grossing band of the seventies.

"Rhino's catalog carries a lot of musicians who were basically teenagers who liked to make a little money and get laid on the road. We pay our advances based on an album doing from three to five thousand copies, which isn't all that much, although most of our records are made from previously recorded material. We're not part of what I consider to be today's world of corporate rock.

"The first time I heard the term 'corporate rock' was years ago from Paul Rappaport (who was, I think, vice-president of promotion at Columbia Records in New York) in specific reference to groups like Emerson, Lake and Palmer, and Kansas. He was referring to the whole organization behind these groups, and it just didn't seem like that was what rock and roll was to me. In the old days if you had a hit record, it more than made up, financially, for ten flops. By the time of the early eighties, it cost companies so much to 'make' a hit, that often sales wouldn't make up the cost of the record, let alone nine flops. Throughout most of Blondie's career, they sold really well. I believe their second-to-last album, *AutoAmerican,* did at least a million units, maybe two million. The album that came after, *The Hunter,* did, I think, somewhere around thirty-five thousand copies. That's the kind of risk that the majors take, and there's really no way to recoup. Another example is Berlin. They were a fairly hip underground band. And then that song they did for *Top Gun,* "Take My Breath Away," became a hit; produced, I believe, by Arthur Barrow, although Giorgio Moroder got the credit. In either case, not their regular producer. He laid all the synthesizers on the record, and it went to the top of the charts. Once that happened, they were no longer that hip underground band, and they lost a lot of their original following. Basically, today, an act is only as good as its last record. As a result, in both cases, Blondie and Berlin, the groups broke up, probably leaving behind some debt to the labels, often making it that much harder to sign with someone else. And most groups' earnings are cross-collateralized, so if they leave a label or break up, they eventually wind up paying back what they owe out of the reserve for royalties due on their hit material.

"Another thing that's significant about today's rock is that a lot of the groups are turning to outside writers, something that hasn't been that prevalent in rock for twenty-five, thirty years. Groups like Heart and Cheap Trick are using outside writers and producers to manufacture hit records, something the Beatles or the Stones or anyone following after in the sixties would never have done."

In order for independent label bands to compete with the majors, promotion has to be at least as thorough, professional and effective, if not more so. One such firm that specializes in independent promotion is the West Coast–based Jensen Communications, founded by Mike Jensen:

"I started out in publicity in 1975 after having done some writing for the Knight-Ridder chain, *Guitar Player* magazine and the Associated Press. I wasn't a critic per se, I was more a feature writer and a personality columnist. When you're a writer you get every publicist's pitch in the world. I found it interesting, fascinating. Eventually I got into doing publicity for a comedy club and really learned the business of press releases, blurbs, how to get attention for an act, that kind of thing. At the same time, I was always involved in politics; I always thought I'd work on Capitol Hill. While still in college in '77 I'd had a couple of offers from various senators to do just that, when I got this offer from Columbia Records to come and develop a publicity department for the touring. The money was right, the autonomy was there, the expense account was there. And I thought, well, that's what I'm going to school for; so I left and went to work at CBS.

"Even though it was almost an accident, choosing music over politics, it was something that appealed to me. Music has always been politics. The way I see it, if a musician is positioned properly, he has just as much impact on the general public as a politician does; maybe more. Whether its Crosby, Stills, Nash and Young and Bruce Springsteen helping cerebral palsy victims, or it's Jimmy Page, Eric Clapton and Jeff

Beck doing a tour for ARMS [Alternative Research into Multiple Sclerosis], or being a part of Live-Aid, or working on the USA for Africa project, all of which I worked on in one capacity or another, these have been the continuing ongoing inspirations for me. Live-Aid kind of triggered a consciousness in this country, to the point where there's a very sixties sound in a lot of the new bands, as well as an increased sense of responsibility towards things other than lining their own pockets.

"I began at Columbia at the tail end of the great years of the record industry, when there was still more money around than anyone knew what to do with. We had a party every other week. It was party/publicity more than anything else. When we opened the West Coast branch of Columbia Records, on Santa Monica [Boulevard], we did the entire ground floor of the building with Astroturf grass and recreated an outdoor party indoors. That party cost over $50,000 for what was basically a three-hour reception. There was a prevailing concept in those days that 'Excess Is Best,' derived from the one rule of publicity: First, Bigger, or Best. Then the crunch came in '79, the famous crash, and we had to think of creative ways to expose acts, because the budgets had been cut dramatically. I saw the publicity department canceled out, and it became increasingly difficult for me to do the kinds of things I wanted to do for my clients. There'd be upwards of thirty releases a month going out, an album a day, and there was just no way to prioritize. Whatever was put in front of you, that's what you had to deal with on any given day.

"Today, publicity in the music business is sometimes viewed as a luxury, and it shouldn't be. Press isn't a luxury, it's a necessity, especially with the independents. If you ignore the press, the press will ignore you. It's like that great slogan of the Ad Council of America: 'Something horrible happens when you don't promote . . . nothing!' I'm keen on event publicity. I like things with a start, a middle and an end, events that herald a specific project. I like to interface my campaigns and become part of an integral part of a band's marketing program. Publicity and PR are two different things. Publicity is like magic, projecting images into people's minds, making them think a certain thing. We're doing that all the time in the music industry, and to a certain extent it's hype. On the other side of the fence there's public relations, which can be anything from the worst nightmare—crisis management where someone dies at a concert or a performer has been thrown in jail for drugs, or has just beaten up his wife or been beaten up by her, and it's all over the front pages of the supermarket tabloids—to the goodwill factors inherent in projects like I mentioned before; the raising of money for charitable causes, that kind of thing.

"In the corporate world, people are paying upwards of five, ten, fifteen thousand dollars a month for publicity and PR campaigns. For an independent, you can start as ridiculously low as thirty-five hundred dollars, and if you can't get that you settle for a little bit less. For the most part, though, for an up-and-coming band it would begin at thirty-five hundred a month plus expenses.

"A typical campaign to promote a rock act by a firm such as Jensen Communications is built around the basic objective of maximizing exposure opportunities. A media kit is almost always the first step, which includes a biography, discography, selected press clippings and what's known in the business as "canned" featured stories; those which serve to promote the best image of a particular client.

"Each client is then assigned a personal publicist whose job it is to implement the planned publicity campaign. The publicist works closely with the client's management and gets involved in photo sessions, interviews, press releases and tour coordination. Costs escalate, depending upon the depth of the campaign and the depths of the client's pockets."[See Appendix A]

Today's "hot" rock is heavy metal, this generation's disco, an apolitical sound more concerned with the conquest of women than the triumph of the spirit. The other "happening" music to have conquered rock's mainstream is rap. While it may not be everyone's bag, there's no denying the pervasive influence of the music, particularly among today's economically disenfranchised urban street youth.

Thirty-one-year-old Russell Simmons is one of the prime players in the world of rap music. His music management company, Rush Productions, handles most of the top rap acts in the business, including Run-DMC, L.L. Cool J, Public Enemy, EPMD, Whodini, Jazzy Jeff and Fresh Prince, Stetsasonic, and Eric B. & Rakim. On any given week, Rush has at least three and sometimes as many as six of the top ten black records on the charts; charts still segregated into such categories as "Dance," "Contemporary Hits," "Rhythm and Blues," or simply, "Black."

Simmons' story is a familiar one: middle-class New York upbringing; murky early background in street politics, which, according to some published stories included selling drugs on the street; self-revelation and ultimate salvation through music. Today, Simmons's organization is strong enough to be able to make a record go gold, even without airplay, something he'd accomplished with a number of his acts. Simmons believes that rap is today's newest tributary off the mainstream. One cut on the Run-DMC *Raising Hell* album was a song called "My Adidas." One of Simmons' stated plans is to buy a radio station for $5 million and program nothing but rap music.

His goals may outlive his empire. Already, there are strong signals that rap has peaked and may be on the way out. Run-DMC's most recent album failed to match the sales figures of its predecessor, and the film the group and Simmons funded to showcase rap music, *Tougher Than Leather,* was a financial disaster. Considered out-of-bounds by MTV and most radio formats except a few urban CHR stations, rap continues to suffer from a lack of competitive exposure, a malady it probably won't survive.

Finally, in a business that today grosses more than $5.5 billion,* no rock star has ever made it onto the *Forbes* 400 list of the wealthiest people in America.†

The highest paid performer in 1988 was Michael Jackson, whose two-year estimated gross was reported by *Forbes* to be $97 million. The next rock performer on the *Forbes* list of entertainers was number 7, Bruce Springsteen, with a two-year gross of $61 million. Number 9 was Madonna with $46 million, number 11 U2 with $42 million, number 13 George Michael with $38 million, number 16 Bon Jovi with $34 million, number 17 Whitney Houston with $30 million, number 19 Pink Floyd with $29 million, number 26 Van Halen with $25 million, number 28 Sting with $24 million, number 31 John Cougar Mellencamp with $23 million, number 32 Grateful Dead with $23 million, number 37 Billy Joel with $18 million.

Impressive numbers, to be sure. However, the professional life span of a rock performer averages out to a two-year run. The above listing contains not a single "new" group, with most having been in the business a minimum of ten years before seeing any significant return on their time. Needless to say, the thirteen acts listed above represent less than one-tenth of one percent of the rock artists who actually release an album. Of those, less than five percent ever make back their label's initial investment. Most only get one shot, and if they fail, they're effectively out of the business.

Almost no rock performers ever make it out of the studio and into the front office of the corporations they keep in business. There are no corporate pension plans for rock stars. Most performers over forty still doing one-nighters are likely

---

*The combined domestic gross for 1987 was $5.57 billion, with 706.8 million records, tapes and discs shipped, short of the all-time high unit sales figure of 726.2 million in 1978. CD sales rose 93 percent to 102 million units, for an estimated $1.6 billion worth of sales.

†On the other hand, Forbes ranking of the richest people in America lists both Laurence Tisch and William Paley in the top twenty, with Tisch's fortune reported to be $850 million and Paley's $440 million.

to be out there because they have to be, needing the money more than the applause. For those too old to truck, it's been left to others, more fortunate, to care for them.

In 1988, Ahmet Ertegun put up $1.5 million in seed money to help establish the Rhythm and Blues Foundation, an organization dedicated to helping track down lost or misappropriated royalties owed to the early R&B musicians.

Another organization was recently formed by Joey Dee, Jimmy Beaumont of the Skyliners, Gary "U.S." Bonds, Leslie Gore, Beverly Lee of the Shirelles, Johnny Maestro of the Crests, Glen Stetson of the Diamonds, Jerry Gross of the Dovells, Joe Terry of Danny and the Juniors, and deejays Bruce Morrow and Wolfman Jack to help those who can no longer help themselves. Dee, shocked by legendary rocker Jackie Wilson's death, after nine years in a coma that left him without enough money for a tombstone, helped initiate the Starlite Starbrite Foundation to raise money for an old-age home for penniless rockers. The purpose of the organization is to help those whose careers failed to provide them with enough money to live out their final days in dignity. Like Big Joe Turner, who recorded the original version of "Shake, Rattle and Roll" before it was covered and became a hit by Bill Haley and His Comets. The song earned for Turner a total of fifty dollars to the day he died. Like Frankie Lymon, who died of an overdose at the age of twenty-six, broke, forgotten and alone in a Harlem bathroom. Like Dee Clark, whose number one hit, "Raindrops," still gets played on radio stations across the country every time it rains, who now lives penniless in a welfare hotel in Georgia.

Like the endless, nameless one-timers and also-rans who never quite grabbed the golden ring; who hit and ran and fell from grace; who made a difference in all our lives. For the rockers with no pensions, no social security, out of sight, out of money, and finally out of their minds, it was never only a song.

Epilogue

I was back in L.A. and thought I'd stop by that Nike store, to thank that girl, even if I wasn't exactly sure for what. Maybe I didn't want to thank her at all. Maybe I just wanted to see her face again and watch her as she so earnestly defended what she believed she believed in.

So I drove my car onto the voluptuous curves of Sunset Boulevard, with my windows down and car radio up. I caught a little Beatles, and then it was time for the news. One of the stories had to do with Elvis Presley. As it happened, that very morning, thirteen years after his death, his estate had finally been settled. The man who sold more records than anybody else in history, who made thirty movies and played 700 sold-out concert performances, left an estate worth less than $7 million; about one week's donation to the Vegas crap tables for the Colonel.

I parked by a meter, got out and headed for the Nike store. I turned the last corner and was practically up against the glass front doors before I realized Nike was no longer there. Gone. Vanished. Out of business. I stared through the empty window at the single blue sneaker left on the floor of the vacant shop.

Victory, I thought to myself. We did it. In an us versus them situation, we'd somehow prevailed. An abandoned sneaker

was all that was left of the corporate dream of a rock empire
that would last a thousand years.

I turned the corner, flushed with my imagined success,
when I first laid eyes on it. I paled at the nearly completed,
greatly expanded Nike shop being industriously built by a
band of workers hustling to the beat of a boom box. I felt like
some off-beat Cinderella, with that blue suede sneak my missing glass slipper to another time and place.

APPENDIX A

El Dorado tour expenses
Alan Freed contract with WINS
Excerpt from Alan Freed FBI file
Peter Yarrow contract
John LaMonte letter
Estimated public relations
expenses for 6 month tour

The bottom line: After 15 cities and 3 months on the road the El Dorados netted a total of $134.62 to be split among 5 musicians. *(Courtesy of the Michael Ochs Archives).*

Gale AGENCY INC

Artists' Representatives

FORTY-EIGHT WEST FORTY-EIGHTH STREET
NEW YORK 36, N. Y.

PLAZA 7-7100

Cable Address:
GALEAGCY NEW YORK

THE EL DORADOS   DECEMBER 31st, 1955

Date	Engagement	Gross	Commissions	Deposits
11/6	South Bend, Ind.	200.00	20.00	50.00
11/10	Boston, Mass.	150.00	15.00	75.00
11/11	Washington, D.C.	300.00	30.00	100.00
11/12	Baltimore, Md.	200.00	20.00	100.00
11/24	Gary, Ind.	200.00	20.00	75.00
11/25	Pittsburgh, Pa.	250.00	25.00	75.00
11/26	Ypsilanti, Mich.	200.00	20.00	50.00
12/7	Atlanta, Ga.	250.00	25.00	--
12/10	Newark, N.J.	200.00	20.00	100.00
12/11	Newport News, Va.	250.00	25.00	125.00
12/17	Mastbaum Theatre, Phila.	800.00	80.00	--
12/24	Canton, Ohio	200.00	20.00	50.00
12/25	Lima, Ohio	225.00	22.50	50.00
12/26	Flint, Mich.	461.80	46.18	75.00
12/26	Detroit, Mich.	300.00	30.00	75.00
	Totals	4186.80	418.68	1000.00

CHARGES -	Commissions as above		418.68
10/3	Western Union charges		3.99
10/6	New York Telephone Co.		6.93
11/6	New York Telephone Co.		1.49
11/14	J. Bracken - Vee Jay - 10%		65.00
	John Moore- balance 11/14		142.25
11/18	John Moore-Mastbaum Theatre advance		100.00
11/23	Moss Photo		9.27
11/28	Lincoln Nat'l Bank - car payment		77.77
12/1	Western Union-John Moore- chicago- on acct.		75.00
12/21	Western Union-John Moore-Chicago-advance		125.00
	Total charges		1025.38

CREDITS -	Deposits as above		1000.00
12/19	Mastbaum Theatre-commission & on account		160.00
	Total credits		1160.00

Balance due EL DORADOS as of DECEMBER 31st, 1955   134.62

Alan Freed's original contract with WINS which specified the station's financial participation in Freed's live shows. When Freed ran into trouble, WINS fired him and refused to participate in his defense.

WINS/28 west 44th street • new york 36, ny • bryant 9-6000

August 10, 1954.

MR. ALAN FREED
36-13 Ingleside Road
Shaker Heights
Cleveland 22, Ohio

Dear Mr. Freed:

This is to confirm the agreement between us as WINS and Artist whereby you are to present radio broadcasts exclusively at and for Radio Station WINS in the City of New York for a period of ten years commencing September 8, 1954.

Performance of this agreement will continue for one year from the above-mentioned date. WINS has the exclusive option to terminate this agreement by giving notice to Artist of such termination on or before sixty days prior to September 8, 1955, and to exercise annually thereafter its exclusive option to terminate this agreement by giving notice thereof on or before sixty days prior to September 8 of each succeeding year up to and including sixty days prior to September 8, 1963.

Any and all notices provided by this contract to be given by either party to the other shall be deemed given when delivered personally to the other party or when deposited in the United States mail addressed to the other party at the addresses set forth at the beginning of this letter or at the last known address of the other party. For the purpose of this paragraph, any officer of WINS or any other person employed by WINS in an executive capacity shall be deemed authorized to receive such notice.

During the entire life of this agreement, you are to perform thereunder as Artist by giving broadcasts for twenty-four hours during every week, except for the annual periods of a two weeks' vacation; during which periods, Artist at his own expense is to supply and pay for the services of acceptable Talent in substitution for his own services. The time of Artist's vacation is to be agreeable to WINS.

In consideration of the extraordinary and unique ability of Artist, WINS promises and undertakes to pay to him for his giving of the broadcasts, twenty-five (25%) percent of the net income derived by WINS from the performance by Artist of the aforesaid broadcasts; this net income to be determined by, and subsequent to, the deduction of the total of the applicable discounts and agency commissions; and WINS guarantees to Artist, as further consideration for his performance of this agreement, the annual payment of Fifteen Thousand ($15,000) Dollars against the twenty-five (25%) percent share of Artist to the net income, computed as aforesaid.

WINS has the right to approve or disapprove in advance each of the programs that Artist will give in the performance of this agreement; and the giving of outside broadcast work by Artist will remain at all times subject to the prior approval in writing by WINS.

WINS will supply Artist with an office and with telephone service.

Artist will supply both office assistance and production help at his own expense.

WINS will afford its facilities for promotion of dances by Artist during the life of this agreement.

In consideration of the affording by WINS as aforesaid of these facilities to Artist, Artist will pay to WINS [Figure deleted]% of the net income, computed as hereinabove set forth, received by Artist from these promotions.

As to the GENERAL CONDITIONS:

A.   With respect to Use of Name and Likeness:

Artist agrees that, for the period commencing with the date of this Contract and ending three (3) months after the termination of this Contract, or any renewal thereof, regardless of the cause of such termination, WINS and the persons, firms or corporations authorized by WINS shall have the right to make or cause to have made likenesses, portraits, pictures, sketches and caricatures of the Artist, and the right to use such likenesses, portraits, pictures, sketches and caricatures, as well as the names, pseudonym and pseudonyms of Artist, it being understood that said use shall be for purposes incidental to the broadcasting and other activities of WINS and such authorized persons, firms and corporations and the sponsors of programs broadcast by WINS, or which use transcriptions owned or sold by WINS. The use of any one or more of the foregoing may, at the option of WINS or those authorized by WINS, be in conjunction with the name, names, pseudonym, pseudonyms, likenesses, portraits, pictures, sketches and/or caricatures of other persons or objects and may be with or without commercial endorsements of products or firms.

B.   With respect to Rehearsals and Incidental Duties:

Artist agrees to take part in all scheduled rehearsals and to perform all reasonable duties in connection with the aforementioned services as may be requested from time to time by WINS, including but not limited to duties related to the preparation and promotion of programs and transcriptions, and the writing, direction and promotion of programs on which he appears as featured artist.

C.   With respect to Proprietary Interest:

(1) Artist agrees that he shall not obtain any right, title or interest in or to any fictitious name, character, program title, theme song, script idea or any material (whether or not originated or suggested by Artist) which Artist may use or which may be used on programs, productions or transcriptions in which Artist renders services during the term of this contract, except as set forth in paragraph (2) of this Section C, it being understood that all such right, title and interest in and to the foregoing shall rest exclusively in WINS or the persons, firms or corporations to whom WINS may assign such right, title or interest; it being further understood that

WINS or such assigns may make any use it or they desire of any or all of the foregoing, both during the term of this contract and thereafter.

(2) Artist shall retain the proprietary right in and to all fictitious names, characters and materials with which he has become identified prior to the commencement of the term of this contract; provided, however, that said names, characters or material are identified in a written memorandum signed by the Artist and filed with WINS on or before the commencement of the term; and provided further that WINS, during the term of the contract and any renewal thereof, shall have a non-exclusive license to use and to permit others to use the same or any part thereof. If, at the termination of this contract or any renewal thereof, irrespective of the cause of such termination, WINS is a party to a contract for the performance of which the use of said fictitious names, character or material is necessary, contemplated or appropriate, WINS shall have the right during the life of such contracts to continue to use or permit the use in connection therewith of said fictitious names, characters or material, provided said use shall not extend more than three (3) months after the termination of this contract or any extension or renewal thereof.

D.   With respect to Indemnification:

Artist agrees not to use any material in the performance of his services hereunder without first clearing the same with the proper WINS supervisory personnel unless such material is furnished to Artist by WINS or through news service to which WINS subscribes. Artist further agrees to protect and indemnify WINS, its agents, servants and employees and other persons, firms and corporations with whom WINS may enter into contract involving Artist's services against any and all loss, cost, liability, damage and expense occasioned by or in connection with any claim, demand, action or cause of action asserted or instituted by any other person, firm or corporation relating to the violation or infringement of the rights of such other persons, firm or corporation in connection with Artist's services or performances or in connection with such names, characters and material as are described in Section C (2) hereof. This warranty, however, shall not extend to claims, demands, actions and causes of action growing out of the violation or infringement of the rights of other persons, firms or corporations occasioned by the use of (1) news material furnished to Artist from news services to which WINS subscribes; or (2) script or material furnished to Artist by WINS (other than fictitious names, characters or material described in Section C (2).

E.   With respect to Use of Company's Name or Call Letters:

Artist agrees that, during the term of this contract, and after the termination thereof, irrespective of the cause of such termination, he will not use or permit to be used, without the prior written consent of WINS, except as an incident to the performance of his services hereunder, the name WINS, any trade-mark of such corporation, any call letters of any broadcasting station owned or controlled by WINS, or any abbreviation or contraction of any of the foregoing, or any title or expression so nearly resembling the same as to be likely to confuse or deceive the public in connection with the name of the Artist or any act or performance with which he is in any way connected or in advertising or announcing the Artist's name, his act or performance, or in giving publicity in any manner to said name, acts or performances.

F.   With respect to Availability of Artist:

The payment of compensation to be made by WINS to Artist as provided in this contract shall be conditioned upon Artist being ready, willing and able at all reasonable times to render services at the request and direction of WINS and, if at any time Artist is not ready, able and willing to perform said services when requested or directed by WINS, upon reasonable notice, WINS shall have the right, at its sole discretion, to terminate this contract immediately or to make such adjustment in Artist's compensation as may be equitable in view of the circumstances; it being understood that the remedies herein granted are in addition to any other legal rights and remedies available to WINS.

G. With respect to Artist's Qualifications and Personal Character:

Artist represents that he now is and, during the term of this Contract, will remain qualified and able to perform competently, in accordance with recognized standards of the industry, the services herein contemplated. Artist further agrees that he will so conduct his personal life as not to reflect discredit on or cause embarrassment to WINS or any of the parties for whom Artist is performing services hereunder, including sponsors of programs in which Artist participates.

H. With respect to Injunctive Relief:

Artist represents that he and his services are extraordinary and unique and that, accordingly, WINS may have no complete and adequate remedy at law for a breach by him of this contract or any provision hereof. Accordingly, in the event of such breach, or an attempted or threatened breach, WINS shall be entitled to equitable relief by way of injunction or otherwise in addition to any legal remedies available to it.

I. Miscellaneous:

(1) No waiver by WINS of the breach of any covenant in this contract shall be deemed a waiver of any preceding or succeeding breach of the same or any other covenant.

(2) This contract shall be subject to, be construed in accordance with, and all the rights and obligations of the parties shall be determined by the laws of the State of New York.

(3) The term "WINS" shall be deemed to include the WINS radio broadcasting station, its successors, subsidiaries and assigns.

J. With respect to Workweek:

Artist shall render services to WINS in accordance with this contract on such days as WINS may require except that Artist shall not be required to perform services on Sundays except in connection with a special broadcast of public service or other unusual interest. Except as provided herein with regard to extra compensation for the sixth day of the workweek, Artist shall not be entitled to premium compensation by virtue of his performance of work for WINS on more than five consecutive days in a week, and Artist's hours of work need not consist of consecutive hours so that the period of time elapsing between his first performance and his last performance in any day need not be used in computing the number of hours worked.

This letter constitutes the entire agreement between the parties hereto and contains all understandings and covenants of said parties, all previous and contemporaneous understandings, covenants and representations not herein contained being expressly waived.

Yours very truly,

RADIO STATION WINS

Information in Alan Freed's FBI file obtained under the Freedom of Information Act.

STANDARD FORM NO. 64

Office Memorandum · UNITED STATES GOVERNMENT

TO : Malcolm R. Wilkey, Assistant Attorney General,   DATE: December 11, 1959
         Criminal Division

FROM : Robert J. Rosthal, Deputy Chief,   RJR:rw
         General Crimes Section

SUBJECT: Request for Investigation in "Payola";
Alan Freed, ████████████ Fraud by Wire

MORRIS LEVY

       As requested, I have prepared a draft memorandum to the FBI requesting investigation into the Alan Freed ████ situation. You will recall it was decided to limit the draft to Freed alone in view of the racketeer influence which appears in this particular matter.

36-012-3

14 | DEPARTMENT OF JUSTICE   FEB 16 1961   RECORDS DIVISION | RECORD

FILE

"Bob Thiele"   2   *Buy CORAL SUNNYSIDE FARMS —*

(1)

Freed

Roulette wanted to go public

     Freed, we gather, is a well known disc jockey in New York. We desire that he be fully interrogated to determine whether he accepted "payola", the amounts of the payment and from whom received. In this connection, we are advised by the Securities and Exchange Commission that Roulette Records, Inc. had under consideration the obtaining of additional financing and conferred with SEC officials with reference to a registration statement. During the course of the conference, representatives of Roulette Records, Inc. stated: (a) that Freed was indebted to Roulette for $18,000, the collateral being a second and third mortgage on his, Freed's, home: (b) that ▓▓▓▓▓▓▓▓▓▓▓▓▓▓▓▓▓▓▓▓▓▓▓▓▓▓ *Ph. KAHL* ▓▓▓▓▓ (c) that ▓▓▓▓▓▓ business manager for a local electrical ? workers union in New York, owned five per cent (5%) of Roulette *Levy* stock; (d) that ▓▓▓▓▓ has a racketeer or gangster background; (e) that Freed once had a stock interest in Roulette, Inc.; (f) that ▓▓▓▓ was allowed to buy stock in Roulette to secure Freed's help in "pushing" Roulette records; (9) that Freed would "push" Roulette records; (h) that Freed received at no expense to himself a twenty-five per cent (25%) interest in a record company from one

     We wish the association of Freed with the Roulette Company, as well as the company in which Freed received a twenty-five per cent (25%) stock interest from ▓▓▓▓▓▓▓▓▓▓▓▓ fully explored with a determination of the "payola", if any, made by them to Freed. — *Morris Levy*

Ben Hoberman? ▓▓▓▓▓▓▓▓▓▓▓▓ manager of station WABC, terminated Freed's contract and it is requested that he be interrogated fully concerning the reason for Freed's dismissal and information known to him (or the station) which suggested that Freed execute an affidavit concerning "payola". If it is developed that record companies made the payments, we desire to know how the payments were carried on their books.

(2)

The Detroit Disc Jockeys

Tom Clay

     We learn from the press that radio station WJBK dismissed disc jockey ▓▓▓▓▓▓▓▓ for accepting "payola" and that station WJBK, TV, dismissed disc jockey ▓▓▓▓▓▓▓ for the same reason. We learn also from the same source that disc jockey ▓▓▓▓▓▓▓▓▓ resigned from radio station WJBK, it being intimated that he had accepted "payola".

Contract Blank

Associated Musicians of Greater New York

LOCAL 802, AMERICAN FEDERATION OF MUSICIANS, NEW YORK 19, N. Y.

THIS CONTRACT for the personal services of musicians, made this ___3rd___ day of ___August___, 19 _61_, between the undersigned employer (hereinafter called the "employer") and ___one___ musicians (hereinafter called "employees").

(Including the Leader)

WITNESSETH, That the employer hires the employees as musicians severally on the terms and conditions below. The leader represents that the employees already designated have agreed to be bound by said terms and conditions. Each employee yet to be chosen shall be so bound by said terms and conditions upon agreeing to accept his employment. Each employee may enforce this agreement. The employees severally agree to render collectively to

the employer services as musicians in the orchestra under the leadership of ___Peter Yarrow___ as follows:

Name and Address of Place of Engagement ___Gerde's Folk City___

Date(s) of Employment ___August 15 through August 27, 1961___

Hours of Employment ___House Policy___

Type of Engagement (specify whether dance, stage show, banquet, etc.) ___Night Club___

The employer is hereby given an option to extend this agreement for a period of _____weeks beyond the original term thereof. Said option can be made effective only by written notice from the employer to the employees, not later than _____days prior to the expiration of said original term, that he claims and receives said option, and a copy of said notice shall be filed with the local in whose jurisdiction the engagement is to be played.

WAGE AGREED UPON $ ___$125.00/Wk___

(Terms and Amount)

This wage includes expenses agreed to be reimbursed by the employer in accordance with the attached schedule, or a schedule to be furnished the employer on or before the date of engagement.

To be paid ___Sunday night ending each week___

(Specify when payments are to be made)

Upon request by the American Federation of Musicians of the United States and Canada (herein called the "Federation") or the local in whose jurisdiction the employees shall perform hereunder, the employer either shall make advance payment hereunder or shall post an appropriate bond.

ADDITIONAL TERMS AND CONDITIONS

If any employees have not been chosen upon the signing of this contract, the leader shall, as agent for the employer and under his instructions, hire such persons and any replacements as are required for persons who for any reason do not perform any or all services. The employer shall at all times have complete control over the services of employees under this contract, and the leader shall, as agent of the employer, enforce disciplinary measures for just cause, and carry out instructions as to selections and manner of performance. The agreement of the employees to perform is subject to proven detention by sickness, accidents, or accidents to means of transportation, riots, strikes, epidemics, acts of God, or any other legitimate conditions beyond the control of the employees. On behalf of the employer the leader will distribute the amount received from the employer to the employees, including himself, as indicated on the opposite side of this contract, or in place thereof on separate memoranda supplied to the employer at or before the commencement of the employment hereunder and take and turn over to the employer receipts therefor from each employee, including himself. The amount paid to the leader shall include the cost of transportation, which will be reported by the leader to the employer.

All employees covered by this agreement must be members in good standing of the Federation. However, if the employment provided for hereunder is subject to the Labor-Management Relations Act, 1947, all employees, who are members of the Federation when their employment commences hereunder, shall be continued in such employment only so long as they continue such membership in good standing. All other employees covered by this agreement, on or before the thirtieth day following the commencement of their employment, or the effective date of this agreement, whichever is later, shall become and continue to be members in good standing of the Federation. The provisions of this paragraph shall not become effective unless and until permitted by applicable law.

To the extent permitted by applicable law, nothing in this contract shall ever be construed so as to interfere with any duty owing by any employee hereunder to the Federation pursuant to its Constitution, By-laws, Rules, Regulations and Orders.

Any employees who are parties to or affected by this contract are free to cease service hereunder by reason of any strike, ban, unfair list order or requirement of the Federation, and shall be free to accept and engage in other employment of the same or similar character or otherwise, for other employers or persons without any restraint, hindrance, penalty, obligation or liability whatever, any other provisions of this contract to the contrary notwithstanding.

Representatives of the local in whose jurisdiction the employees shall perform hereunder shall have access to the place of performance (except to private residences) for the purpose of conferring with the employees.

The performances to be rendered pursuant to this agreement are not to be recorded, reproduced, or transmitted from the place of performance, in any manner or by any means whatsoever, in the absence of a specific written agreement between the employer and the Federation relating to and permitting such recording, reproduction or transmission.

The employer represents that there does not exist against him, in favor of any member of the Federation, any claim of any kind arising out of musical services rendered for any such employer. No employee will be required to perform any provisions of this contract or to render any services for said employer as long as any such claim is unsatisfied or unpaid, in whole or in part. If the employer breaches this agreement, he shall pay the employees, in addition to damages, 6% interest thereon plus a reasonable attorney's fee.

The employer, in signing this contract himself, or having same signed by a representative, acknowledges his (her or their) authority to do so and hereby assumes liability for the amount stated herein, and, if applicable to the services to be rendered hereunder, acknowledges his liability to provide workmen's compensation insurance and to pay social security and unemployment insurance taxes.

To the extent permitted by applicable law, there are incorporated into and made part of this agreement, as though fully set forth herein, all of the By-laws, Rules and Regulations of the Federation and of any local of the Federation in whose jurisdiction services are to be performed hereunder (insofar as they do not conflict with those of the Federation), and the employer acknowledges his responsibility to be fully acquainted, now and for the duration of this contract, with the contents thereof.

The undersigned, whether signing this contract as principal, agent or otherwise, in order to induce Local 802, A. F. of M., to approve this contract, personally undertakes to pay, and will be principally responsible for the payment of all sums required to be paid hereunder.

Mr. Mike Porco, Owner	Peter Yarrow
Employer's Name	Leader's Name
Michele Porco	*Peter Yarrow*
Signature of Employer	Signature of Leader
West Fourth Street, XXXX	50 Central Park West, XXXX
Street Address	Street Address
New York, N.Y.	New York, N.Y.
City State	City State

Local No. ___802___

Membership Card No.

Phone

Booking Agent

If this contract is made by a licensed booking agent, there must be inserted on the reverse side of this contract the name, address and telephone number of the collecting agent of the local in whose jurisdiction the engagement is to be performed.

802 Steady Engagement

Form B-3a 1-1-59

John LaMonte's bid for freedom. His cooperation with the government added strong support to The Beatles lawsuit against Capitol and would eventually help convict Morris Levy.

U.S. DEPARTMENT OF JUSTICE
ORGANIZED CRIME STRIKE FORCE
EASTERN DISTRICT OF NEW YORK
35 Tillary Street
Brooklyn, New York 11201

February 23, 1979

Mr. Donald J. Goldberg
Two Girard Plaza, Suite 1420
Philadelphia, Pennsylvania 19102

Re: John LaMonte

Dear Mr. Goldberg:

Mr. LaMonte appeared before a special grand jury on January 25, 1979. Prior to his appearance before the grand jury, he spent several hours with FBI agents discussing his involvement in the counterfeit sound recording industry. Agents familiar with the industry tell me that Mr. LaMonte was extremely helpful and candid concerning his knowledge of the business.

Pursuant to our understanding Mr. LaMonte will not be prosecuted for any transactions he discussed with the FBI, myself or the grand jury.

Mr. LaMonte agreed to be a witness in any future proceedings this office institutes including trial testimony.

Based upon the above, I can state that he has been of great assistance to our investigation. I would prefer not to set forth the details and specifics of his cooperation due to the sensitive nature of the information and grand jury secrecy; however, feel free to inform any appropriate bodies of his total candor and cooperation.

I will be happy to provide additional information if you desire.

Very truly yours,

THOMAS P. PUCCIO
Attorney-in-Charge

By: _____
JOHN H. JACOBS
Executive Assistant

EXHIBIT "B"

April 13, 1988 estimate by Jensen Communications (leading rock and roll public relations firm) for office expenses associated with 6 month tour by established group. All expenses "from the road" would be in addition to this estimated $17,164.34 total.

BREAKDOWN OF BUDGET FOR SIX MONTH PROJECTION

PHONES:

Local calls $75.00 × 6 = $450.00
Long Distance $300.00 × 6 = $1,800.00

FAX:

$20.00 × 6 = $120.00

PHOTO DUPLICATION:

B&W 2 poses 1000 ea = $776.80
Color slides 5 poses 40 ea = $224.87

PRESS CLIPS

50 a month × 6 = $300.00

FEDERAL EXPRESS:

6 a month × 14.00 = $504.00

MESSENGERS:

6 a month × 11.00 = $396.00

MAILING SUPPLIES FOR EVERYDAY USE:

labels   450 × .02 = $9.00
8 × 10 cards   450 × .18 = $81.00
9 × 13 env.   450 × .16 = $72.00
12 × 12 card   450 × .19 = $85.50
13 × 13 env.   450 × .22 = $99.00
#10 env.   450 × .08 = $36.00

XEROXING:

average copies per month 4000 × 6 × .05 = $1,200.00

NATIONAL MAILINGS:

copies 6750 × .05 = $337.50
postage 2250 pcs × .65 = $1,462.50
supplies 2250 pcs × .16 = $360.00 (most mailings go in a
      9 × 13 env.)
labels 2250 pcs × .02 = $45.00

POSTAGE:

450 pcs × .25 = $112.50 letters etc.
500 pcs × 2.40 = $1,200.00 press kits
250 pcs × 2.40 = $600.00 albums
175 pcs × 1.85 = $323.75 video mailings
misc mail $250.00

MISC.

Entertainment for 6 months $600.00
Outside writing $1,000.00
Artwork $1,500.00
Audio Video Duplication $1,500.00

PRESS KITS OPTIONAL:

1000 kits w/foil lettering & printing on inside flap $1,718.92

APPENDIX B

The following is an informal log of rock songs used in commercials, compiled during the writing of this book. Songs listed in capitals denote original (master) hit versions. The names of the original artists are in parentheses.

1. "MY BLUE HEAVEN" (Fats Domino)—Labatt's beer
2. "TONITE TONITE TONITE" (Genesis)—Michelob beer
3. "WOOLY BULLY" (Sam the Sham and the Pharaohs)—California Cooler
4. "HAPPY TOGETHER" (Turtles)—Golden Grahams cereal
5. "Witch Doctor" (David Seville)—Noxema
6. "Everything Old Is New Again" (original hit version written and recorded by Peter Allen, Fats Domino sings in the commercial)—Fruit Drink
7. "Short Shorts" (Royal Teens)—Nair
8. "Tutti-Frutti" (Little Richard)—Fruit Scoops ice cream
9. "BAD CASE OF LOVIN' YOU" (Robert Palmer)—Dr. Pepper
10. "SLOW HAND" (Pointer Sisters)—Shick Plus razors
11. "LIES" (Knickerbockers)—Grand Gourmet dog food
12. "Just My Imagination" (Temptations)—Canada Dry
13. "LAND OF 1000 DANCES" (Cannibal and the Headhunters)—Subaru
14. "CHERRY OH CHERRY" (UB40)—Cherry Coke
15. "FREEWAY OF LOVE" (Aretha Franklin)—Burger King
16. "CAN'T HELP MYSELF" (Four Tops)—Duncan Hines
17. "New York, New York" (Frank Sinatra)—Philadelphia cream cheese
18. "Get Closer" (Linda Ronstadt)—Close-up toothpaste

19. "YAKETY YAK" (Coasters)—American Dairy Association
20. "Who Do You Love" (George Thorogood)—Honda
21. "GOOD LOVIN' " (Young Rascals)—California Cooler
22. "WILD THING" (Troggs)—California Cooler
23. "Da Doo Ron Ron" (Crystals)—Energizer Batteries
24. "EVERYBODY HAVE FUN TONIGHT" (Wang Chung)—Michelob
25. "SPLISH SPLASH" (Bobby Darin)—Great Adventure amusement park
26. "BILLIE JEAN" (Michael Jackson)—Pepsi
27. "YOU BELONG TO THE NIGHT" (Glenn Frey)—Pepsi
28. "DO THE CONGA" (Miami Sound Machine)—Pepsi
29. "JUST THE TWO OF US" (Bill Withers)—Dentyne gum
30. "ONLY YOU" (Platters)—Armor-All
31. "REVOLUTION" (Beatles)—Nike sneakers
32. "Oh Boy" (Buddy Holly)—Buick
33. "SUNSHINE OF MY LIFE" (Stevie Wonder)—Minute Maid orange juice
34. "LAZY HAZY CRAZY DAYS OF SUMMER" (Nat "King" Cole)—Monmouth Park racetrack
35. "HERE'S TO THE WINNERS" (Frank Sinatra)—Holiday Inn
36. "SOMETHING" (Beatles)—Chrysler
37. "IT'S SO EASY" (Buddy Holly)—Toyota
38. "(EASY AS) ABC" (Jackson 5)—ABC Technical Schools
39. "FOR YOUR EYES ONLY" (Sheena Easton)—G.E.
40. "(YOU MAKE ME FEEL LIKE A) NATURAL WOMAN" (Aretha Franklin)—Chic Jeans
41. "WALK THIS WAY" (Aerosmith)—Sun Country wine cooler
42. "(THEY CALL ME) THE BREEZE" (ZZ Top)—Ford
43. "DO YOU BELIEVE IN MAGIC" (Lovin' Spoonful)—Lemon Dash detergent
44. "STRUT . . ." (Sheena Easton)—Holiday Spa
45. "ADDICTED TO LOVE" (Robert Palmer)—Sun Country wine cooler
46. "LOVE IN MY TUMMY" (Ohio Express)—Schlitz beer
47. "SHORT PEOPLE" (Randy Newman)—Sesame Place
48. "SUMMERTIME SUMMERTIME" (Jamies)—Chico San
49. "WIPE OUT" (Surfaris)—Stridex
50. "Mack the Knife" (Bobby Darin)—McDonald's
51. "MODERN LOVE" (David Bowie)—Pepsi

52. "I HEARD IT THROUGH THE GRAPEVINE" (Marvin Gaye)—California raisins
53. "TURN TURN TURN" (Byrds)—*Time* magazine
54. "NOWHERE TO RUN" (Martha and the Vandellas)—Holiday roach spray
55. "LITTLE BITTY PRETTY ONE" (Thurston Harris)—Chicken Tenders
56. "Hunk of Burnin' Love" (Elvis Presley)—Hershey's chunk chocolate candy
57. "I CAN SEE CLEARLY NOW . . ." (Johnny Nash)—Glass Plus glass cleaner
58. "SHOUT" (Isley Brothers)—Shout cleaner
59. "LOOK WHAT THEY'VE DONE TO MY RAIN" (Melanie)—oatmeal raisin cereal
60. "LITTLE DARLIN' " (Diamonds)—Kentucky Fried Chicken
61. "WHOLE LOTTA SHAKIN' GOIN' ON" (Jerry Lee Lewis)—Burger King
62. "ROCK AROUND THE CLOCK" (Bill Haley and His Comets)—Shield soap
63. "HAVEN'T GOT TIME FOR THE PAIN" (Carly Simon)—Medipren
64. "LOOKIN' FOR SOME TUSH" (ZZ Top)—Busch beer
65. "MOONDANCE" (Van Morrison)—Country Sun Cooler
66. "PAPA'S GOT A BRAND NEW BAG" (James Brown)—Success rice
67. "MAMMA SAID" (Shirelles)—Granola Dipps
68. "LEGS" (ZZ Top)—Hanes panty hose
69. "Do Wah Diddy Diddy" (Manfred Mann)—Kentucky Fried Chicken
70. "AMERICAN PIE" (Don McLean)—public service announcement for drunk driving
71. "TIME OF THE SEASON (Turtles)—Noxema
72. "La Bamba" (Ritchie Valens)—Pop Secret microwave popcorn
73. "TOSSIN' AND TURNIN' " (Bobby Lewis)—Almond Delight cereal
74. "BREATHLESS" (Jerry Lee Lewis)—Sunlight dishwashing liquid
75. "MAMA DON'T LET YOUR BABIES . . ." (Willie Nelson)—Burger King
76. "STAND BY ME" (Ben E. King)—Anheuser Busch

77. "SHOP AROUND" (Miracles)—Pacific Yellow Pages
78. "Hey, Good Lookin' " (Hank Williams)—CARL'S Jr.
79. "RHAPSODY IN BLUE" (George Gershwin)—United Airlines
80. "The Way You Look Tonight" (Frank Sinatra)—Michelob
81. "OUR HOUSE" (Crosby, Stills, Nash and Young)—Pacific Yellow Pages
82. "OUR HOUSE" (CSNY)—Emerick Sausage
83. "THE MAGIC TOUCH" (Platters)—Hyatt Hotels
84. "OPERATOR" (Jim Croce)—AT&T
85. "FOR YOUR PRECIOUS LOVE" (Jerry Butler)—The Gold Industry
86. "BONEY MARONEY" (Larry Williams)—Puparoni dog food snacks
87. "MICKEY" (Toni Basil)—Mickey Mouse Products (Disney)
88. "DANCING IN THE STREETS" (Martha and the Vandellas)—ABC-TV
89. "WHO PUT THE BOMP" (Barry Mann)—Hi-C Cooler
90. "REMEMBER THEN" (Earls)—Subaru
91. "BETTY LOU GOT A NEW PAIR OF SHOES" (Little Richard)—Soos foot comforters
92. "GO WHERE YOU WANT TO GO" (Mamas and the Papas)—Mazda
93. "BLUEBERRY HILL" (Fats Domino)—Hyundai
94. "WHEN A MAN LOVES A WOMAN" (Percy Sledge)—Subaru
95. "COME GO WITH ME" (Dell-Vikings)—Chicken Littles
96. "YOU'RE SIXTEEN" (Johnny Burnette)—Dole fruit bars
97. "HIGHER AND HIGHER" (Jackie Wilson)—Arrow shirts
98. "I'M WALKIN' " (Fats Domino)—Fisher Price toys
99. "Let the Good Times Roll" (Shirley and Lee)—CBS-TV network
100. "JUST A GIGOLO" (David Lee Roth version)—Marty's Physical Fitness Emporiums
101. "THINK ABOUT ME" (Aretha Franklin)—Burger King
102. "ON THE ROAD AGAIN" (Willie Nelson)—Valvoline
103. "PRETTY WOMAN" (Roy Orbison)—Diet Center Inc.
104. "THE GOOD OLD DAYS" (Carly Simon)—Heinz ketchup
105. "I LIKE IT LIKE THAT" (Chris Kenner)—Coco's food chain

106. "TAKE GOOD CARE OF MY BABY" (Bobby Vee)—Carters baby care products
107. "SPLISH SPLASH" (Bobby Darin)—Drano
108. "DUKE OF EARL" (Gene Chandler)—Vanish
109. "LA BAMBA" (Ritchie Valens)—Subaru
110. "TEQUILA" (Champs)—Velveeta cheese
111. "RESCUE ME" (Aretha Franklin)—Slim Mint
112. "LITTLE DEUCE COUPE" (Beach Boys)—Pacific Bell
113. "GOOD VIBRATIONS" (Beach Boys)—Sunkist
114. "WOULDN'T IT BE NICE" (Beach Boys)—Lincoln-Mercury
115. "FUN FUN FUN" (Beach Boys)—Southwest Airlines
116. "DANCE DANCE DANCE" (Beach Boys)—Delco
117. "WALK ON THE WILD SIDE" (Lou Reed)—Honda
118. "JUMP" (Pointer Sisters)—Bounce dryer sheets
119. "I LOVE L.A." (Randy Newman)—Nike
120. "WHAT THE NIGHT CAN DO" (Steve Winwood)—Michelob
121. "AFTER MIDNIGHT" (Eric Clapton)—Michelob
122. "GREAT PRETENDER" (Platters)—Red Lobster
123. "CITY OF NEW ORLEANS" (Arlo Guthrie)—Oldsmobile
124. "Teddy Bear" (Elvis Presley)—Teddy Grahams cookies
125. "America" (Ray Charles)—Life Magazine.

The following artists performed jingles written especially for the products being advertised:

The Blasters, Belinda Carlisle, Albert Collins, Jerry Garcia, Journey, Leon Redbone, Leon Russell, Ringo Starr, Narada Michael Walden and Looters, Starship, Richie Havens, David Clayton Thomas, Manhattan Transfer, Dobie Gray, Debby Harry, Al Jarreau, B. B. King, Buskin and Batteau, and Carl Perkins

ACKNOWLEDGMENTS

There is no adequate way I know of to thank everyone who helped with the writing of this book. The rock community was more than generous and open with me; and almost without exception, everyone I contacted willingly cooperated in my efforts to tell this story. A chain of communication developed which led from one contact to another in what amounted to a continual flow of information.

Hundreds of interviews were conducted over a period of fifteen months, with a number of people requesting anonymity. That request was and shall continue to be honored. I wish to thank the following for their important contributions: Andy Bamberger, Harold Bronson, Artie Butler, Kip Cohen, Bob Emer, Steve Fleischman, Lance Freed, Gil Friesen, Bob Gaudio, Barry Goldberg, Danny Goldberg, Andrew Goldsmith, Harlan Goodman, Arthur Gorson, Michael Horner, Michael Jensen, Ben E. King, Kevin Kennedy, Art Laboe, Arthur Levy, Leonard Marks, Stan Milander, Bob Neuwirth, Michael Ochs, Irwin Pincus, Paul Rothchild, Stephen Soles, John Storyk, and Josh White.

I would also like to thank Gaye Weaver for her research assistance, which included the setting up of appointments, the photocopying of documents, library research, and endless nights spent discussing the implications of the material we discovered. On the West Coast, Bonnie Halpern was a key research coordinator, arranging meetings with people it would have been difficult, if not impossible, for me to otherwise have interviewed. On the East Coast, a similar function was fulfilled by Nina Streich. To this trio I am extremely grateful.

My thanks to my agent, Mel Berger, and my editor, Kent Oswald, a couple of terrific and able men.

Wherever possible, facts were double- and triple-checked for accuracy. In an undertaking of this type, errors are almost inevitable, and I apologize in advance for any that may have gotten by. If verified, every effort will be made to correct misinformation in future editions.

As I worked on this sometimes depressing history, the words of Alfred Bester continued to play in my head. As he wrote, "There has been joy before. There will be joy again."

BIBLIOGRAPHY

Ackroyd, Peter. *T.S. Eliot, A Life.* New York: Simon & Schuster, 1984.

Archer, Gleason L. *History of Radio.* New York: American Historical Society, 1936.

Bangs, Lester. *Psychotic Reactions and Carburetor Dung.* Edited by Griel Marcus. New York: Knopf, 1987.

Bazin, Andre. Trans. *What Is Cinema.* Translated by Hugo Gray. Berkeley and Los Angeles: University of California Press, 1967.

Bloom, Allan. *The Closing of the American Mind.* New York: Simon & Schuster, 1987.

Booth, Stanley. *The True Adventures of the Rolling Stones.* New York: Vintage, 1985.

Brand, Oscar. *The Ballad Mongers.* New York: Funk and Wagnalls, 1962.

Bronson, Harold. *Rock Explosion: The British Invasion.* Los Angeles: Rhino Books, 1984.

Brown, Peter, and Gaines, Steven. *The Love You Make.* New York: McGraw-Hill, 1983.

Bush, Ronald. *T.S. Eliot, A Study in Character and Style.* New York: Oxford University Press, 1983.

Cantor, Norman. *The Age of Protest.* New York: Hawthorne Books, 1969.

Ceplair, and Englund, *The Inquisition in Hollywood.* New York: Anchor Press/ Doubleday, 1980.

Chapple, Garofalo. *Rock and Roll Is Here to Pay.* Chicago: Nelson, Hall, 1977.

Clark, Dick. *Rock, Roll & Remember.* New York: Thomas Y. Crowell & Co., 1976.

Dachs, David. *Anything Goes.* New York: Bobbs-Merrill, 1964.

Davis, Clive, with James Willwerth. *Inside the Record Business.* New York: William Morrow, 1975.

Denisoff, *Tarnished Gold.* Transaction Books, 1986.

DiLello, *The Longest Cocktail Party.* Chicago: Playboy Press, 1972.

DiOrio, Al. *Borrowed Time.* Philadelphia: Running Press, 1981.

Ellis, *A History of Film.* Englewood Cliffs, N.J.: Prentice-Hall, 1979.

Erickson, Halloran, Hearn. *Musician's Guide to Copyright.* New York: Scribner's, 1983.

Ewen, David. *All the Years of American Popular Music.* Englewood Cliffs, N.J.: Prentice-Hall, 1977.

Farnol Group, Inc., eds. *The ASCAP Biographical Dictionary of Composers, Authors and Publishers.* New York: ASCAP, 1966.

Flippo, Chet. *Your Cheatin' Heart.* New York: Doubleday, 1985.

Fox, Ted. *In The Groove.* New York: St. Martin's, 1986.

Frascogna, and Hetherington. *Successful Artist Management.* New York: Watson-Guptill, 1978.

Freedland, Michael. *JOLSON.* New York: Stein and Day, 1972.

Garfield, Simon. *Money for Nothing.* Winchester, Ma.: Faber and Faber, 1986.

Gelatt, Ronald. *The Fabulous Phonograph.* Philadelphia and New York: Lippincott, 1955.

Gillett, Charlie. *The Sound of the City.* New York: Pantheon, 1983.

Goldman, Albert. *Elvis.* New York: McGraw-Hill, 1981.

Goldrosen, John. *Buddy Holly: His Life and Music.* Bowling Green, IN: Bowling Green University Popular Press, 1975.

Green, R., ed. *Protestantism and Capitalism.* Boston: D.C. Heath and Co., 1959.

Greenfield, Jeff. *Television: The First Fifty Years.* New York: Harry N. Abrams, 1977.

Groia, *They All Sang on the Corner.* New York: Phillie Dee Enterprises.

Guralnick, Peter. *Lost Highway.* New York: Vintage Books, 1979.

Guralnick, Peter. *Sweet Soul Music, Rhythm and Blues and the Southern Dream of Freedom,* New York: Harper & Row, 1986.

Hammond, John. *Hammond on Record,* New York: Summit Books, 1977.

Harris, Jay, and Editors of TV Guide. *TV Guide: The First Twenty-five Years.* New York: Simon & Schuster, 1978.

Harrison, George. *I, Me, Mine.* New York: Simon & Schuster, 1980.

Haskins, Benson. *Nat King Cole.* New York: Stein and Day, 1984.

Hebdige, Dick. *Subculture: The Meaning of Style.* London and New York: Methuen, 1979.

Hendler, Herb. *Year by Year in the Rock Era.* New York: Praeger, 1987.

Hilburn, Robert. *Springsteen.* New York: Rolling Stone Press/Scribner's, 1985.

Hirshey, Gerri. *Nowhere to Run.* New York: Penguin, 1984.

Hounsome, and Chambre. *Rock Record.* New York: Facts on File, 1981.

Jackson, Michael. *Moon Walk.* New York: Doubleday, 1988.

Jahn, Mike. *Rock: From Elvis to the Rolling Stones.* New York: Quadrangle Books, 1973.

Kelley, Kitty. *His Way*. New York: Bantam Books, 1986.

Kent, Antony. *Kemp's Music and Record Industry Yearbook 1965*. London: Kemp's Printing and Publishing, 1965.

Kiersh, *Where Are You Now, Bo Diddley*. New York: Doubleday, 1986.

Klein, Joe. *Woody Guthrie, A Life*. New York: Knopf, 1980.

Lampell, Millard, ed. *California to the New York Island*. New York: The Guthrie Children's Trust Fund, 1960.

McGowan, *Here Today, Here to Stay*. St. Petersburg, Fla.: Sixth House Press, 1983.

Marcus, Griel. *Mystery Train*. New York: Dutton, 1976.

Marsh, Dave. *Born to Run*. New York: Dell, 1981.

Martin, George. *All You Need Is Ears*. New York: St. Martin's, 1979.

Meyer, Hazel. *The Gold in Tin Pan Alley*. Philadelphia: Lippincott, 1958.

Miller, Jim, ed. *The Rolling Stone Illustrated History of Rock and Roll*. New York: Rolling Stone Press/Random House, 1976.

Nite, Norman. *Rock On*. New York: Crowell, 1974.

Norman, Philip. *Shout*. New York: Simon & Schuster, 1981.

Paley, William S. *As It Happened*. New York: Doubleday, 1979.

Passman, Arnold. *The Deejays*. New York: Macmillan, 1971.

Phillips, Michelle. *California Dreamin'*. New York: Warner Books, 1986.

Pollock, Bruce. *When Rock Was Young*. New York: Holt, Rinehart, Winston. 1981.

Rockwell, Don, ed. *Radio Personalities*. New York: Press Bureau Inc., 1935.

Shaw, Arnold. *Black Popular Music in America*. New York: Macmillan, 1986.
———. *The Rockin' Fifties*. New York: Hawthorn Books, 1974.

Shelton, Robert. *No Direction Home: The Life and Times of Bob Dylan*. New York: Ballantine, 1987.

Shemel, Sidney, and M. William Krasilovsky. *This Business of Music*. New York: Billboard Publications, 1977.

Shepherd, and Slatzer. *Bing Crosby: The Hollow Man*. New York: St. Martin's, 1981.

Simon, George. *The Best of the Music Makers*. New York: Doubleday, 1979.

Spitz, Robert. *Barefoot in Babylon*. New York: Viking, 1979.
———. *The Making of Superstars*. New York: Anchor Press/Doubleday, 1978.

Stein, Howard, and Ronald Zalkind. *Promoting Rock Concerts*. New York: Schirmer Books, 1979.

Summers, comp. *Radio Censorship*. New York: H. W. Wilson Co., 1939.

Tosches, Nick. *Unsung Heroes of Rock 'n' Roll*. New York: Scribner's, 1984.

Ulanov, Barry. *A History of Jazz in America*. New York: Viking, 1955.

Uslan, Michael, and Bruce Solomon. *Dick Clark's the First 25 Years of Rock and Roll*. New York: Dell, 1981.

Vaughn, Robert. *Only Victims,* New York: Putnam's, 1972.

Wagner, Walter. *You Must Remember This.* New York: Putnam's, 1975.

Ward, Ed. *Michael Bloomfield: The Rise and Fall of an American Guitar Hero.* New York: Cherry Lane Books, 1983.

Ward, Ed, Geoffrey Stokes and Ken Tucker, eds. *Rock of Ages: The Rolling Stone History of Rock and Roll.* New York: Rolling Stone Press/Summit Books, 1986.

Weber, Max. *The Protestant Ethic and the Spirit of Capitalism.* Translated by Talcott Parsons. New York: Scribner's, 1958.

Weiner, Rex, and Deanne Stillman. *Woodstock Census.* New York: Viking, 1979.

Whitburn, Joel, comp. *Billboard—Top 1000 Singles, 1955–1986.* Milwaukee: Hal Leonard Books/Record Research, 1985.

Whitcomb, Ian. *Tin Pan Alley.* New York: Paddington Press, 1975.

Wilder, Alec. *American Popular Song.* New York: Oxford University Press, 1973.

Wiener, Jon. *Come Together.* New York: Random House, 1984.

Williams, Roger. *Sing a Sad Song: The Life of Hank Williams.* Chicago: University of Illinois Press, 1980.

Wilson, Earl. *Sinatra.* New York: Macmillan, 1976.

Various issues of the following periodicals were used as references:

BAM, The California Music Magazine
Billboard
BMI
Business Week
Forbes
Fortune
Los Angeles Times
Musician
New Musical Express
New Republic
People
Performance
Rolling Stone
The Village Voice

Some of the research for this book was done at the New York Public Library, the music library at UCLA, the library at USC, and the Michael Ochs Archives.

Some of the material pertaining to the Beatles' lawsuit against Capitol/EMI was obtained from official court documents and the 1980 report by the Pennsylvania Crime Commission entitled "A Decade of Organized Crime."

The FBI transcripts concerning Alan Freed were obtained through the Freedom of Information Act and given to me by Lance Freed.

Index

Page numbers in *italics* refer to photos.

Bearsville Records, 240
"Beatlefests," 205
Beatlemania, 128, 129, 184
Beatlemania, 205
Beatles, 44, 88, 99, 125, 126–29,
    131–36, 161, 173, 179, 219,
    222–23, 239, 244, 266
  breakup of, 153–60
  CDs and, 209–10, 216
  commercials and, xi–xiv, 203–9,
    251–52
  Klein's luring of, 133–35, 155–56
  royalties of, 132–33, 157, 158–59,
    206, 209, 210–16
Bee Gees, 151, 179, 186, 220, 225
Bell and Tainter, 14–15
Bell Laboratories, 16
Bennett, Tony, 33, 40
Berlin (band), 244
Berlin, Irving, 10, 61
Berliner, Emile, 16
Berry, Chuck, 41, 44, 53, 56, 81, 86
Bertelsmann, 224
Big Audio Dynamite, 232–33
Big band music, 9–11
Big Brother and the Holding
    Company, 138, 139, 140
Billboard, 29, 33, 40, 53, 54, 57, 61,
    63, 68, 69–70, 72, 83–84, 98, 105,
    121, 166, 240
Billings, William, 3–4
Bitter End (New York City), 111,
    141–42
Blackboard Jungle, 54
Blacklists, 73, 113
Blackwell, "Bumps," 39
Blondie, 186, 244
Blood, Sweat and Tears, 136, 143,
    148
Bloom, Allan, 201
Bloomfield, Michael, 162
Bluebird, 42
Blues, 9, 17, 24, 39, 118
BMI (Broadcast Music Inc.), 23–26,
    31, 32, 38, 42, 66, 67, 72, 73, 75,
    83, 94
  anti-trust action against, 56–57
  formation of, 23
BMI Awards, 56
Booker T. and the MGs, 166
Born in the USA, 194, 197, 233
Boston Ventures, 223
Bowie, David, 184, 202
Bradley, Owen, 60

Branca, John, 236
Branson, Richard, 236
British Invasion, 125, 126
British Marconi Company, 7
Bronson, Harold, 242–45
Bryce Hammer Ltd., 154
Budweiser, 202
Busby, Jheryl, 236
Butler, Artie, 97–98
Paul Butterfield Blues Band, 118

Calloway, Cab, 37–38
Cameo Records, 135
Canterino, Dominick ("Baldy Dom"),
    219
Capitol/EMI, 231, 239
  Beatles' lawsuits against, 206–16,
    266
Capitol Records, 30–31, 38, 42, 53,
    100, 101, 128–29, 130, 134, 136,
    139, 150, 157, 159, 172, 239
  Beatles' royalty dispute with, 206,
    209, 210–16
  Nike "Revolution" commercial and,
    206–9
Carmichael, Hoagy, 37
Caruso, Enrico, 17
Cash, Johnny, 60
Cassettes, 168, 189, 195
Cat Records, 42–43
CBS (Columbia Broadcasting System):
  acquisition attempts and, 190–92
  divisions sold by, 190, 192, 195–99
CBS Records, 172, 178, 184–85, 188,
    189, 191, 192–99, 204, 209, 222,
    224, 228, 232–33, 241, 245
CBS-TV, 190, 192
CDs (compact discs), 194–95, 209–10,
    216, 233–34
Cellar, Emanuel, 66
Champagne Records, 47, 56
Chaplin, Ralph, 102
Charitable donations, 214
Checker, Chubby, 83
Chess Records, 40–41, 98, 124
Chickering, Jonas, 4
Chords, 42
CIO (Congress of Industrial
    Organizations), 104
Citro, Sam, 214
Clapton, Eric, 151, 202
Clark, Dee, 250
Clark, Dick, 81–85, 87–88, 99, 100,
    122, 135, 144, 175

Rothchild, Paul, 109, 235–36
Roulette Records, 219
Rounder Records, 231
Royal Teens, 121–22
Royalties, 48, 51, 108, 119–20, 131,
  136, 163, 165, 220–21, 250
  ASCAP and, 21–23, 24, 25
  of Beatles, 132–33, 157, 158–59,
    206, 209, 210–16
  copyright laws and, 19–20
  on folk music, 105–6
  for radio airplay, 13, 22–25
  tour expenses and, 171, 188
Rubsam, Edward, 18
Rupe, Art, 39
Rush Productions, 248

Sabit, Dr., 50
San Francisco Mime Troupe, 137
H. G. Saperstein and Associates, 64
Sarnoff, David, 8
Satellite Records, 166
Satin, Tenenbaum, Eichler &
  Zimmerman, 211
Saturday Night Fever, 179, 186, 187–88,
  194
Scheck, George, 99
Scher, John, 146
Schulhof, Michael P., 197
Scott, Marty, 230–31
Scrapping, 210–12, 213–14
Screen Gems, 162
Securities and Exchange Commission
  (SEC), 135
Seeger, Pete, 73, 104, 105, 106–7
Sengstack family, 20n
SESAC, 23n
Seven Arts, 150–51
Sex Pistols, 184–85, 189
Shanachie Label, 239
Shannon, Del, 127
Shapiro, Ben, 138
Sharpton, Rev. Al, 218
"Sh-Boom," 42–44
Sherman Anti-Trust Act, 25
"Sherry," 123–24, 128
Sholes, Steve, 60–61
Silver Beatles, The, 223
Simmons, Russell, 248
Sinatra, Frank, 28–31, 39, 40, 51, 53,
  57, 62, 63, 64, 66, 68, 96, 100,
  128, 150, 151
Singles, studio costs for, 93
Skiffle, 130–31, 132

Sky, Patrick, 239
Sledge, Percy, 203
Smith, Joe, 81, 87, 239
Smith, O. C., 198
Snow, Jimmy Rodgers, 59
Somer, Abe, 138
Songwriting, 19–20, 94–96, 245
Sony Corporation, 189, 196–99, 222,
  224
Soul music, 166
Sousa, John Philip, 17
Spark Records, 61
Special Projects, Inc., 64
Specialty Records, 39
Spector, Abner, 97–98
Spirituals, 5
"Splish Splash," 99, 100
Springsteen, Bruce, xii, 68n, 177–78,
  193, 194, 197, 198, 220, 225, 226,
  232, 233, 236, 237, 245, 249
Starlite Starbrite Foundation, 250
Starr, Ringo, 155, 156, 158, 160, 205
Stax, 166
Stax-Volt, 166
Steele, Tommy, 131
Steinberg, Sue, 237
Stewart, Jim, 166
Sting, 221, 237, 249
Stoller, Jerry, 95, 98
Stoller, Mike, 61, 220
Stone, Jesse, 38
Subsidiary labels, 42n, 172
Sullivan, Chuck, 218n
"Ed Sullivan Show, The," 128
Clayton F. Summy Publishing
  Company, 20n
Sun Records, 58, 60–61
Supreme Court, U.S., 22
Swan Records, 82, 83, 127
Swan Song, 240
Swid, Stephen, 196
Swit, Bandeer, and Koppelman, 209
Synchronization rights, 207–8

Tams-Witmark Publishing, 21
Tashjian, Ralph, 217
Taxe, Richard, 214
Tax reform, 196
Teenagers, 27–28, 66
Teichiku Records, 223
Television quiz shows, 74–75
Teller, Al, 193, 230, 232
Temptations, 164, 165
"There Goes My Baby," 96–97